MARTIAL ARTS
BEST OF CFW
2000

MARTIAL ARTS
BEST OF CFW
2000

By Paul Vunak Copyright © 2025 I&I SPORTS SUPPLY.
All rights reserved. Published by I&I SPORTS SUPPLY
ISBN 978-0-934489-77-5

Dedication

To all of you—those who deserve the most of the credit, the writers who supply us with an enormous amount of material every year to fill the pages of our magazines.

Acknowledgements

Our special thanks go out to the usual suspects, our staff editors, for taking time and effort to make every article better and comprehensive for the reader.

Contents

Foreword 10
   Jose M. Fraguas

A One-Armed Wonder 12
   Dave Cater

Byung In Lee's Inverted Blade 18
   Jane Hallander

Caine Comes Home 22
   Mike Leeder

Tai Chi's Lethal Weapons 30
   Mark Cheng

Ernie Hudson—Crossing the Line 36
   Todd Hester

The Higher Teachings 42
   Steve Tarani

Wong Fei Hung's 10 Killing Hands 50
   Bill Fong

The Fighting Prince 60
   Todd Hester & Kid Peligro

Seeking the Softness of Hung Gar 66
   Calvin Chin

Heal Pains, Strains Instantly 72
   Thomas Richard Joiner

Muay Thai: The National Sport of Thailand 78
   Terry L. Wilson

Ryoki Abe 84
   Sue McGlynn

Wai Hong's Words of Wisdom 90
   Julian K. Duran

The Art of the Flow 96
   Jose G. Paman

Wing Chun Trapping 102
   Alan Lamb

The Makiwara 108
   Michael J. Lorden

The Karambit: The Curved Blade of West Java Steve Tarani	114
The Unstoppable Richard Norton Todd Hester	120
Pai Lum Tao's White Crane Glenn C. Wilson	128
The Legacy of Professor Vee Robert Dreeben	134
A Quarter-Century of Capoeira Sergey Gordeev	140
It's Shanghai Noon for Jackie Chan Ric Meyers	146
Mande Muda: The JKD of Pencak Silat Mike Young	152
Choy Lee Fut's Steel Fan Howard Choy	160
Thai Boxing in JKD Paul Vunak	164
Chang Tung Sheng's Training Secrets Mark Miller	170
The Secret Behind Chang's Strength Mark Miller	176
Cary Tagawa, The Martial Artist Athlete Todd Hester	182
Hung Gar's Unbeatable Tiger Joseph Plante	188
Turning Fear into Power Dr. Will Horton	196
Paul De Thouars' Serak/Bukti Negara Danny Huybrechts	200
Flying High with the Jet Dr. Craig D. Reid	208
Gerald Okamura, Damage Control Todd Hester	214
Qi Gong: The Power to Cure Cancer Wen Mei Yu and Theresa Marie Hoff	220

Foreword

To say we get a lot of mail at CFW Enterprises would be quite an understatement. Every year we receive literally hundreds and hundreds of story submissions for all of our various magazines. These manila envelopes contain works ranging from fascinating to—well, to put it diplomatically, "fanciful." Yet we open nearly each and every piece of mail to separate contents from the envelope while doing our best not to commit an eco-crime.

Kidding aside, what we look for in the mail is the best martial arts writing in existence. To be considered "the best" there are some basic criteria which must be met. The editors at CFW Enterprises carefully evaluate the articles they receive to finally decide those which will be published. It is not an easy task since many variables are involved in the process.

Needless to say, while we receive a lot of good submissions we also, as an occupational hazard, have to read a lot of "really bad stuff." Fortunately, after years of working as an editor you develop an instinct and can quickly identify an unusable submission.

That's what this series is all about: bringing you the "Best of CFW" for each year, without prejudice in terms of the writer, the source, or the subject. Our aim is to provide the readers with a wide selection of styles and systems. The collection includes many different authors who offer their own perspectives of the arts and the influences of their respective arts in the field. All of them have expressed their ideas in a very different way. But whether expressed in the language of the teachers, the language of the students, or the language of the thinker, there is truth in concepts, philosophies and techniques that so many martial artists have believed and lived by for decades.

Here at CFW, we have made every effort to present each article and work as accurately as possible within the limitations of the book format. In addition to being a resource for researches, writers, students and teachers, we hope this collection of works will provide comfort and inspiration for all those who love the martial arts. There are many excellent books about the martial arts with more on the way. My hope is that this book of collective works and articles will prove a worthy companion to them in two main ways: first, in its size and scope; second in its practicality and ease of use.

There have been many changes in the martial arts but some things are still the same. A well-written article is one of them. Our job and responsibility at CFW as the world leaders in the publication of martial arts magazines, videos, and books is to inform and educate the reader, promoting all the styles and approaches without being limited by any of them.

As early as I can remember. My house was filled with martial arts magazines from around the world. For many years, I gathered publications and became curious about many of the authors who wrote for them. The more I researched, the more I realized that those "great people" were a lot more like you and me than they were different. Today I have written hundreds of articles in magazines around the world, more than a dozen of books under my own name and a couple under some else's. At CFW, our editors have read, written, edited and re-written more articles and books than one could possibly imagine. Although it is unlikely any of us will ever be awarded the Nobel Prize, the writing that we like is the writing that we like. Nothing can change that.

I bring all this up because I believe all the writers who have submitted material to be published in the different magazines owned by CFW Enterprises have followed similar paths.

Walk on!

—**Jose M. Fraguas**
General Manager
CFW Enterprises

A One-Armed Wonder

Nicknamed the "one-arm bandit," world kickboxing champion Baxter Humby hasn't let a missing right arm hold him back.

Dave Cater

Baxter Humby didn't ask to be born without a right hand. It just happened. Baxter Humby never asked that his affliction be met with pity. It just happened.

Baxter Humby never asked his kickboxing opponents to treat him differently in the ring because all he had left was a left.

It just happened—but only once. Only until Humby peered into the eyes of the man across the canvas, blocked an incoming left and then retaliated with one of his own.

Baxter Humby didn't have to explain.

It just happened.

For Humby, what happened Oct. 26, 1972 can be reasoned as easily as why he was born with brown eyes or brown hair. It's the natural disorder, which sometimes evolves from natural order. Trying to rationalize only leaves you feeling more powerless, less able to make sense of why.

"A couple of times I asked, 'Why me?' he explains. "But then I figured I'd show people that the only limits you have are the limits you place on yourselves. In the end, it made me a better person. I respect people more, I respect myself more. I understand how to take a negative situation and

No Quit In Him

It could have been easy for Humby to see the negative situation for what it was and quit living—plain and simple. Plenty of people choose that path and get away with it. No questions asked.

But that wasn't how his parents were going to raise their son. They weren't about to lend him a helping hand, no matter how much he needed one. Instead, they gave him encouragement, they gave him hope, and they gave him a reason to try.

"The only limits you have are the ones you impose on yourself."

"They never said I couldn't do anything," Humby related of his upbringing in Winnipeg, Manitoba, Canada. "In fact, they actually encouraged me to try different things. They didn't try to shelter me from what people might think of you because you only had one hand."

Instead, Humby grew up like any other kid—right hand or not. He played baseball, basketball, and football and ran track right along side those who were physically complete. Track turned out to be his forte and led him to consecutive berths on the Canadian Para-Olympic team for the 1992 Games in Barcelona, Spain, and the 1994 Games in Berlin, Germany.

In Spain, he finished fourth in the 1,500 and 10,000 meters and sixth in the 5,000 meters. He added a fourth and fifth in the 5,000 and 10,000 meters, respectively, in Berlin.

"Sometimes when people told me I couldn't do it I wanted to show them I could. I never said, 'I can't do it.' I played all the sports where people had to have two hands. I just persevered and had no problems with it. Basically what might have brought me down actually made me stronger."

Put Up Or Shut Up

Of course, there was the occasional bully who wanted to show why two hands were better than one. Humby decided early on to meet each challenge head on.

"I never got teased too much about (the missing hand)," he recalled. "But when it happened, I'd fight them and they could see I could take care of myself, see that it was no problem. That earned me respect."

It also earned him an appreciation of the battle, which had been simmering through years of watching Bruce Lee movies—including his favorite, *Enter The Dragon*. In 1987, a 17-year-old Baxter Humby finally got his wish when he began training in tae kwon do.

"I loved the discipline, loved the way you could perform all those amazing moves you saw on television," notes Humby. "And martial arts are more open to everything."

But what really caught his eyes was kickboxing, muay Thai style. "I loved the competition, I loved the thrill of competition," remembers Humby, who holds black belts in tae kwon do and sik tai (Filipino martial arts).

And he loved the ring.

Bandit On The Loose

Carrying the moniker of the "One-Armed Bandit," a tag placed on him early in life by his father, John, Humby never felt more at home than between the ropes.

The same could not always be said for his opponents.

Some laughed. Some taunted. Some stepped back. Some threw punches with trepidation. Some simply stared. Let's face it: fighting a one-handed boxer is not easy. If you win, you were supposed to. If you lose, you're going to hear about it for months.

"The reaction was hard for me at first," admits Humby, a 5-foot-ll, 154-pounder. "I remember what it felt like when people backed up. There were times when no one wanted to fight me. I felt bad that because of my arm I couldn't achieve my dreams. But once I overcame that and started winning some titles, people wanted to fight me. They wanted to fight for my titles."

There have been plenty of opportunities because for Humby, there have been plenty of titles—five in all since he captured the Canadian Super Welterweight Kickboxing Champi-

onship in 1996. He followed that up with the IKBA International Kickboxing title and the IKKC California Kickboxing Championship in 1998 and the IKKC USA Boxing Championship and the WMTF World Kickboxing crown earlier this year.

He's For Real!

For a guy with only one hand, he's doing a pretty good job of holding onto his titles. With a record to 32-3-1, he has established himself as one of the country's top junior middle-weight full-contact fighters.

"Fighters don't take me lightly anymore," insists Humby, who calls Malibu, Calif., his home following a 1997 move. "They're more aware that I'm for real instead of some one-armed guy they have to take it easy on."

Lacking a right hand does not pose as many problems as one would think. Humby covers up his "perceived" deficiencies with strong block-and-counter tactics. Attacking his vulnerable left side leaves one open to a sudden and often violent counterattack.

"Once he throws to my right, I try and counter with three or four combinations and get out," he adds. "I leg check block and throw a hook or kick to the body."

If you think that's easy, try wrapping your right arm to your side and Thai boxing an opponent full force. The fact that Humby is competitive is admirable. That he's winning at every level is testament to how talent and perseverance are an unbeatable combination.

Ably trained by 1996 Muay Thai light heavyweight champion Maurice Travis and master Tom Khamvongsa, Humby lets his power make an early statement. All it takes is a hard punch or kick to wake up even the most doubting giant.

Humby's daily training regimen consists of sparring for an hour in the morning followed by an hour of working the weights. He alternates between two and a half hours of muay Thai or kickboxing and grappling work. A night bike ride or jog keeps the muscles loose and ready for the next day. Humby also is particular about what he eats, preferring to consume five smaller meals a day. He stays away from sweets but supplements his diet with plenty of fruit.

"They find out very early they have to respect me," he notes.

From a fighting stance (1), jab so the opponent weaves back (2). As the opponent follows with a right cross, lean back and drive the knee into the abdomen (3). Keep your hands up and the knee will stop the attack before the cross connects (4).

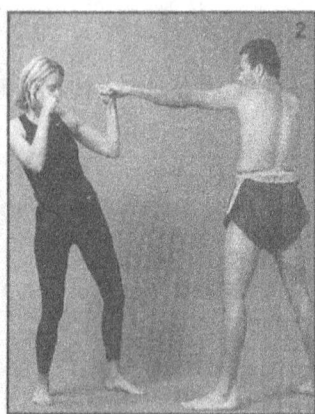

Laughing No More

A case in point is his world title fight against reigning No. 1 contender Ray Gonzalez, easily the toughest test of Humby's career. Gonzalez came in expecting to win, taunting the challenger at the outset. He left wondering how he could have been so wrong.

"Basically, I went in there strong and focused, but all he did was taunt me," relates Humby. "I hit him hard but he kept laughing at me and taunting." A steady diet of knees to the midsection and lefts to the face wiped the smile right off Gonzalez' face.

"My dream was to win the title, but winning that way made it more special," he said after breaking Gonzalez' left leg in the fourth round.

Special is a perfect way to describe Humby's outlook on life. "I remember thinking one day that life isn't that bad. In fact, I'm missing a right hand and my life is great."

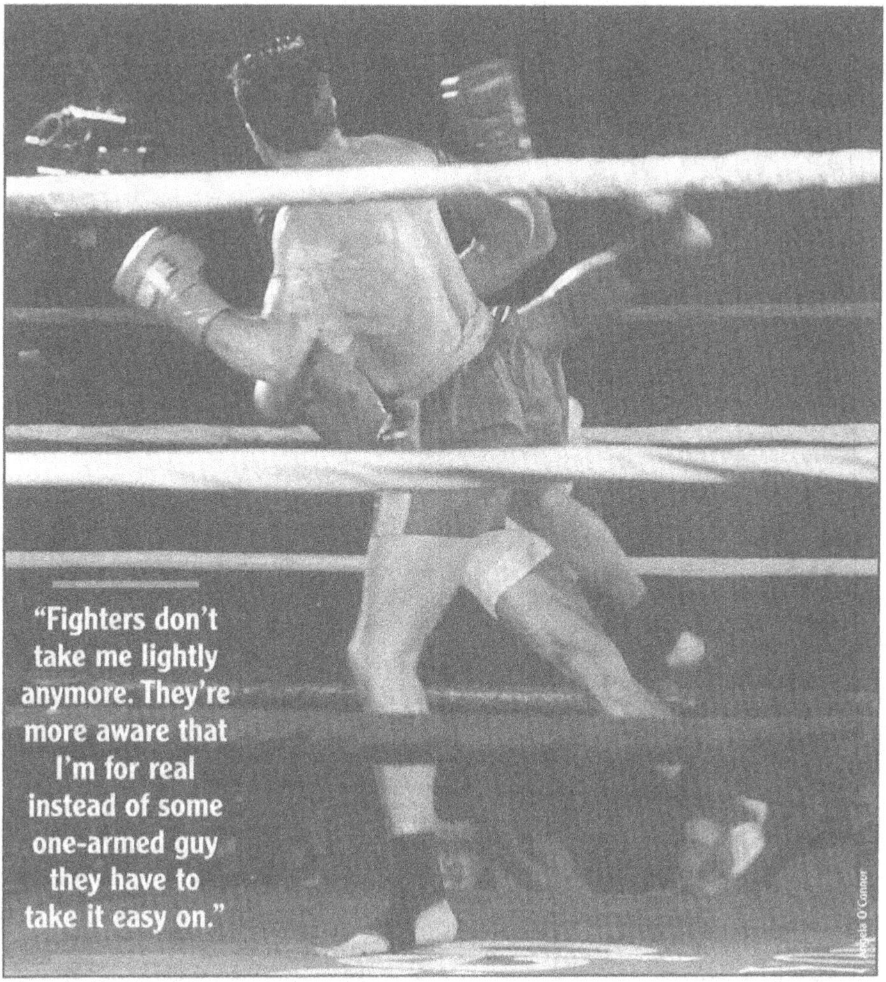

> "Fighters don't take me lightly anymore. They're more aware that I'm for real instead of some one-armed guy they have to take it easy on."

It's this same philosophy he'd like to give youngsters who have similar disabilities.

"I want to show kids who are challenged that there are no limits, that they can do anything they can put their mind to."

Take it from a guy who saw his missing right hand not as a limit to what was possible, but as a reason to do the impossible. ®

Byung In Lee's Inverted Blade

Another Dimension in Swordsmanship

Jane Hallander

Martial arts were originally structured around the use of weapons, not empty hands, because weapons, such as swords and staffs, were more efficient in a fight than just bare hands. Since ancient martial arts were based on life and death combat situations, an important part of any martial artists skill was the ability to keep using his weapon, no matter how the fighting conditions changed.

Swords were the primary weapons of Korean martial artists and military men. Unlike their Japanese counterparts, Korean swordsmen wielded their blades both single-handed and with two hands, cutting in wide, circular patterns as well as straight thrusts. This versatility was good as long as there was plenty of room in which to maneuver the heavy fighting blades. But what if they were forced into a corner, were fighting indoors, or were attacked from behind?

Korean fencing masters developed special techniques to handle close-quarter combat. They simply reversed the sword direction and continued with the fight, without losing any of the sword's effectiveness. Known *as yuk gum* (inverted sword), these techniques, made popular by the fierce Silla warriors (about AD 600), added a new dimension to the art of swordsmanship.

Today, the Korean martial art of kuk sool won continues with the study of yuk gum techniques, considering them as important to traditional Korean weapons' knowledge as any other sword technique. Byung In Lee, an eighth dan kuk sool won master, teaches in Austin, Texas and is considered one of kuk sool's foremost experts at yuk gum technique.

Inverted sword techniques are said to have had their origins with one of Koreas oldest martial arts, *sado mu sool* (tribal or family martial arts). Later, during Korea's Three Kingdom period (about AD 600), yuk gum techniques were adapted for military usage and made popular by the Silla Kingdom's legendary *wha rang* warriors, who were looked upon as Korea's version of Japan's samurai class.

Yuk gum techniques were used for close-in fighting, when a swordsman had little or no room to swing his weapon in the powerful, broad, reaching arcs that cut through anything in the blade's path. Yuk gum principles also applied to situations where many enemies attacked at the same time.

"Coupled with the defender's spinning body motion, one slice could cut down several enemies. This was called *sal sa sool*—one motion can kill many," explains Lee.

Yuk gum techniques are well suited to use with only one hand. It was possible for a soldier with an injured arm to continue defending himself by holding his sword in the inverted position with his good hand. The same applied to a warrior with damaged vision. Since yuk gum spinning techniques can cover large areas, there was little need to have precise aim. Therefore, if a fighter had to seek out his enemies

"Yuk gum techniques are always circular actions, arcing in any direction. The yuk gum practitioner doesn't even have to face the direction in which he cuts"

by sound alone, his yuk gum cuts would work equally well for offensive cutting or defensive blocking movements. Not only could he effectively keep enemies away from his front and back with inverted sword actions, but a blinded defender could also defend his sides with figure-eight slicing motions.

Since they are short-range techniques, inverted sword movements were strictly for use on foot, rather than horseback. They were man-to-man defense tactics that couldn't be jammed by other weapons, as could straight sword techniques. A good swordsman trained in yuk gum techniques could draw and cut before his opponent's blade was even out of its case.

As far as the technique itself, yuk gum is the opposite of the more common *jung gum* (straight sword technique). Jung gum is the often seen two-handed or single-handed (tip forward) chopping, slicing, and stabbing techniques associated with most swordsmanship arts. Jung gum places the fighter facing front, always striking to the front and side with straight, forward movements.

On the other hand, yuk gum techniques are always circular actions, arcing in any direction—to the front, rear, or either side. The yuk gum practitioner doesn't even have to face the direction in which he cuts. According to Byung In Lee, yuk gum techniques are just as versatile and fast as straight sword (jung gum) movements.

An inverted sword stylist doesn't need to move his body as much as one who thrusts and chops with straightforward sword techniques. Instead, his footwork is stable and solid, designed to give him the maximum strength his body can produce.

The weapon's handle is always grabbed sideways by the yuk gum practitioner, with either one or both hands, exposing the blade's cutting edge horizontally. Slices are made in one of five directions: cross body, out forward from the body, straight upward, downward, and backward. X-shaped cuts are done by slicing up, angling across the body, bringing the sword around to one side, or cutting upward again in the opposite direction. If the yuk gum stylist wants extra strength, for instance, to brace against a powerful force, he might line up his forearm and elbow against the back of the blade.

When cutting to the side, the yuk gum stylist twists his waist, producing a quick whip-like power. This is important, since he doesn't have the entire length of his blade to use as an extension of his hands.

Korean straight sword techniques use both single and double-handed grips on the weapon. Inverted sword actions are no different. Although the single-handed grip is preferred with most yuk gum techniques, double-handed gripping is done whenever extra power is needed, such as with a straight downward thrust. Both hands are also used when cuts to either side are made—when the sword is not braced against the forearm. Straight stabs to the rear can be either with one or two hands controlling the sword. Yuk gum techniques are flexible enough that the deciding factor of whether or not the swordsman uses one or both hands for gripping is his own individual strength.

No matter how many hands hold the sword, the actual method of controlling the blade remains the same. The sword practitioner's arm and wrist must be flexible enough to maintain the constant circular, twisting, and rolling motion necessary to bring the blade into striking position. Those same wrist and arm movements also enable quick changes from straight sword techniques into inverted techniques, and back again, according the situation.

Yuk gum techniques include fast spinning motions, where the swordsman's entire body makes a complete 360-degree turn, cutting as many close-in opponents as possible. Called the motionless sword, this technique requires only the swordsman's body to move. The sword is carried tight against the body, as if it were actually part of the body, with the blade hidden from the opponent's view until the spin begins.

In the old days of Korea's fighting past, yuk gum spinning techniques often involved kicking while the sword cut its targets. Not only did kicks fit well with inverted sword movements, but since the weapon was carried close to the body, other acrobatics (such as cartwheels, handsprings and front flips) could also be used effectively.

Since Korea contains a wide variety of different terrain, and since the sword was primarily a soldier's weapon, ancient Korean swordsmen practiced their sword techniques under all types of conditions.

"One of the best times to practice sword techniques is in the early mornings when everything is calm," explains Lee. "If you want to improve your balance go to a beach. In the sand it's easy to lose your balance. In Korea we used the soft, sticky sand to improve our balance and footwork."

Different types of terrain provided expertise in all kinds of footwork. Rocks, sand, and wet grass all effect balance and footwork, and should be used for practice.

Even moonlight and complete darkness played important roles in the training of Korea's swordsmen. In the dark, sword practitioners were required to rely upon their sense of hearing and feel for contact with their enemies. It they practiced enough under those circumstances, the lack of daylight proved to be no problem at all.

Also wind often comes up at night, challenging the yuk gum swordsman to develop his sense of hearing to an acute stage. Mornings, on the other hand, are good times to use the eyes for superior concentration. The final result combines hearing and sight, together with mind control, to produce an invincible fighter.

Climate made no difference either to ancient Silla swordsmen. It snows in Korea, making the winters cold and foreboding for outside practice. Yet that did not deter Korean swordsmen, who practiced year-round without jacket or shoes. They also used Korea's heavy rains and accompanying winds to further develop their hearing and sight. As rainwater seeped into their eyes, they improved their vision and balance. The winds made their hearing more acute.

Perhaps the greatest self-defense benefit to modern-day martial arts practitioners of inverted sword techniques is the versatility derived from this type of training. No longer needing to rely on the full length of a several-foot-long weapon, the martial artist can learn to use his or her body for power and mobility and can effectively defend with even a short stick or rolled-up magazine. ®

Caine Comes Home

David Carradine's first journey to the Shaolin Temple was a spiritual experience for both the man and the character he played.

Mike Leeder

I've pretty much spent the greater part of my adult life living and working in Hong Kong, and it was my interest in martial arts and martial arts related film and television that brought me here. My heroes include most of the usual suspects, and while I'm a die-hard Jackie Chan fan and can credit an afternoon doublebill of the old Rank Video releases with the classic Neil Adams artwork, of *Snake in the Eagles Shadow & Drunken Master* starring the man himself for really getting me hooked. I do have a confession to make: Jackie wasn't my first martial arts or kung-fu hero, and sorry folks but it wasn't Bruce Lee either. My first real introduction to the martial arts can be traced back to the BBC back in England on Saturday afternoons in the early 1970s when I would tune in for the weekly adventures of everybody's favorite wandering Shaolin monk, Kwai Chang Caine as played by David Carradine in the classic TV series "Kung Fu."

I loved that show, the characters, Blind Master Po and his young student Grasshopper! the philosophy, "I do not wish to know all the answers, I seek only to understand all the questions." I even liked the action back then!

Rebirth of Caine

Jump-cut to 25 years or so later in Hong Kong's Peninsula Hotel, where courtesy of an introduction by the blonde fury herself, action actress Kim-Maree Penn (*Knock Off, Death Games*), Australian producer/director Harold Weldon invites me to work as associate producer (among other things!) on his latest project, "A Martial Arts Journey." The project is to be a documentary co-production between Harold's own company Asiavision, and Freemantle International (producers of a little-known show called "Baywatch"), focusing on the history of martial arts both real and reel to be

filmed on location at the birthplace of the martial arts, Shaolin, and to finish up in the birthplace of the martial arts movie, Hong Kong.

I readily accepted Harold's offer, and set about assembling a few key personnel to work on the project, notably ace cameraman and cinematographer Henry Chung (DOP on *Bishonen &Slow Fade,* both of which were well-received at this year's Berlin Film Festival) and soundman extraordinaire, Mark Roberts. I also set about arranging various interview subjects to participate in the Hong Kong end of the project including a certain Jackie Chan.

As we prepped the project, Harold and myself kept in communication by phone and fax, several possible presenters were discussed for the project but nobody seemed ready to commit, until about a week to ten days before we were to set out for the shoot. Harold called me to let me know that the host of the show has been confirmed, and will be accompanying us to Shaolin and Hong Kong. Who was to be the host? None other than Kwai Chang-Caine himself, David Carradine.

Coming Full Circle

The concept of having the man whom pretty much introduced Shaolin and kung-fu to the world travel to the real Shaolin was the obvious, if slightly surreal choice. And if Kwai Chang-Caine was going to make his first trip to the real Shaolin Temple, I was more than happy to be accompanying him.

The time to go was soon upon us, and Henry, Mark and I were to make our own way from Hong Kong to

David Carradine, seen with his "Caine-like" flute and hat, poses with Xialong (Little Dragon), the "Kung-Fu" kid from the Shaolin Popeye movies who at the tender age of 10 is considered the future of martial arts movies.

all traveled on to Shaolin together. Loaded down with equipment, we had quite an easy, uneventful journey and soon arrived at the Zhengzhou Holiday Inn. And there he was. Sitting in the hotel coffee shop was the man himself, Harold Weldon, and seated with him was David Carradine and his lovely wife Marina.

Brief introductions were made, before we quickly grabbed dinner and set off on a wild white-knuckle three-hour journey through the nighttime Chinese countryside and our destination, the Shaolin Temple—well, okay the nicest hotel in the town of Donguan about five minutes drive from the Temple itself.

The next few days were to be a flurry of activity at Shaolin, with little or no sleep as the main order of the day. We'd wake up about 4 a.m. and go to the Temple before dawn to being filming, capturing the monks' early morning rituals and chanting on film, before capturing interviews and demonstrations with the top fighting monks at the temple including Xiaolong (Little Dragon), the "Kung-Fu" kid from the Shaolin Popeye movies who may only be ten years old but without a doubt is the future of martial arts cinema. He carries himself with great presence and is a humble and sweet kid, and did I mention that the boy could move! We also recorded a fantastic demonstration by the Temple's premier team of fighting monks, as well as a great discussion and interview with Shaolin Demonstration Team Captain De Yung, who plays a form known as The Way Of The Heart to David in the Pagoda Gardens. Each of the 247 pagodas contains the remains of past monks and abbots

An Audience with the Abbot

We were also granted an audience with the Abbot of Shaolin, Shi Yongxin, who agreed to discuss a variety of subjects on camera with David. As the Abbot arrived in full robes and regalia, he seemed somewhat solemn and a little reluctant to talk despite the valiant work of our translator, Le Dong. How could we break the ice? It was then that I pulled an ace from my sleeve, well from my bag actually. I had brought my handy Sony Hi-8 Sc55 Handycam (plug, plug!) with monitor and a copy of David's performance in the pilot of "Kung Fu." After watching a few moments of the young Carradine's performance in the pilot, he smiled, exclaiming; "You played a Chinese monk! How interesting!" The ice was broken and we recorded a great interview/conversation between the two.

Interweaving with our interviews and the demonstrations by the monks, we captured David's thoughts and preconceptions about Shaolin both before and after he visited the Temple. We asked how he had thought it would be, and if it had measured up to his expectations. "It surpassed them!" exclaimed a smiling Carradine. We also managed to record great footage, which really captures the spirit of the old series and allowed us to cut back and forth between our footage and the original

Carradine and a young monk work in a musical moment for the documentary.

David Carradine looks right at home with these young students who train at the Shaolin Temple (top). As the cameras roll, David shares lunch and philosophical discussions with some of the monks (left).

series. As David in Caine-esque attire (hat, satchel and flute), he strolls through the Chinese countryside with the Song Shan Mountains in the background, passing temples and shrines, before arriving at the hallowed halls of Shaolin.

Now we were shooting at a breakneck pace during our time at Shaolin, very long shooting days, late nights, early mornings. I have the highest respect for David for being a trooper of the top level. We were staying at a 5 Star Hotel—by Mainland Chinese standards—and had to deal with interesting toiletry facilities and choices of food. Let's just say that my respect for David grew during the shoot: not even food poisoning could keep this man down. David also deals with his fans very well. Throughout the Hong Kong leg of the shoot fans from several countries besieged him. And even at

Shaolin, he had to deal with some recognition, particularly from one young Frenchman studying there. This fellow might have spent just a bit too long at the Temple, or possibly sat too close to the TV all those years ago, as despite Davids protests, he was convinced that David had once actually lived and trained at Shaolin himself.

Historic Meeting

Eventually our stay at Shaolin had to come to an end, and we prepared to return to Hong Kong for the final days of shooting. We eventually arrived back across the border from China, a little after 8 a.m. Monday, and ready for a full day of shooting, starting off with David performing tai chi in the rain alongside the Tai Chi Statue among the skyscrapers of Hong Kong's Exchange Square, ending the day with our interview with Jackie Chan.

Jackie was hard at work on his latest project for Media Asia, *Jackie Chan—My Stunts.* Thanks to Willie Chan and Solon So at JC Group, an interview had been scheduled and confirmed for that afternoon. But rather than disrupt Jackie in the midst of shooting and have him travel to meet us, *My Stunts* writer/ producer Bey Logan had kindly offered us the opportunity to conduct our interview with Jackie on the *My Stunts* set at Sai Kung. We arrived at the Sai Fong studios in the late afternoon, and the location was a hive of activity, as Jackie and his stunt boys were revealing some of the secrets of their stuntwork. Once we were set up and ready to rock, Jackie and David met for the first time. The historic encounter was captured on camera.

Shi Yongxin, Abbot of Shaolin, was a bit reluctant to speak in front of the camera until he saw the pilot episode of "Kung Fu."

"When the Kung Fu television show premiered in 1972, no one could have imagined its impact."

David plays tai chi in Hong Kong's Exchange Square.

Jackie looked fitter than ever, fresh from *Rush Hour,* and his English was now more fluent. Both David and Jackie expressed their knowledge of and admiration for each other's work, with Jackie even quoting a few Caine-isms from memory.

Their discussion is magical television. Jackie and David describe at length their various injuries, both film and martial arts related, as well as their martial arts background. Jackie reveals how he has yet to visit Shaolin himself, and how he was so impressed that a Western show could reveal so much of the spiritualism of kung-fu, while Hong Kong movies were so much more fighting orientated. Jackie also revealed his interest in doing another *Drunken Master* or traditional kung-fu movie. David and Jackie even discussed the possibility of working together at some point.

The rest of the documentary includes demonstrations and interviews with such lethal leading lights of the Hong Kong movie industry as Jackie's *Project S* co-star Fan Siu-wong, wing chun master

"Both David and Jackie expressed their knowledge of and admiration for each other's work, with Jackie even quoting a few Caine-isms from memory."

and *Crime Story* villain Stephen Chan, *Knock Offs* Michael Miller (who faces off and does away with stand-in opponent *moi!*), *Double Team* bad guy and former Jet Li stunt double Hung Yan Yan, stunt-man-turned-director Ridley Tsui Po-wah, Jackie's longtime producer Chua Lam, and much more.

When the "Kung Fu" television show premiered in 1972, no one could have imagined its impact. The program immediately introduced an entire culture to the physical and spiritual side of Chinese martial arts. David Carradine, like Jackie Chan, remains one of the central figures responsible for kung-fu's current popularity. His visit to the Shaolin Temple, and the welcome reception from its inhabitants, only solidifies his position as a leader in the traditional movement.

When "Caine" returned to his roots, he found himself more deeply entrenched than he ever could have imagined. Kung-fu is alive and well—at the Shaolin Temple and in David Carradine's heart. ®

Mike Leeder is a Hong Kong-based actor/writer and occasional martial artist. His work regularly appears in Combat, Impact, Screen Power, Inside Kung-Fu, Femme Fatales, *and many other magazines.*

Tai Chi's Lethal Weapons

Understanding tai chi's combative side and the principles that make it work.

Mark Cheng

Snap, crackle, pop! If you thought those sounds were reserved for the little guys on the cover of the Rice Krispies box, think again. Those are the sounds an attacker's joints make when he's joint locked, launched into the air, and sent crashing into the ground head-first. Sound rough? This is the combat effectiveness of Yang style tai chi. Despite tai chi's current reputation, its original purpose wasn't as a geriatric exercise routine.

Tai chi's history is a mixed bag. While the modern era sees tai chi as a mostly soft, smooth form of exercise, its birth was anything but peaceful. Yang style tai chi founder, Yang Lu-Chan, went through incredible hardship, not only in his studies with the Chen family, but also during the full contact trial-and-error process of synthesizing his own system. Yang and his heirs fought many matches to prove the worthiness of the system they boldly named the "Supreme Ultimate Fist," eventually winning the favor of the Qing Dynasty royal court.

Many modern-day students and "instructors" are shocked to hear and see that tai chi is a full-fledged combat art. The kicks, punches, throws, and locks of the system are versatile weapons, especially when the applications of the form are understood properly. However, most modern practitioners see the motions as an exotic dance and fail to comprehend the combat value of each and every movement in the form.

The locking and throwing techniques contained in tai chi are of special interest to the combat-minded student of the art. In keeping with tai chi's philosophy of maximum efficiency, a joint lock or throw allows for the maximum response from an opponent while requiring the minimum force from the defender. Compared to a strike, a throw requires far less accuracy and power to put an opponent on the ground. A throw allows the defender to strike their opponent with the full force of gravity and surface area of the ground, surpassing the damage that could be inflicted by a strike.

For example, a technique such as "Cross Hands," can be applied as a blocking or deflecting technique, as is often taught. However, the real power of this technique lies when it applying it as a throw. This example doesn't hold true for every movement in the long form, so tai chi enthusiasts can't be indiscriminate in choosing throws to include in their combat arsenal. A clear understanding of the logic behind tai chi's applications is essential to understanding this facet of the art.

There are two main differences between a simple takedown and a combat throw. First of all, as any physics major can tell you, the "drop zone," or height from which an opponent falls, is a major com-

ponent of a throw's potential energy—the higher up the defender releases the throw, the greater the attackers impact velocity. Secondly, the attackers landing skill is an essential factor in a throw's combat effectiveness. A judoka, aikidoka, hapkido, shuai-chiao, or high-level jiu-jitsu practitioner will most certainly have an intimate knowledge of proper falling and countering techniques. Anyone who saw Rickson Gracie in *Choke* knows full well that he was set up for a big fall yet cleanly maneuvered out of the throw in mid-air. Thus, intelligent "weapon selection" is important for the technique's success.

Joint-locking techniques are an interesting concept in efficiency as well. For combat usage, they allow a fighter to seriously damage his opponent with a higher likelihood of keeping him out of the fight. For instance, a punching and kicking fight between two equally skilled (or unskilled) fighters can drag on for a while. Punches and kicks might land with sound impact, but not guarantee that the receiver is going down. Whereas a fight where one fighter employs a full-force joint-lock or joint destruction is over as soon as the technique is used. Once an elbow is hyper-extended, a shoulder pulled out-of-joint, or a cervical trauma created, the fight is over.

A technique like "Hands Play the Pi-Pa" can be a double joint-destruction, depending on how it's applied. The tai chi practitioner's right hand shoots out to deflect an incoming strike, then seizes and twists it, while pulling inward. This is the yielding and re-directing theory in action. Then the left hand swings upward to create a hyper-extension of the opponent's elbow. The small turn and swing in the technique pulls the opponent even further off-balance, and the returning move can either slide his shoulder out of the socket or propel him backwards.

This was the first application my father did on me as a youngster. One afternoon while my father was practicing, I sat on the side watching him and snickering. Children

"The principles of yielding to an opponent's force, and redirecting him down to the ground or into a submission hold are clearly found in both aikido and tai chi."

Facing an attacker, (1), Cheng slips a punch (2), attacks the legs (3), upends the opponent (4), and slams him to the ground (5).

Cheng simultaneously blocks and kicks to defend a punch (1). Trapping the attacker's neck (2), he cranks the neck (3) and turns the attacker over (4).

can't immediately comprehend the power of such slow motions in fighting, and I remember thinking that his form looked like a slow-motion replay of a kung-fu movie. Clearly annoyed with me, he called me over and told me to punch at his face as hard as I could. Since he'd already taught me how to punch and kick years before, I was eager to see how this slow-motion stuff would keep my fist from landing on him. In an instant, he received my punch, pulled me off my base, and with a smoot, lifting motion, locked out my arm and shot me 4 feet through the air and right into the wall. I was an instant convert, and my mother just walked by shaking her head.

These two concepts of joint-locking and throwing, along with maximum output from "soft" techniques, bear such similarity to aikido that several articles and books have been published on the subject. Not too long ago I saw an academic text written by a Japanese aikidoka and a Chinese tai chi player on the similarities of the two arts. The principles of yielding to an opponent's force, and redirecting him down to the ground or into a submission hold are clearly found in both arts. This, however, is often misunderstood by tai chi practitioners who are stuck knee-deep in the "push and shove" mindset.

With a proper understanding of the logic of tai chi applications, modern-day practitioners can breathe life into an otherwise dead form. Simply practicing a tai chi form doesn't bring it to life. The form itself is a lifeless series of movements. Life comes into the form when a practitioner understands the spirit and intent of each movement, the subtle nuances of each posture, and the transitions between them. Mimicking the motions in a monkey-see, monkey-do fashion is fine if one is studying tai chi for exercise alone, but even then, the full benefits cannot be reaped without a better understanding of the combat applications. This is not to say that every tai chi student must be ready to be joint locked and thrown. Instead they should strive to understand visually how each movement of their body relates to a self-defense application. This kind of understanding makes the correct form easier to remember and allows the student to apply *yi* or "intention" to every move. Tai chi's joint locks and throws are an exciting part of Chinese martial arts combat. Understanding them will help your form, and might save your life. $

Mark Cheng is a Chinese martial arts researcher and instructor based in West Los Angeles and Pacific Palisades, California. For seminar information, e-mail Sifu Cheng at MJCSifii@aol.com.

Ernie Hudson—Crossing the Line

Todd Hester

Ernie Hudson knows what it's like to grow up tough—but on the surface you'd never know it. One of the most recognizable faces in American cinema, Hudson possesses an undeniable comic flair, appearing as everything from Winston in *Ghostbusters* to Agent Gus Anders in *Mr. Magoo*. Sprinkled into his three-decade body of work, however, have been roles in darker films such as the martial arts classic *The Octagon* with Chuck Norris, *The Crow* with Brandon Lee, and the recent *Best of the Best IV*. Very familiar with martial arts, Hudson has studied "off and on" for several years with taekwondo expert Simon Rhee. Hudson's current hit, HBO prison-drama *Oz*, contains vicious fight scenes and darkly emotional characterizations.

Beneath Hudson's comic veil, there seems to be a deep well from which, seemingly at will, he can dredge up edgy, angry, and violent characters. A casual glance at Hudson's Ivy League pedigree might give one the impression that the Yale-educated performer had been born into a privileged family, and that his harsh enactments are nothing more than evidence of his powerful acting ability. In reality, however, Hudson's "edge" comes from deep inside and is a result of his surprisingly difficult childhood.

"I never knew my father," Hudson recalls, "and my mother was dying from tuberculosis. I was born at home, when my grandmother was at church. When she came home, there I was. No one thought to call the doctor or to go to city hall to record it—so I had no birth certificate. A few months later my mother died. Years later, when I tried to get my first passport, it was nearly impossible because I had no immediate blood relations. I had an aunt swear out an affidavit and I had to get my school records to show the passport office. On them were some comments my third grade teacher had made." Hudson laughs. "She said I had a terrible temper but that I was a great storyteller."

While Hudson's talent for storytelling wouldn't turn into his life's work until years later, his temper helped him to survive—especially in his poverty-stricken hometown just outside of Detroit. "Ben-

ton Harbor is a little place," Hudson says. "It was very depressed and there were no jobs, so even as a kid it was tough. When Detroit went through that big recession in the '60s and '70s, Benton Harbor got hit really hard. It never really recovered and unemployment rose really high. So that meant a lot of crime."

Adding to the stress of growing up in a depressed area was that fact that not only was Hudson from the wrong side of the tracks, but the tracks also split his family down the middle. "I've always had the mindset to be able to take care of myself physically, in a fighting way," Hudson states. "I think it's natural when you grow up the way I did. I was raised by my grandmother, who was really into church—a very Pentecostal, hellfire-and-brimstone, God-fearing, the-devil-chasing-you-around type of woman—which took me a long time to get past. So I was very much into going to church every day. But on the other hand, I would fight at the drop of a hat—so I was isolated within myself. I was too churchy to hang-out with the guys on the street, but I was too street-wise to be accepted totally within the church. I was in this weird childhood no-man's land—I didn't quite fit in anywhere."

If Hudson's grandmother was "churchy" though, his uncles were just the opposite. "My Uncle Charles was a total gangster," Hudson recalls, "drove a Cadillac, gambled, carried a gun, did the whole thing. My other uncle, Isaiah, was a physically powerful guy, but he was sweet in a crazy way. I mean, if he saw a sad movie he'd cry, but then if you messed with him he would kill you. Just the littlest thing would set him off—but when he wasn't killing people he was very sweet. So from each of them I got a little bit."

From his uncles, the young Ernie quickly learned the law of the street—and these lessons would stay with him for the rest of his life. "My Uncle Isaiah knew a Brazilian style of fighting that came from Africa—capoeira. I don't know where he learned it but he used it. He was a fighter and a gambler and was always on the edge. He always told me that the only way to survive a fight was to make your opponent believe that you're deadly."

For a young boy learning his way around the neighborhood, those words became gospel. "When that if you fight, you have to totally dominate the other person; and then you spare him—but only after you totally dominate him—otherwise he's still a danger to you in the future. You also have to make him, and everyone around you, believe you're crazy—that you'd rather die than lose. If at any point you're not willing to die, then fighting is pointless because you're already beaten before you start. So as a little kid, and I'm talking three years old here, I had this African warrior mentality thrust upon me."

Starting school, Hudson soon found that he would have to use the advice much sooner than he had anticipated, and against much bigger foes. "My first fight," he recalls, "was when

"Hudson has studied off and on for several years with taekwondo expert Simon Rhee."

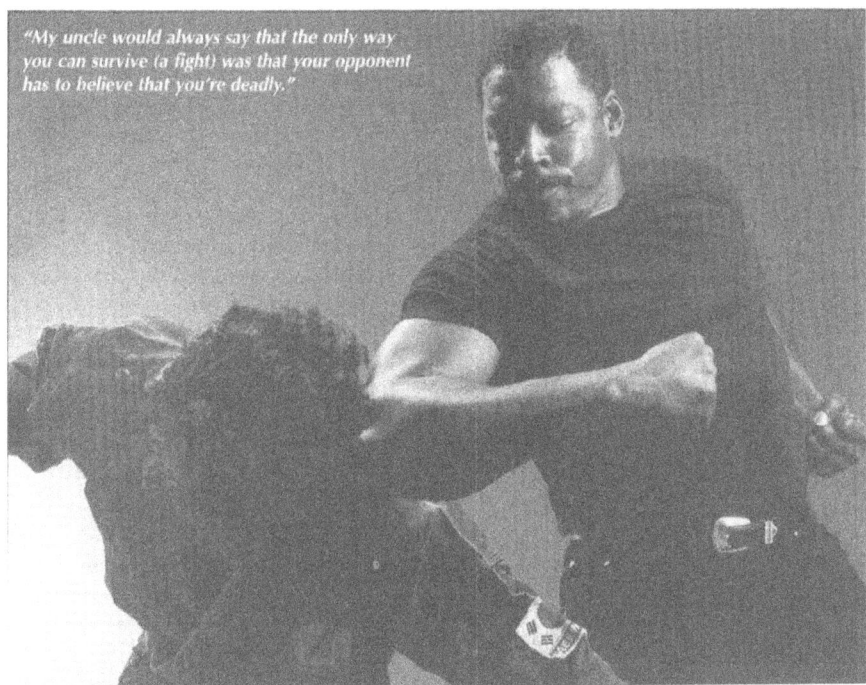

"My uncle would always say that the only way you can survive (a fight) was that your opponent has to believe that you're deadly."

I was in the first grade and my half-brother was in the third grade. There was a kid who was picking on him, who had a reputation as a fighter. My brother was always a leader, but he was never a fighter. So I got tired of him being picked on, so one day I just walked up to this third-grader and I beat him up really badly. As I was fighting, I remembered my uncle saying, Act like you're crazy' So after I beat up this tough kid I started acting nuts in front of his friends, screaming at them and hitting myself, because I didn't want to have to fight them later. I scared them so badly that they ran off crying. So I got this reputation for not being all there. And that helped me to get into less fights. I could stand up for other kids just by intimidating whoever was picking on them."

If Hudson intimidated the bad kids, though, he also scared the good ones. "As I got older I got into boxing and I started to fight in the Golden Gloves. I was the toughest kid in school—or at least I thought I was—and nobody ever challenged that. The other kids always had a kind of respect for me. I wasn't a bad kid, but I was a tough kid. I would always take-up for those that were being picked- on. But even though I would take-up for them they were still afraid of me and wouldn't play with me. So I was a little lonely but I survived, you know?"

As Hudson grew up, he had several close calls with the violence of the streets. "As I started to get older, into my late teens, I started to realize that fighting is not glamorous. You have to believe that all fights are deadly—how do you 'kind of' fight? I mean, it's like pulling a gun on someone. If you're not going to shoot the person, don't pull the gun. You don't pull a gun and make a speech because there's always a potential for going to the bottom line very fast. So you avoid fights, but if you have to fight, you totally commit to it. You need to try to stay away from that bottom line because if you get close to it, you might have to cross it. And crossing the line means going all the way.

There was this time in Detroit when a guy came and threatened that he was going to shoot me. So I went to a friend's house and got his gun. So I go downstairs and now I've got my gun, and he's

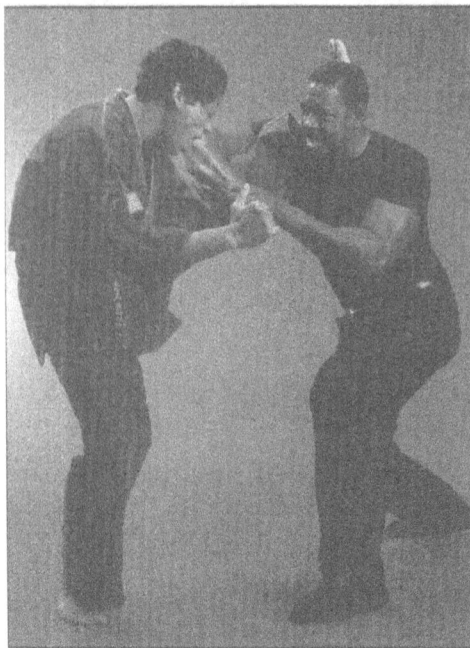

got his gun. The whole thing is stupid to begin with, but I just found myself getting closer to that line. So luckily when I went downstairs, he had his hand in back of him. So I have my gun in my pocket, aimed at him, and I'm thinking that if this guy makes any kind of sudden move I'm going to shoot him. But we talked it out and got through it. He didn't make any sudden movements and things calmed down. But what scared me afterwards, was that I was too close to that line. I was committed to shooting him. If that would have happened you would not be seeing the Ernie Hudson you see today. That one moment of self-control, where I didn't cross the line, defined the rest of my life. I realized that I didn't want to go to jail—I wanted to be someone."

Hudson went on to graduate from high school—but definitely not with honors. "I was from a family that was not at all into education," he laughs. "In fact, I was the first person to graduate from high school. That's why just was such a big thing. If I came home with Fs or whatever, my grandmother didn't know the difference because she couldn't read or write."

Married with a family upon graduation, Hudson found that his D grade-point average wasn't enough to get him any kind of decent job—much less into college. "I was always told to just go to high school. No one ever told me I had to study. But I wanted to make something of myself and the only hope I saw was by going to college. I tried everywhere but no one was interested in me and my D average.

"In my life I've always found that you deal with things directly. If I have a problem with somebody, I sit down with them and say 'Look, this is where I'm coming from.' The more you distance yourself from a problem, the bigger that problem becomes. So I went to the admittance council at Wayne State and I sat down with them and said, 'I know my grades are screwed-up, but I've got a wife and I've got a kid and I'd like to make something of myself' And they said, 'If you go to a junior college and do well, we'll look at you again.'

"So I went to Highland Park Junior College, which had also turned me down, and talked them into letting me take two classes; which was the best thing that could have happened. I took a class in English and one in History. The first day in school, I had it in my mind that people who went to college were somehow brighter, and smarter, and had all their stuff together—you know, a step above me. But I got there and I went, 'Wait a minute, these guys aren't all that, I can do this.' So I attended Highland Park for a year, did well, and then transferred to Wayne State. Once I was there, someone told me that if I maintained a B average I could get a scholarship. So I got a scholarship and hustled some jobs to made ends meet.

"I just kind of stumbled into the theater program. I was writing back then—I was always writing—and a friend of mine who was with a local theater read a play I had written and did a production of it. So once I got into the theater I really felt like I had found my home. After I graduated I applied at Wayne State, the University of Iowa, and several others, got accepted, and decided to go to

> "Avoid fights, but if you have to fight, totally commit to it. Try to stay away from that bottom line because if you get close to it, you might have to cross it"

Iowa on a scholarship, where I should have gone, actually, because they have a very good writing program. But based on several plays I had written, I got offered a scholarship to Yale. So I went there— it was just too hard to pass up the Ivy League."

Hudson only stayed at Yale for year, though, because he found its "stuffy" atmosphere unbearable. After winning the lead parts in nearly all of the Yale plays, however, and having already been noticed in L.A., Hudson soon landed the lead role in a Minneapolis-based production of *The Great White Hope*, which thrust him into the permanent limelight. Hudson toured the country to critical acclaim, ending up in L.A. *Ghostbusters* came several years after and Hudson's life was never the same again.

Having met with success after success, Hudson finally reached an area as far away from the mean streets of Benton Harbor as he could get—the upper class enclave of Southern California's Hidden Hills. "I was moving in and I thought I had left that entire part of my life behind me," Hudson says. "Then as I'm walking into the house, I hear this voice coming from one of my new neighbors and I realize who it is—Sinbad—who also just happens to be from Benton Harbor. Maybe we carry part of who we are, and where we came from, around with us forever. Maybe we never escape from it— and maybe we shouldn't try."

"I still think about what my uncles taught me," Hudson reflects, "and even today, it's very hard for me to drop my guard with people because I want them to take me seriously—to believe I'm someone to be reckoned with. I don't want them to get close enough to lose respect for what I might do; uncertainty is a powerful tool—people fear the unknown. Once you lose that grip of uncertainty on your opponent's mind, what have you got? Uncertainty can be the thing that keeps violence at bay, and that makes someone back off—it can keep you from crossing the line." ®

The Higher Teachings
A Special Interview with Dan Inosanto

Steve Tarani

In today's technologically advanced societies, the martial arts have predominantly developed into a physical training system. Aside from the more obscure corners of the globe, such as the remote provinces of the Indonesian Archipelago and the Philippine Islands, the once-common concept of "totality of training" resides with the warriors of antiquity and the ancient temples and battlefields of long-forgotten times.

According to the ancients, it was believed that man was comprised of mind, body, and spirit. Thus, in order to fully train oneself, the totality of a warrior had to be developed to the highest level of performance. The ancient Greeks considered it an honor to serve the gods in battle.

In more recent times (400 A.D. through the mid-18th century), various temples in China and Japan were built on the concept of preservation of knowledge, and the physical, mental, and spiritual understanding of self. Unfortunately, due to the tremendous amount of personal dedication and discipline required, only a select few became "masters of self." As time went on, and invading armies persisted, the ruling class became more focused on rapid methods of developing fighting skills—it was much quicker to train a soldier to kill than to train him to think. Take a hard look at our modern armed forces today. In just a few months of boot camp, a modern warrior is equipped with the basic knowledge required for maximum efficiency in the art of destruction.

Throughout history, various groups migrated from their indigenous regions and brought with them food, dance, music, philosophies and fighting systems—but what of the ancient principles and teachings of the masters? If the physical aspect was only one-third of the total training package, then what happened to the remaining spiritual and mental knowledge required for a fighter to develop on all three levels?

In today's martial arts community, we are most fortunate to have the opportunity to ask one of the greatest martial artists of modern times about this. In this very unique interview about the lost "higher teachings" of the martial arts, Guro Dan Inosanto gives us a rare glimpse at the age-old and revered knowledge of the ancient masters.

Q: I'd like to discuss the spiritual perspective of the arts, not in the sense of a belief in God, but in the sense of a higher level of human awareness. From your 40 years of worldwide training and teaching, do you feel the martial arts contain spiritual elements?

A: Yes, I would say so, especially at the higher levels. All the way from upper-level aikidokas to the majority of the old Malaysian, Indonesian, and Filipino teachers. They have always preserved this spiritual element. And Filipinos, particularly in the Villabrille system, have always considered that to be the highest element of the art: that which is your particular relationship to the Creator, whatever you may conceive that to be.

The Indonesian, Malaysian and Filipino arts usually don't separate the physical, mental, or spiritual elements of training—at least as far as the older generation goes. I don't know about now, what with the arnis and escrima tournaments coming about because that's more into the tournament aspect of it. But the old—say the first pioneering people from Asia—yes, that was a very main part of their belief and training.

Q: The word "religion" was derived from the Latin word "relegere" which means "to bind" or "hold together," as in the Japanese term "budo." In Asia, one can readily observe the relationship of this in the martial arts through such cultural practices as Zen and Budo. Is there such a relationship in the Filipino martial arts?

A: Yes. Throughout most of the Philippines, the first pioneering peoples that came to the Philippines brought with them the *septagurog*. In their belief system, they taught the word "bahala" (Guro Inosan- to draws on my notepad). This is "ba," the symbol for female, or feminine energy from the word "babahi." This word is "ha," this is the symbol of the sun, or creative energy. This is "la," the symbol for man or male energy. So you have male and female energy (similar to the ancient Chinese Yin and

Yang) and you have creative energy (represented by the sun—similar to the ancient Egyptian Ra). When you put these three symbols together, "ba," "ha," and "la," it means God, or the creative element. You can see by this small example that the combined concepts of physicality and spirituality are integrated into the mechanics of their thinking.

So if you always think of that (the highest creative aspect) first, that's what they're thinking of: you know, that the Creator is always first. In the Villabrille system, this is what we call "Supreme Being." This is you and this is your opponent, [again Guro Inosanto sketches on the notepad]. In the thinking of the Villabrille system, this dictates whether you are going to win or lose so you just go for it because it's their understanding that the outcome of battle has already been predestined. So this is called the "universal triangle" in the Villabrille system. In several other systems, the other part of the triangle is God, the Son, because many of them are Catholic, and the Holy Ghost. This is what they refer to as the "spiritual triangle," and this is the universal triangle. These are the two main triangles in the Villabrille system. God, the Son and the Holy Ghost or the Holy Spirit. This is called the "Supreme Being." That's the term they use, however, whether you want to call it Nature or God, Allah, Yahweh or Elohim, or even Mother Nature, it still represents this highest creative aspect.

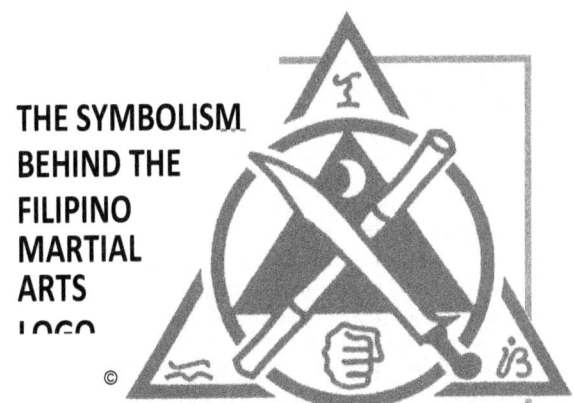

THE SYMBOLISM BEHIND THE FILIPINO MARTIAL ARTS LOGO

©

1. The Universal triangle
2. The circle represents the Creator: form with continuous motion.
3. The Kali triangle: love, compassion, humility
4. The stick: the core of the Filipino martial art. The first weapon taught, from which to learn all other weapons
5. The blade (points upward toward "Life"); the blade is taught after the stick
6. The fist representing the empty hand art of the Philippines
7. The half moon symbolizes the "half" of the Philippines (Southern Philippines) which were never under Spanish rule, and also the "moonlight," which was the only time kali practitioners could safely practice their art during Spanish rule
8. The four parts of the circle represent the four saints called upon by Kali practitioners: Saint Michael, Saint Gabriel, Saint Uriel and Saint Raphael
9. Ancient "K" for kali, kaliradman
10. Ancient "E" for eskrima, estocada and estoke
11. Ancient "S" for silat

© Inosanto Academy

Q: And the root from which these perspectives arrived?

A: This is the basis of the older generation understanding. This is when you have what the Chinese masters call *qi* (or chi) and the Japanese masters call *ki*—it is spiritual energy which is controlled by the mind. I'll show you how this works. [Guro draws another traingle on the note pad]. And this is what they call "the seat of power," which the Hindu masters call "prana." This is what you might call "the mind," the ancient Filipino term for this is "Huha huna." And this is your opponent. So it has to go back and forth between the two—mind and power. But this "Huha huna" really dictates the game—so the mind directs power.

Much of the spiritual aspect was already integrated into the old fighting systems. Along with this, went much symbolism. For example when they take a stick and go like this [Guro Inosanto gestures with a rattan stick in his hand], in the name of the Father and of the Son and of the Holy Ghost, amen, and then they cut the stick. That's their [the old ones] belief. A lot of the training emphasis is placed upon constantly focusing the mind, gearing the mind up toward, putting the subconscious mind into what it's all about. Because the fighting [physical] is just one aspect of the art.

Q: Are there comparable techniques which have survived which can help develop the awareness of the mind and perception?

A: Yes. Each system has developed what we call "breathing exercises" and nowadays you might call it "visualization." I have found this to be very common in many of the Filipino systems. A lot of people were, at one time, concerned about the totality of man. Some say it came from an age of "enlightenment" from Europe and spread to Asia via explorers and various naval powers. Others say, because of the training of the yogis that arrived from India and Tibet, these ideas were never present in the minds of the ancients. The first of the pioneering people came from India, Tibet, and Persia, and they mixed with people of Southeast Asia which changed the physical features and a little bit of the culture, and they proceeded into the Philippines. And this co-mingling of cultures had much to do with the development of these ideas.

There are many, many sources in which they [the old masters] explain that. Visualization is probably one of the most powerful training tools that they taught and still teach to this day, passed down from generation to generation.

Q: Due to technology, there's a certain lack of creative energy in our society, which in turn, renders it further dependent on technology. How do you feel about the martial arts as a tool for the development of creative energy?

A: It is one of the best tools because it's the only "tool" where you are self-testing yourself all the time. Any time you self-test yourself, you have to question yourself, and when you question yourself, you question your purpose in training in the martial arts—what is it for? Is it for power, admiration of your friends, or for gaining money? It could be anything. So you definitely have to question yourself.

Facing-off espada y daga (sword and dagger) against an opponent (1), Inosanto attacks to the neck (2), which is blocked (3), forcing him to attack low (4). Blocking the return thrust (5), Inosanto traps the weapon (6), and attacks the arm (7). Following this up with a neck attack (8), Inosanto immobilizes both of his opponent's arms (9), and thrusts to the chest (10).

Eventually, questions blossom into those such as "what is my place in the universe?" or "why is this universe?" And then, according to the old masters, when we think about it, meditate on it, we may have some idea there was something which was a primal cause in creating it, like a formula. You just kind of "pop out." Man, in general, was like a formula.

The ancient thinking was that you can't just happen to have nothing and throw around random products and hope that they'll form some kind of amalgamation which, given several billion years, will happen to mutate into some type of self-sustaining, perfectly-balanced ecosystem. They believe there was a creator behind that plan. So definitely, specific thinking and minute, contemplative meditation—breaking things down to their smallest common denominator—brings us closer to understanding the "upper levels." Whatever that thing is that draws us closer to understanding self—whatever you conceive it to be—whether you call it Mother Nature or whether it is just realizing your place in the universe.

"The martial arts are a vehicle for self-growth... it teaches you a lot about who you are, what you're capable of doing."

> "We come to realize our physical limitations and we eventually seek a higher meaning in the training, rather than just physically being able to 'kick butt'"

Q: So the martial arts can actually cause you to introspect?

A: It causes you to inspect yourself internally, externally, and realize no matter how much you train, you can lose it. So there's got to be a better goal because we lose it. We can never get as strong as the tiger no matter how much we pump iron; we can never defeat the grizzly bear with our bare hands, right? So we come to realize our physical limitations and we eventually seek a higher meaning in the training rather than just physically being able to "kick butt" and things of that nature.

Q: Many times, the term "higher level" has been used by masters and grandmasters. Could you elaborate on some examples of this term?

A: If you train in the martial arts, I think the first thing you're going to do is to grow physically and martial art-wise. But later on, you'll begin to see that it will help you emotionally, and also mentally—because you can transfer the learning in one field to another field. It will definitely promote personal mental growth. Third and final is that it will help you grow spiritually because you'll realize that the mental, emotional, and physical education cannot possibly be the end.

It's just like the thinking of the ancient Greeks: you have to educate the whole person, you have to develop it's entirety. You must come to expose this higher common creative spiritual element. This is one thing, the physical body, but there are other bodies that we're talking about, more subtle bodies. I won't go into that here because it gets into the mystical teachings. But definitely people can see you grow emotionally, and you're definitely going to grow socially. You need to know how to interact with different people—sometimes a little bit more violently to one group and sometimes more harmonious to another group. You must learn how to deal with it. And then the last part is the spiritual aspect. And then, of course, in-between that is the mental aspect. The mental aspect is that you can use your process of thinking. It can transfer over into other fields—

Q: So then the martial arts in your opinion is...?

A: The martial arts are a vehicle for self-growth. It's like a mirror to look at yourself in—how you're growing, how you're doing. It teaches you a lot about who you are, what you're capable of doing, what you have not achieved, and what you're capable of achieving.

Q: So by using the martial arts, one can form this marriage of the higher self and the physical self?

A: Yes, definitely. Because the belief is that we possess a higher and lower self at the same time. The last of the upper-level training deals with the "flowering" or development of the higher self. You have the subconscious, which is a kind of a lower self, and then you have the higher ability to direct the subconscious, more or less. The upper and lower selves are inclined in one direction or the other. This type of training instills the discipline necessary to move oneself closer to mastery of both selves, and this will then help you in daily life. That is their [the old ones] belief.

Q: If it were your responsibility to initiate this understanding on a grand scale, what do you feel would be necessary to accomplish this task worldwide?

A: I think it is a process of educating different people. You could do it in other ways. It could be other fields; it doesn't have to be martial arts. Martial arts, I think, is quick because it questions you daily

Facing an attacker with a single stick, Inosanto blocks the strike (1), counters to the head (2), then reverses to the chin (3). Trapping the attacker's wrist (4), Inosanto pressures upward against the joint (5), and disarms his opponent (6).

and straight away, so it's a better vehicle in my opinion. You can do it through music—I think you can do it through any art form—but I think in martial arts it deals with it more upfront and personal. When you get into the martial arts you can reach a level of understanding right away because it demands continual self-questioning.

Q: Is that because it involves your eyes and ears and other physical senses?
A: It puts all the senses into play and also goes beyond the senses—and I think that's where it's at. $

Wong Fei Hung's 10 Killing Hands

Bill Fong

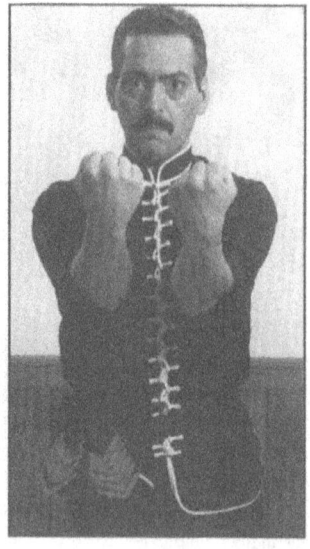

Of the many legends throughout martial arts history, there may be no greater than that of the great grandmaster Wong Fei Hung. During his lifetime (1850-1933) Wong Fei Hung achieved an unsurpassed reputation for martial skills and feats. His life and accomplishments have been portrayed in over 100 movies, usually starring the late and revered Kwan Tak Hing.

Wong Fei Hung began his martial arts training at the age of five under the guidance of his father, Wong Kay Ying. Being a direct disciple of south sil lum master Luk Ah Choy, Wong Kay Ying had much to offer his young son. From his father, Wong Fei Hung had learned the techniques of the dan gong and cern gong kuen (single and double strong hard fists), fuk fu kuen (controlling the tiger fist), gi mo cern do (mother and son double swords), man fu kuen (angry tiger fist), ng long bat gwa gwun (fifth brother eight diagram pole), fei tong (flying hook), and the hak fu kuen (black tiger fist).

But, it was not until master Wong Fei Hung met renowned sifu Tit Kiu Sam that he eventually reformed and refined the southern hung kuen we know today. Both masters had exchanged their techniques, knowledge and experience, since their lineage traced back to the Nam Siu Lam Temple to an individual monk there, Gok Yuen. With the knowledge of Tit Kiu Sam's hand bridge and horse stance, along with the original nam kuen (southern fist) Gee Shim's fat ga lo han kuen (Buddha style abbot fist) and his own fighting techniques, Wong Fei Hung had finally created the fu hok cern ying kuen (tiger/crane double pattern fist form), the trademark of the hung ga style. It was this form that made Wong Fei Hung the most famous nam kuen sifu (southern siu lum master) in China.

The sup juet sao (ten killing hands) comes from the fu hok cern ying kuen. The sup juet sao is a series of ten principles that Wong Fei Hung thought were the most effective killing methods in hung kuen. Because of its effectiveness and practicality, master Hung became a hero in China because he never lost a fight. The main principles are: strike the eyes; stop the breath; break the face; explode the ears; crush the groin; twist the tendons; break the fingers; dislocate the joints; break the elbow; and

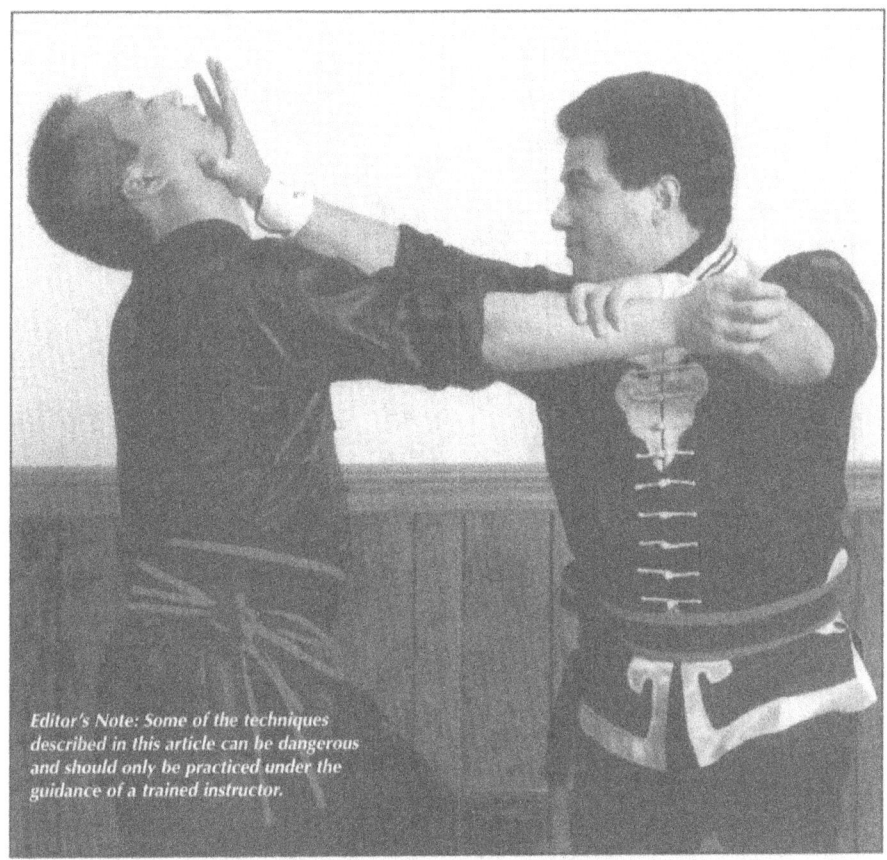

Editor's Note: Some of the techniques described in this article can be dangerous and should only be practiced under the guidance of a trained instructor.

dim mak (nerve points). It should also be noted that without the proper hung ga training (foundation, basics, conditioning, ging, body connection) and comprehension of the style, the ten killing hands would be simply reduced to basic blocks, strikes and grabs.

The techniques accompanying this article demonstrate some of the most common ways to achieve the ten killing hands.

Po Pai Sao—Side Tiger Claw

This technique emphasizes the use of the side tiger claw (jut ming fu). The key points of this technique are: Use the tiger claw to lock and crush the throat (fung hau), which will stop the breath; poke the opponent's eyes, which causes blindness. The object of po pai sau is to block and grab your opponent's punch while stepping back into a side bow stance, then at the same time use your side tiger claw to strike the throat or chin.

These movements accomplish two things—stepping back and sinking—which keep your body away from your opponent's other hand. And by grabbing your opponent's punch and simultaneously locking his throat, it elongates and holds his position so he can neither move forward nor backward.

Side Tiger Claw *The attacker throws a right punch (1). Sifu Tony Franco intercepts with a left grab (2). Franco twists into a bow stance and applies (3) a side tiger claw to lock the throat, pulling the opponent's punch and pushing with the tiger claw. Using the same techniques, instead of locking the throat, apply a tiger claw to the face (4). Strike the chin, push the head back, and then claw the eyes.*

Double Backfist

Sifu Bill Fong attacks with a right-handed collar grab (1). The opponent counters by exploding forward into a bow and arrow stance, with his left hand in a clenched fist (2). He also attacks with a hooking fist. He then sinks into a mid-level cat stance (3), before exploding into a bow and arrow stance and smashing (4) downward with a cern gwa choy faht technique to destroy the facial structure.

Cent Gwa Choy Faht—Double Backfist

The emphasis is on the double fist (cern gwa choy faht) smashing downward upon your opponents face, which causes multiple fractures to the facial structure including the cheekbone, bridge of nose and eye sockets. This technique counters well against a collar grab. As with all hung ga techniques the cern gwa choy faht will only work when used in conjunction with the hung ga footwork.

Key points of this technique are: Remembering to keep your fists close together. This will help you hit your intended target; only by rising, sinking and violently exploding forward into your stances, as well as opening and closing your torso with speed and power, will you be ensured maximum effectiveness.

Heaven Piercing Fist
Bill Fong attacks with a left-handed collar grab (1). John counters (2) with his left foot and sinking into a horse stance, breaks the foe's hold with a golden scissor hand technique. John quickly explodes into a bow and arrow stance (3), simultaneously attacking his opponent's temple and side of his face with a rising backfist. John then delivers the tong tin kueh faht techniques (4) two inches below the floating ribs.

Tong Tin Kuen Faht—Heaven Piercing Fist

This technique emphasizes the uppercut (heaven piercing fist) to the floating ribs. Speed, power and violent aggressive transition from stance to stance is essential for maximum effectiveness of tong tin kuen faht, as with all techniques such as, gum gao gin sao (golden scissor hand) and gwa choy faht (backfist).

Key points include:

- Sealing the breath by attacking the floating ribs two inches below the nipple.
- To obtain maximum power and ensure effectiveness when executing this technique, you must pull back one fist while simultaneously delivering the tong tin kuen faht. Also, you must pull your upper torso back in an erect position at the time of impact, simultaneously advancing with a sliding mouse step.
- Only by sinking into sai ping ma (horse stance) and simultaneously trapping your opponents attacking arm with the gum gao gin sao (golden scissor hand) will you bring your attacker down to set up for the gwa choy faht (backfist).
- Use of the hung ga footwork is essential for the effectiveness of the tong tin kuen faht.

Ngaw Fu Cum Yang—Hungry Tiger Catches The lamb

In this technique, the hung ga tiger claw is emphasized. This is shown by the vise-like grip used to crush the groin and the tearing by the hands to seal the chi and gouge the eyes. When the fingertips of the tiger claw dig into the particular accupoints in the face, you can cause disruption and blockage of chi and blood flow into the opponent's brain, as well as severely damaging the eye organs.

Hungry Tiger Catches the Lamb

John Velasquez executes a left straight facing punch (1). Bill Fong intercepts the attack with his right tiger claw forearm and sinks into a horse stance (2). The defender reaches down with the right tiger claw and crushes the groin of the attacker (3). Fong steps forward into a bow and arrow stance and drives (4) his left tiger claw into the opponent's face.

The important points regarding the ngaw fu cum yang technique are:
- The defender must develop quick hands to block the incoming punches.
- Both hands must work together in unison.
- The body must sink in stance.
- Concentrate on the target.
- Like a tiger, step in strong.

Angry Tiger Descends the Mountain
Velasquez throws a straight facing punch at Fong, who is standing in the on-guard stance (1). Fong intercepts (2) the attack by using the golden scissor hand motion to snap the opponent's elbow joint. The defender sinks his stance (3), twists the left arm of the opponent and applies the right tiger claw onto the elbow to destroy the joint.

Man Fu Ha San—Angry Tiger Descends The Mountain

In this particular grappling technique, the tiger claw is used to exert tremendous pressure onto the opponents elbow joint. By sinking the stance, coupled with the lock onto the joint, the opponents elbow can be seriously and permanently destroyed. The important points to note about the man fu ha san technique are:

• The defender must intercept the incoming attack with the golden scissor hand motion.

• You must step forward and sink into a bow and arrow stance (ging ma) for greater leverage. Remember, this technique can only be executed with proper stancework.

• The rear hand twists the arm until the elbow points up and must pull the opponent's arm back while the top tiger claw presses downward to exert immense pressure on the elbow to break the joint.

San Ban Dan Gwai—Squeeze and Crush the Dan Gwai

This technique puts emphasis on stancework, using pulling, twisting and sinking. Sau ban dan gwai is also known as dai ma gwai cho (take the horse back to the stable). The key points of this technique are:

• Stop the blood flow to the brain by squeezing the neck.

• Dislocate or break the neck by twisting and sinking after squeezing. The object of sau ban dan gwai is to parry or block the opponent's strike as you step in to apply a chokehold. By squeezing the carotid artery, the oxygen supply to the brain is cut off. When your opponent goes limp, step forward and at the same time twist and sink in your stance. This will break or dislocate the neck.

Won Won Bao Hok—Reincarnation of the Fulfilled Crane

In this particular technique, the crane's beak is targeted to the opponent's eye. By using the whipping motion of the attacking arm, the "beak" essentially pierces into the ocular cavity of the skull, thereby destroying the eye. It is important to note that to effectively execute the won won bao hok (reincarnation of the fulfilled crane) technique, you must observe the following:

• The whipping energy, or "bin ging," must be executed with the turning of the waist at the same time to achieve a greater impact. Also, the striking hand must be kept relaxed to acquire the whipping power.

• The escaping of the grip on the wrist, using a snake motion, must flow immediately into the won won bao hok strike unleashed to the opponent's eye in a fluid, quick and continuous manner.

Squeeze and Crush the Dan Gwai
The opponent attacks with a right punch (1), which is deflected downward with a circular block (2). A grab brings the opponent in and off balance (3). Franco applies a chokehold and checks the opponent's arm (4). Franco locks the arm, twists and sinks, breaking his opponent's neck (5).

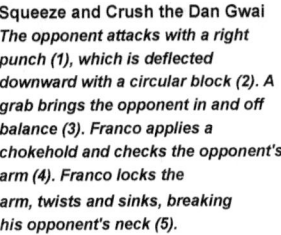

Hau Gi Tao Toe—Monkey Steals the Peach

This technique is used to twist tendons and break bones (usually fingers and collarbones). The key points here are to grab, squeeze, twist and lock on to your opponent's attack. By grabbing the fingers and twisting up (also called tiger climbs up mountain) you will subdue and break the fingers.

When attacking the collarbone and using all four key points, you will not only cause the bone to break, but also cause severe nerve and tendon damage. Hung gas tiger claw training will condition the hands to make this technique effective.

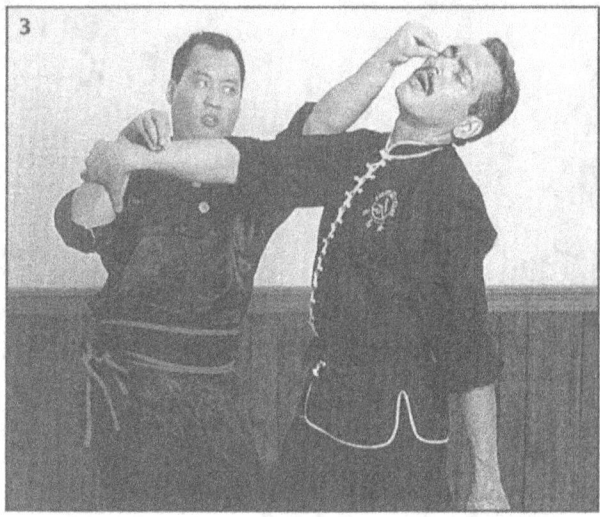

Reincarnation of the Fulfilled Crane

The opponent grabs Fong's right hand (1). Using a snake-like coiling motion, Fong circles his hand around in a clockwise direction to release the grip (2). Fong then unleashes his counterstrike (3) with his left-hand crane's beak to destroy the opponent's eye.

Cern Fei Wu Dip—**Double Flying Butterfly**

This technique is used to damage and dislocate the tailbone. The key points here are to use a strong tiger claw for grabbing and low twisting stances to develop power for striking. Double flying butterflies got its name because the hand and foot positions are open and form the shape of a butterfly.

Fu Pao Cern Kuen—Tiger Leopard Fist

In this technique, emphasis is placed on slapping the ears with double leopard paw strikes. This forces air into the ear drums, which causes them to explode and disorients the opponent.

You can also use fu pao cern kuen to attack your opponent's eyes. This technique counters well against a double-handed collar grab. Key points of this technique include:

• You must sink into the diu ma (cat stance) while simultaneously executing the man fu yan ngam (hiding tiger) to create an opening.

• The use of ging (inch power) is extremely important for maximum effectiveness. Also key is exploding forward into yee jee kim yeurng ma (crane stance).

• You can finish your opponent by stopping the flow of oxygen to the heart and brain by wrapping your arm around the opponent's neck.

• Use of the hung ga footwork, as well as speed and power, is essential for the sup juet sao to work.

In hung kuen, Wong Fei Hung dedicated his life to the research and study of this art. As a result, grandmaster Wong preserved the traditional hung style and raised it to the next level. The sup juet sao is among the famous series of techniques supplemented within the fu hok cern ying kuen, tiger crane double form. Other techniques and philosophies are also incorporated with the structure of this famous form, such as ten tiger and eight crane techniques.

Bill Fong (Kwong Wai Lum) is director of the Staten Island branch of Yees Hung Gar-Fongs Hung Ga Kung Fu Association and an inner room disciple of master Frank Yee (Yee Chee Wai). He is a former deputy secretary general of the United Kung Fu Federation of North America.

The Fighting Prince

Sheik Tahnoon Bin Zayed of the United Arab Emirates is a real-life Arabian prince, one of the Middle East's most dynamic young leaders, and one of the best friends the martial arts have ever had.

Todd Hester & Kid Peligro

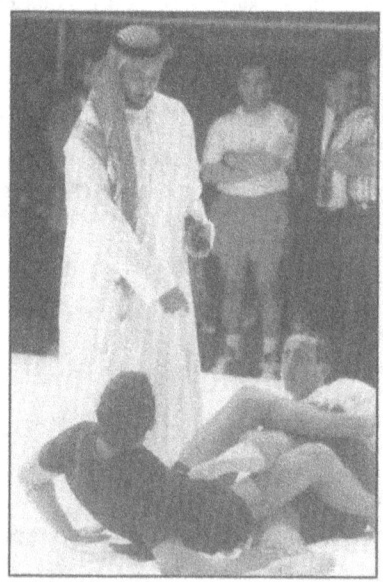

If you were lucky enough to be enrolled in San Diego State University in the late '80s, and just happened to study Brazilian jiu-jitsu from Nelson Monteiro, you might remember a classmate named "Ben" who was quiet, courteous, unassuming, and always more than happy to spend an hour or two after class cleaning the mat. But if you think that Ben was just another face in the crowd, you'd be sadly mistaken. In reality, Ben was Sheik Tahnoon Bin Zayed, the son of the President of the United Arab Emirates, one of the planet's wealthiest men, and one of the Arab world's most dynamic young leaders.

"I still remember the first time he walked into the school," classmate Gerry Costa says. "He was with an Englishman named Guy Neivens and they both wanted to study jiu-jitsu, so Nelson made an appointment for the following afternoon. But when we showed up the next day there was a note on the door from Guy, saying that he and Ben had come by but that no one was there—Nelson had forgotten the appointment. So Nelson called them and rescheduled for the next morning. When we showed up the next day there was another note on the door from them—Nelson had forgotten two days in a row." Costa laughs. "But Ben was very even tempered and didn't seem to mind, which in retrospect, considering who he is, is a little amazing. They came back again and finally got hooked up."

The class soon learned that Ben had a background in karate, judo, and several other styles, and had been studying martial arts since childhood. He told his classmates that he had become interested in submission grappling from watching Royce Gracie fight in the UFC and was amazed that some-

one could take on, and defeat, men so much larger. He also said he was interested in all the grappling arts and simply wanted to learn what worked.

In addition to Brazilian jiu-jitsu, he also started studying the instructional tapes of Oleg Taktarov, whom he saw in the UFC and greatly admired. "Tahnoon really liked leg locks," Costa recalls. "He watched Oleg's sambo tapes and started going after everyone's ankles and knees constantly. We used to complain to him, "You're watching too many of Oleg's tapes. Stop it!"

Tahnoon also enjoyed training at different schools and traveled throughout Southern California with Neivens, seeking to gain the most knowledge he could from his time in America. On one occasion he went to a well-known grappling school and inquired, in his typical low-key manner, about the possibility of taking private classes. The owner looked at the modestly-dressed foreigner and said, "I don't think that you can afford privates. They are very expensive. You had better consider training elsewhere." Tahnoon simply nodded and said, "Perhaps you are right. I probably belong somewhere else."

For two years, Prince Tahnoon trained regularly with Monteiro, not revealing his true identity. Usually the first to show up for class, he would often stay late to help Monteiro clean up and close down the school. All the time, no one suspected they had an undercover prince in their midst.

"Guy always seemed like he was in charge," Costa recalls. "When we went out to dinner, he did most of the talking and would pull out the cash—he wasn't flashy but he always paid all the bills himself." It soon became apparent that the two definitely weren't your typical pair of college roommates. An outspoken Englishman and an earnest Arabian are not two people you see hanging out in San

Tahnoon and Jerry Costa

Diego everyday. After a while, everyone in the class decided that Neivens was simply a rich Englishman and that Ben was his bodyguard.

"Because I thought that Tahnoon worked for Neivens," Costa recalls, "I always tried to give him extra hints. Guy was pretty good at jiu-jitsu, so I would always take Tahnoon aside and tell him, 'I'm going to show you some new moves so you can kick your bosses butt and make him tap.'" Costa smiles at the memory. "Tahnoon always nodded at me with a simple smile, without much expression, even though he had to be laughing inside. But because I knew him from the beginning as just a fel-

low student and a friend, I got to see the true side of him—which was unassuming, modest, friendly, helpful, and very patient with people."

"He was tough as nails, though," Costa continues, "don't get me wrong. During one of his first classes, Nelson slammed him to the mat and he landed awkwardly on his thumb. Nelson told Tah- noon that it was just dislocated and then yanked on it like crazy to set it. Then he told Tahnoon to keep training. So Tahnoon went ahead and trained for another hour, his thumb getting bigger and bigger. Finally, his entire hand swelled to the size of a football and Nelson told him to go get it checked. When Tahnoon came back the next day his entire hand was in a cast—the thumb had been badly broken." Costa shakes his head. "To this day we don't know if Tahnoon broke it when he fell, or if Nelson broke it when he tried to fix it."

On another occasion, one of the senior students in the class was telling "Ben" about a new car Dodge had just come out with named the Viper—which was not yet commercially available. Tahnoon, who also loved cars, became very enthusiastic. "Yes, I have a Viper."

The student just shook his head. "Yes, I'm sure in your country that you have a lot of snakes— you probably keep them as pets—but I'm talking about a car."

Tahnoon, excited to talk with a fellow auto enthusiast, wouldn't quit though. "No, I have a Viper, a red one. I'll show it to you. You can play with it."

The student just nodded condescendingly. "You can paint your snake any color you want, buddy, but I'm not going to touch the thing. I don't like snakes."

Fhe next day at class, as they were training, a horn sounded outside the school, loud and long. The car buff looked out to see what was going on and then called the others to the window with a trembling voice. "You're not going to believe this!" There, sitting outside in a bright, red Dodge Viper, was "Ben," eagerly waving at his friends to come outside so he could take them for a spin.

Soon after that, Tahnoon told his classmates that he was preparing to return home. "I was very sad," Costa recalls, "because he was like family to me. He asked Nelson to go out to dinner with him one night.

Sheik Tahnoon spends time with the press before the 1999 World Championships at Abu Dhabi.

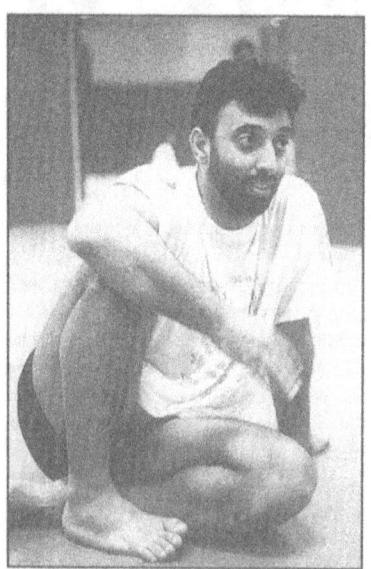

At about 1:00 in the morning I get a breathless phone call from Nelson: 'Gerry, you're not going to believe this, but Ben is the boss and Guy works for him—a lot of people work for him—an entire country! And he wants me to go there and open up a school!' I was shocked at first but then I didn't believe him—no one did until Tahnoon told us himself. But then you could see it in him. I mean, Tahnoon was a leader without ever claiming to be one. He never asked anyone to do anything that he wouldn't do himself and he always led by example."

Tahnoon and Neivens (the real bodyguard) returned to the emirates shortly afterwards. A few months later Monteiro followed and opened the first school of Brazilian jiu-jitsu in the entire Middle East. For Sheik Tahnoon, though, this was only the beginning. He immediately adopted over twenty homeless orphans, got involved in several charities to take care of many more, and began training the children in martial arts, inviting teachers of all disciplines to come to Abu Dhabi to teach classes. With large groups of children needing a place to train, Tahnoon built the Abu Dhabi Combat Club, a state-of-the-art training center where the children, and serious martial artists from both inside and outside the country, could train.

From all over the world, Tahnoon invited such noted fighters as jiu-jitsu champions Royler and Renzo Gracie, American mixed-martial artist Matt Hume, Russian world champion wrestler Alexandre "Sasha" Savbo, and world judo champion Kareem Barchalov to either follow in Monteiro's footsteps and move there to teach, or come and give guest instruction.

"I have been all over the world," three-time world jiu-jitsu champion Royler Gracie says. "I have been in the U.S. Olympic Training Center in Colorado Springs and the best gyms in South America, Europe, and Japan, and I have never seen anything like the Abu Dhabi Combat Club—nothing is even close."

Royler's cousin, no-holds-barred fighter Renzo Gracie, agrees. "Prince Tahnoon has spared no expense to make a facility where world-class fighters can train in world-class surroundings. He didn't have to share it with anyone, but he did. He wants to advance the martial arts by having a place where the top experts can come and offer instruction and also learn from each other through friendly, intense competition."

To this end, Tahnoon started the Abu Dhabi World Submission Wrestling Championships. Now

"He immediately adopted over twenty homeless orphans, got involved in several charities to take care of many more, and began training the children in martial arts."

in its third year, the year 2000 championships are slated to go off March 1,2, and 3 in the 3,000- seat Abu Dhabi Combat Club Arena. Attracting top fighters from all over the world, the list of past and present competitors reads like a who's who of grappling and includes such stars as Mark Kerr, Mario Sperry, Royler and Renzo Gracie, the Inoue brothers, the Machado brothers, John Lewis, and the Chinese National Judo Team—and that is just a small sampling. All told, over 100 fighters will travel to Abu Dhabi this year to compete for the title of World's Greatest Grappler.

Last years standout, Raptor Team member Jean-Jacques Machado, winner of the Best Technique Trophy, puts it this way. "If you want to compete against the best, you have to go to Abu Dhabi. Everyone who is anyone in submission wrestling is invited. If someone is not there, it isn't because they weren't invited—all the top guys are asked—it's just because they don't want to face the best."

Costa, still living in San Diego but now an advisor to Tahnoon on the Abu Dhabi championships, is perhaps best suited to offer an insight into the mind of the Fighting Prince. "In order to understand what motivates Tahnoon you just have to keep in mind one thing—he loves the martial arts and he loves the fighters. It's very simple. He wants to give top martial artists a place to train and compete that is worthy of their skills."

"And don't think that the world championships are the end of his plans," Costa says mysteriously. "I have a feeling that it's only the beginning." He laughs. "Just remember the story of the Viper— there's always more to Sheik Tahnoon than meets the eye."

Seeking the Softness of Hung Gar

The average student will tell you hung gar is the most external martial art on earth. But dig a little deeper and you'll find a soft, subtle side known to only advanced stylists.

Calvin Chin

Much of what I've seen of hung gar supports the popular notion that the style is an external martial art. This classification is a misnomer and does not begin to characterize this traditional multifaceted system.

When my students exhibit hung gar, they are often misunderstood and considered to be practicing a hybrid system. Our use of natural strength is in conflict with what is perceived to be strength in martial arts. However, taken to a higher level, hung gar is both an internal as well as external martial art. In fact, all martial arts must be refined to the level of internal as well as external to fully appreciate their practical application.

Just as hardness in the sense of stiffness is not what creates external power, softness in the sense of flaccidity is not what creates internal power. In fact, hard and soft are two extremes we never want to reach. The external aspects of all martial arts must be guided by internal principles to develop explosive executions. However, internal principles are not achieved simply by practicing in slow motion.

Divide And Conquer

Too often, the hardness prevalent in hung gar comes from stiffness resulting in brute force or dead strength. This is because movements are being isolated. Isolation of movement is what we strive to overcome at the higher levels. The internal aspect of all martial arts is achieved when mind and body become integrated and movements become totally connected with balance and strength and total body coordination. It is not easy to see the soft side of hung gar at its higher levels because the subtleties of the movements are camouflaged within their transitions. Softness comes from the ability to yield to movements through sequential coordination of body components. This is considered live strength, yielding and pliable. The body works together as a connected unit, not as separate isolated movements.

All hung gar is noted for its bridges and low stances. There may be slight variances in form sequence, but more often the difference is in the execution of techniques. The strength and stiffness of execution will vary in practitioners, depending on their level of understanding. Beginners view power as strength so they have difficulty practicing a martial art without using strength. Because beginners do not understand how to use their strength, their movements are done with too much

Hung gar's Dragon Waves Tail

force and postures become stiff. Their tendency to use excessive strength in the arm requires their bodies to be rigid. This is reactive tension created to compensate for the excessive force generated by the arm. In this rigid state, the practitioner loses balance when stepping is incorporated. The irony is that using excessive strength leads to stiffness, which becomes a hindrance rather than an asset in the execution of technique.

Hung gar has a history of hardness. The early martial artists were vagabonds who traveled and learned from different teachers. They tended to become attached to the hard side of the martial art because it was more easily attainable. Today's society is not much different. People want to learn things fast. By learning things fast, they misinterpret strength and are misguided through their learning experience. Hung gar is not often practiced to the soft stage of refinement because not everyone trains for a long period of time or has the opportunity to study with the great masters.

To Another Level

Taking martial arts to more advanced, softer levels require time to develop muscle memory and programming of the sequential events that underlie motor skills. What most practitioners have attained

Hung gar's Lion Plays with Ball.

is the hard or external level. The agility of footwork and the softness comes with years and years of training and enough time to understand the principles of hung gar.

The use of natural strength is contrary to our perception of power. Power as brute force is more commonly accepted. However, once this concept of hard execution is adopted, it is very difficult to change until the methods change. And the methods can't change until the understanding of the movement changes. At that point, the teacher has to offer guidance to soften the movements.

Hardness can also be learned through assimilation. If a teacher exhibits dynamic power, then the students will pick up the hardness through mimicry without understanding the true execution. This lack of understanding can manifest itself into stiff execution and over time it becomes habit. Breaking that habit is a process that

Black Tiger Claw
Chin uses vertical elbow to redirect Kalaitzidis' punch (1). Chin sinks and Kalaitzidis is diverted downward (2). While sticking to Kalaitzidis' arm, Chin turns and follows through with a left palm push while locking Kalaitzidis' leg (3). This is the connection between upper and lower body.

Its the training approach that makes the difference. The goal is to attain a naturalness in the postures that is inherent in the geometry of one's skeletal make-up. Levers and fulcrums play an important role in body mechanics, which help maximize the efficiency of the strength used to create a force. Using natural strength, students develop soft movement without the stiffness that is apparent in many styles and learn to create the same force without excessive strength. Once this concept is understood, then the student is ready to evolve to the next stage of development, whereby the same process is followed.

Natural Movements

In traditional systems such as hung gar, characteristics and principles are built into the forms. The guidelines that control the characteristics of the system are further governed by the principles in martial art theory. This helps a practitioner achieve a high level of martial skill. Until the principles are absorbed into the body and mind and become natural, the movements will be forced. The founders of these styles had the insight and depth to create the forms as a mapping of footwork and strategies and as a means of preserving their systems. They are the textbooks of traditional kung-fu systems and equivalent to the precepts of the *Tai Chi Classics*.

Crane Beak, Hook and Strike
Turning waist is the key as Chin intercepts Kalaitzidis[1] punch with hook hand and deflects with his forearm at Kalaitzidis' elbow (1). In a continuous motion, Chin strikes Kalaitzidis[1] face with an explosive fingerjab (2).

Lion Plays With Bull
Chin sinks with a corner backfist using a forearm bridge to redirect Kalaitzidis[1] punch (1). While sticking to Kalaitzidis[1] arm, Chin turns and follows through with a punch to his chest (2).

Hung gar
elbow press

Double Bow Posture

Chin blocks and uses a forearm in an oblique angle to deflect (1). Kalaitzidis follows with a right punch while Chin adjusts his position to defend (2). Chin turns and follows through with a double palm strike (3).

Hung gar heel kick to knee and palm strike to neck.

"Too often, the hardness prevalent in hung gar comes from stiffness resulting in brute force or dead strength."

Many people practice form without knowing its true purpose. Built into the form are imagery, fundamental principles and martial guidelines and through the stages of refining the form, a student evolves into the higher levels. The 12 bridges of hung gar categorize the methods of the hand maneuvers. They are guided by other principles in what is termed as the five coordinates: hand, eye, body, waist and stance. These coordinates must work in unison to achieve a higher skill level. The summation of components, the five coordinates result into total body movement, a concept that is more evident in the internal systems, but is inherent in all martial arts in its advanced stages.

The hard and the soft theories should be prevalent in all systems of martial arts. At the higher levels where hard and soft meet, the distinction between external and internal cannot be detected. Hardness and softness are not what appear on the surface. However, hardness works even when it is not generated from natural strength. But softness is ineffective without a deeper understanding of

Rising block with uppercut

within softness there is hardness. Ultimately, there should be a
the hard, never the other way around. To execute a movement
elaxed. A movement has to be
on of opposing groups of
there is tension that creates

n direct the movement better
'd not as being rigid, but
loes not mean that movements
In our hung gar training, we
ise of hard and soft execu-
pparent and the focus should
power. Developing good tran-
g correct body alignment
allows the practitioner to use innate strength and to use it efficiently. It is more difficult to make the transition from hard to soft, but once you have developed softness, you can never be rigid.

There is no secret formula in finding the softness in hung gar. The soft stage evolves over time through the understanding of the
the mechanics of the movement and the body's understanding of the principles that guide it.

Palm strike with leg sweep

Principles are subjective through interpretation. If the practitioner is not at a level where the principle can be interpreted as a concept of integration and the unification of body components, the movement remains stiff. When the principles are in place, the sequence of postures in a form should be fluid. Fluidity comes from the linkage of postures through the transitions. The postures may be similar, but the transitions are varied, all of which are guided by martial arts principles. Any practitioner who wants to seek the soft level has to analyze and re-learn many of the movements. Taking a single form to its highest level is how a student achieves in martial arts.

Balancing Hard And Soft

guidelines and principles of a traditional system. Fundamental guidelines and principles are the true differences between what is traditional and what is eclectic. Hybrid systems are created when complex concepts and theories are extrapolated and then simplified from traditional systems. In their fragmented and eclectic state, they do not contain the depth of information found in whole traditional systems.

The knowledge gained in a traditional system taught by a qualified teacher is boundless because evolution is endless. You constantly discover and reinforce your understanding of what is attainable in martial arts.

Heal Pains, Strains Instantly

These ancient Chinese herbal remedies will keep you off the shelf and on your feet.

Thomas Richard Joiner

Over the years I have known many misguided martial artists who, as a result of their preoccupation with muscle development, paid little attention to strengthening and developing the supporting structures, ligaments and tendons. The frequency of this oversight is substantiated by the high number of injuries involving sprained, strained, pulled, twisted, and torn ligaments and tendons. These fairly common injuries usually occur during training.

Ligaments, the fibrous tissues that connect bones to bones, undergo two common injuries: minor sprains and tears. Minor sprains are treated with ice to reduce swelling, then bandaged for support, followed by physical therapy when needed.

Safflower

Reprinted with permission from The Warrior As Healer by Thomas Richard Joiner, published by Healing Arts Press, an imprint of Inner Traditions International, Rochester, VT 05767; ©1999 by Thomas Richard Joiner. To order call (800) 246-8648.

The more serious torn ligament usually requires surgical repair, after which it is immobilized in a soft cast (to allow proper healing). Like a broken bone, a torn ligament requires a lengthy healing time, usually six-to-eight weeks.

Tendons, on the other hand, are fibrous cords connecting muscle to bone. Common injuries include ruptures and inflammation—what is called tendonitis. Occasionally tendons are severed; surgery is required to reconnect their torn ends. In some cases it is necessary to graft tendon from elsewhere in the body or from a donors tendon to reconnect them.

Treatment for ruptures and tendonitis consists of resting the affected body part, applying ice packs, and using herbal therapy to reduce inflammation, alleviate swelling, and restore normal blood flow.

Increased amounts of stretching, practicing tai chi chuan, and using herbal supplements are some of the techniques recommended to develop and strengthen ligaments and tendons to avoid injury.

Herbal Formulas That Aid Recovery from Torn Ligaments or Tendons
Raw Form Preparation
Qi Li San *(Seven Thousandths of a Tael Powder)*
Pang Xie Lao Wo Nui Tang *(Prescription for Treatment of Injury to Tendons)*
Shaolin Shuang Jin Xue Gu Dan *(Shaolin Strengthen the Sinews and Connect the Bones Elixir)*
Shaolin Zhan Jin Dan *(Extend the Sinews Elixir)*
Patent Formula
Qi Li San *(Seven Thousandths of a Tael Powder)*

Martial artists know well that to excel they must spend an equal amount of time developing strength and flexibility. The body of the karateka and kung-fu practitioner must be flexible. Such suppleness can be acquired through a program of prescribed stretching exercises. Unfortunately, one of the features of rigorous flexibility training is the occasional sprained or torn ligament.

Qi Li San is renowned for reducing the healing time of a torn ligament. This formula will invigorate the blood, promote the movement of chi, and reduce swelling and pain.

Qi Li San is also available in a prepared patent formula for those who prefer the convenience of using

Injury-Management Formulas
Prescription for Treatment of Injury to Tendons

In this formula traditional Chinese medicine has an excellent remedy for the treatment of injured tendons and ligaments that, regrettably, many in Western culture find repulsive. I hope this aversion can be overcome, since the remedy is famous for providing quick relief.

A freshwater soft-shell crab, what the Chinese call pang xie, and a large snail known as lao wo nui, are used. To prepare this formula, the snail is removed from its shell and then smashed. The crab, although left in its shell, is smashed as well. Then the two are mixed and applied to the affected area. The area is covered with a broad, cloth bandage and then wrapped firmly with white gauze. This formula will quickly reduce the swelling from strained tendons and ligaments. Discard it after the swelling is reduced.

Qi Li San Herbal Ingredients

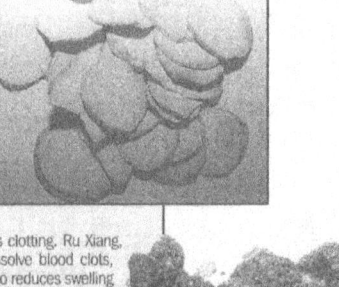
Dragon's blood resin

Grams Needed	Chinese Name	English Translation
30	Xue Jie	dragon's blood resin
4.5	Hong Hua	safflower
4.5	Ru Xiang	frankincense
4.5	Mo Yao	myrrh
.36	She Xiang	deer gland secretions
.36	Bing Pian	camphor resin
7.5	Er Cha	cutch paste
3.6	Zhu Sha	cinnabar

Frankincense

Analysis of the herbs in this formula

Hong Hua circulates the blood and prevents clotting. Ru Xiang, She Xiang, and Bing Pian all alleviate pain, dissolve blood clots, reduce swelling, and promote healing. Mo Yao also reduces swelling and alleviates pain. Er Cha primarily clears infection and has the minor ability to stop bleeding. Xue Jie can be used either internally or externally to stop bleeding; it will strengthen the sinews as well as being useful for treating symptoms related to injuries from falls, contusions, fractures, and sprains. Zhu Sha has a sedative effect.

Recommended Method of Preparation
Mix the herbs and then grind them into a fine powder.

Recommended Dosage
Mix 1.5 grams of powder with 4 ounces of sweet rice wine or warm water.
Drink daily until healing is complete.

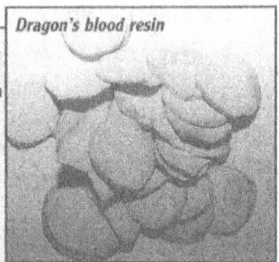
Myrrh

Shaolin Shuang Jin Dan Herbal Ingredients

White peony root

Grams Needed	Chinese Name	English Translation
60	Dang Gui	tang-kuei root
30	Chuan Xiong	lovage root
30	Bai Shao	white peony root
30	Shu Di Huang	wine-cooked Chinese foxglove root
30	Du Zhong	eucommia bark
60	Wu Jia Pi	five-bark root
90	Gu Sui Bu	mender of shattered bones rhizome
30	Gui Zhi	Saigon cinnamon twig
30	Tian Chi Ginseng	pseudo ginseng
30	Hu Gu	tiger bone*
60	Bu Gu Zhi	scuffy pea fruit
60	Tu Si Zi	dodder seeds
60	Dang Shen	relative root
30	Mu Gua	quince fruit
60	Liu Ji Nu	Liu's residing slave
90	Tu Bie Chong	wingless cockroach
30	Huang Qi	milk vetch root
60	Xu Duan	teaselroot

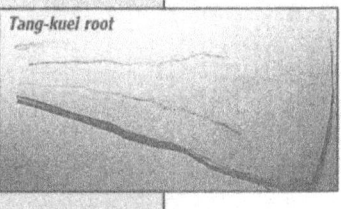
Tang-kuei root

* Tiger bone is an illegal substance in the United States.

Analysis of the herbs in this formula

The herbs Dang Gui, Bai Shao, and Shu Di Huang all enrich the blood and stop pain, while Chuan Xiong, Gui Zhi, and Mu Gua circulate the blood. Du Zhong, Wu Jia Pi, and Hu Gu all strengthen bones and sinews. Xu Duan heals fractured bones. Tian Chi Ginseng and Bu Gu Zhi stop bleeding. Tu Si Zi assists in stopping bleeding, but its main function—along with Dang Shen and Huang Qi—is circulating the chi. Liu Ji Nu, Gu Sui Bu, and Tu Bie Chong all relieve pain, prevent blood clots, and accelerate healing.

Recommended Method of Preparation
Mix the herbs and grind them into a fine powder to be used as pills. Traditionally, this formula was intended to be made into pills; if you prefer, however, you may prepare the herbs in capsule form.

Recommended Dosage
Take 1 pill twice a day, drink with sweet rice wine at room temperature, until healing is complete.

Caution: Any formula containing Tian Chi Ginseng should not be used by pregnant women. It could harm the fetus!

 Best of CFW Enterprises, 2000

Shaolin Shuang Jin Xue Gu Dan *(Shaolin Strengthen the Sinews and Connect the Bones Elixir)*

A useful formula for those who might be turned off by the preceding one is Shaolin Shuang Jin Xue Gu Dan. It strengthens the tendons and ligaments and shortens the healing time after an injury.

Extend the Sinews Elixir

This last formula used to treat ligaments and tendons is like a combination of all those previously mentioned. It was well-known among ancient martial artists for its abilities to aid in the healing of strains and tears. Shaolin Zhan Jin Dan is considered especially useful for martial artists practicing styles that require a more rigorous stretching regimen, such as wushu acrobatics, which require astounding physical agility. Strains and tears of ligaments are likely to occur more frequently in these styles.

Extend The Sinews Elixir Herbal Ingredients

Grams Needed	Chinese Name	English Translation
60	Dang Gui	tang-kuei root
60	Chuan Xiong	lovage root
45	Hong Hua	safflower
45	Tao Ren	peach kernel
90	Zi Ran Ton	pyrite (dip in vinegar 7 times)
60	Tu Bie Chong	wingless cockroach
90	Ma Qian Zi	nux vomica seed (remove the hairs)
90	Xue Jie	dragon's blood resin
30	Jiang Huang	tumeric rhizome
60	Bai Zhi	angelica root
30	Mu Xiang	costus root
30	Chen Pi	ripe tangerine peel
15	Chen Xiang	aloeswood
15	Xiao Hui Xiang	fennel fruit
60	Tian Chi Ginseng	pseudo ginseng
90	Ru Xiang	frankincense
90	Mo Yao	myrrh
90	Chi Shao	red peony
90	Xiang Fu	nut grass rhizome
90	Er Cha	cutch paste
12	Ji Xue Teng	chicken blood vine
30	She Xiang	deer gland secretions
30	Chuan Wu Tou	processed aconite appendage
60	Feng Xian Hua	impatiens flower
60	Ma Huang	hemp yellow
9	Zhu Sha	cinnabar
3	Bing Pian	camphor resin

Analysis of the Herbs in This Formula

Dang Gui enriches the blood and stops pain. Chuan Xiong, Hong Hua, Ji Xue Teng, Tao Ren, and Chi Shao circulate the blood. Zi Ran Ton, Tu Bie Chong, Ru Xiang, Xiao Hui Xiang, She Xiang, and Bing Pian all dissolve blood clots and alleviate pain. Chuan Wu Tou, Mo Yao, and Feng Man Hua reduce swelling and resolve infection. Tian Chi Ginseng and Xue Jie stop bleeding. Chen Xiang, Jiang Huang, Ma Qian Zi, and Xiang Fu circulate chi. Mu Xiang and Chen Pi calm the stomach. Er Cha clears infection. Zhu Sha has a mild sedative effect. Ma Huang and Bai Zhi accelerate healing.

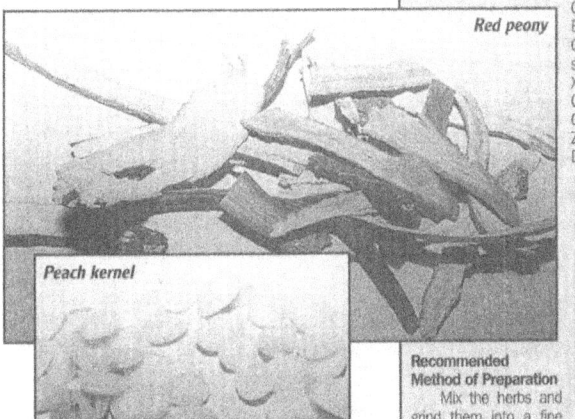

Red peony

Peach kernel

Angelica root

Cutch paste

Recommended Method of Preparation

Mix the herbs and grind them into a fine powder to be made into pills. Traditionally, this formula was prepared as pills; if you prefer, however, you may put the herbs into capsules.

Recommended Dosage

Take 1-to-2 pills (each containing 4.5 grams of powdered herbs) twice daily with room-temperature sweet rice wine until healing is complete.

Caution: Any herbal formula containing Tian Chi Ginseng should not be used by pregnant women. It could harm the fetus.

Herbal Oils, Liniments and Salves

> "Tieh Ta Yao Gin is effective for treating sprains, torn ligaments, strained muscles, and bruises. It will reduce swelling and repair broken blood vessels; it can be used for cuts and abrasions."

Regular participation in any athletic activity invariably results in occasional injury, and martial arts are no exception. Admittedly, the potential for serious injury (such as broken bones) does exist to a somewhat greater degree in martial arts than in many other activities, primarily because of the amount of sparring or simulated fighting that is necessary to perfect technique and improve skills. However, when the importance of controlling technique is emphasized, serious injury can be kept to a minimum.

By far the most common injuries seen in martial arts are the minor aches and pains that occur as a result of strenuous daily training. These minor injuries have always been accepted as a normal part of development by martial arts practitioners. Anyone who seriously embarks on the study of martial arts soon becomes familiar with the expression "No pain, no gain."

At one time a standard part of martial arts training was informal instruction in the use of herbal oils and liniments to effectively manage sore muscles and strained ligaments. Such formulas are considered important not only for treating existing injuries but also as a way to avoid any long-range side effects, such as arthritis and rheumatism, that can develop many years after an original injury has occurred.

Patent Formulas

Zheng Gu Shui *(Rectify Bone Liquid)*
Tieh Ta Yao Gin *(Traumatic Injury Medicine-Essence)*
Hsuing Tan Tieh Wan *(Bear Gallbladder Traumatic Injury Pills*)*
Te Xiao Yao Tong Ling *(Specific Lumbaglin)*

Rectify Bone Liquid *(Also known as Zheng Gui Shui Analgesic Liniment)*

This is without a doubt one of the most powerful liniments available in Chinese medicine. It is especially effective for deep bone bruises and hairline fractures.

When using Zheng Gu Shui special care must be taken by those with fair or delicate skin; prolonged contact can cause blistering or irritation. (If either develops, immediately discontine use.) However, if you can get past this side effect, this herbal liniment is one of the most effective available.

How to Use This Patent Formula

To properly use Zheng Gu Shui soak a square piece of gauze in the liniment and place it over the injury. Cover the gauze with plastic wrap, making it as airtight as possible. Zheng Gu Shui should start to "heat up" the injured area. Leave it on for 20-to-30 minutes, then remove the gauze and discard.

Caution: Zheng Gu Shui is for external use only. It should not be taken internally.

Traumatic Injury Medicine—Essence *(Also known as Die Da Yao Jing)*

While not as powerful as Zheng Gu Shui, Tieh Ta Yao Gin is excellent and can be used for a variety of traumatic injuries. It is effective for treating sprains, torn ligaments, strained muscles, and bruises. It will reduce swelling and repair broken blood vessels; it can be used for cuts and abrasions. It also eliminates dark purple bruised blood and invigorates the chi and blood, thus expediting healing.

How to Use This Patent Formula

Rub this liniment into the injured area, then cover the area with a towel. Keep the towel over the injured area for at least 30 minutes.

Bear Gallbladder Traumatic Injury Pills* *(Also Known as Xiong Dan Die Da Wan)*

This formula is very popular in China for the treatment of martial arts injuries. It invigorates blood circulation, reduces swelling, and breaks up stagnant blood while promoting the healing of broken blood vessels. Martial artists use it for all kinds of bruises, sprains, and swelling from the trauma of punches, kicks, and falls.

HsuingTan Tieh Wan comes in boxes of 10 pills. Dissolve 1 pill in hot water and drink it like tea. Take a second pill and dissolve it in rubbing alcohol; this should then be rubbed onto the affected area.

Caution: Do not use Hsuing Tan Tieh Wan if there is bleeding or an open wound. Also, the formula should not be used internally by a pregnant woman. It could harm the fetus.

* *Bear gallbladder is an illegal substance in the United States.*

Te Xiao Yao Tong Ling Patent Formula *(Specific Lumbaglin)*

Te Xiao Yao Tong Ling is a famous patent medicine, available in pill form, that is used to relax pulled muscles or tendons and to relieve inflammation. The formula can be used for muscle strain or constriction anywhere in the body. It is excellent for long-term use and can also be considered for use in the early stages of training (for relaxing or warming up muscles and tendons), thereby avoiding some of the soreness and discomfort that normally occur before the body becomes fully conditioned.

How to Use This Patent Medicine

Te Xiao Yao Tong Ling comes in boxes of 24 capsules. Take 1-to-3 capsules daily as needed, according to the instructions included in each package. ®

Muay Thai: The National Sport of Thailand

To the people of this Southeast Asia nation, muay Thai, or Thai boxing, is a combination of the NBA, the NFL, and Major League Baseball.

Terry L. Wilson

The ancient art of muay Thai is synonymous with Thailand. In Bangkok, huge stadiums are packed nightly with exuberant fans that treat each fight as if they were at an NBA playoff game. The highest-rated television show is the weekly one-hour muay Thai telecast in addition to a daily radio talk show dedicated to muay Thai. With all this adulation, the popularity of muay Thai goes unchallenged as the nation's most loved sport.

Aside from the traditional ties muay Thai has with Thailand, another reason for its popularity is the gambling that surrounds the fights. Thais treat a muay Thai fight the same way Americans do a day at the track. There are, however, no betting windows or bookies, instead barkers holding handfuls of cash take bets from excited spectators. With each round a fighters odds may go up or down depending upon how he is doing. It's sort of like handicapping a horse race as the race is in progress. Once the winner is decided, the money is distributed to the various winners in the crowd. Don't ask me how they keep track of who gets what, I have no idea. I just watched in awe as thousands of dollars passed from hand to hand without a single dispute.

"Many people make much money from the fights," explained one of the gamblers. "This is fun for us but it is also serious business. That is why we listen to the radio so we can find out how the fighters are feeling and to learn if someone is fighting with an injury."

When I asked him about the way the money changes hands and if they ever get ripped off in the exchange his answer didn't surprise me, "No one would intentionally cheat or pocket another person's money. That would be very bad karma."

No where is muay Thai more honored than on the island of Phuket. At the recently opened Fan- taSea Cultural Theme Park in the Palace of the Elephants, the history of Thailand and muay Thai is presented in a state-of-the-art live stage show. Costing more than 100 million dollars (US), FantaSea is an experience of unparalleled excitement. "Fantasy Of A Kingdom" is a Las Vegas-style show complete with hundreds of performers, muay Thai fighters, stuntmen, more than 30 elephants and a dozen high flying acrobats on bungee cords performing high atop the one-of-a-kind theater. All of this is wrapped around lasers, pyrotechnics and special effects, creating an unforgettable theatrical experience.

In the process of enacting the history of Thailand, the story of the origin of the country's fighting art unfolds during a breathtaking battle-sequence pitting Burmese soldiers against Thailand's army of muay Thai trained warriors. Brilliantly staged and choreographed, the fight scenes feature muay Thai at its best. Kicks, punches and weapons are all used with stunning results, and when the battle is in question, the Thai's call upon the nation's symbol for help. Moments later, like the Calvary coming to the rescue, in rushes more than a dozen elephants to aid the muay Thai fighters. Together they defeat the invaders and vanquish their enemy, thus saving the country.

This alone makes "Fantasy Of A Kingdom" a must-see experience. Muay Thai is, however, only one part of the fabric that when stitched together makes up the complex history of Thailand. To understand muay Thai, you must understand the roots from which it grew, and this show offers a wonderful insight to the art and the country itself. This task is magnificently accomplished through the shows traditional dances, performed by beautiful women in colorful costumes, magic and music. While you're visiting FantaSea stop off at the Golden Pavilion located across from the Palace of the Elephants. This is the world's largest buffet, seating more than 4,000 visitors, and the food is great. A taste of Thailand is the perfect set-up for the show and the excitement of muay Thai.

At each turn of the road one can't help but feel the influence of muay Thai as you tour around the island of Phuket. The warrior creed got its start more than two hundred years ago with a famous battle between an invading Burmese army and a group of islanders led by the wife of the Phuket

As much a cultural heritage as it is a sport, muay Thai permeates nearly every facet of Thai society. Here, fighters rehearse for a Thai Village show.

Muay Thai and Western boxing legend Samart Payakaroon recently visited the Los Angeles area for several fighting seminars, exhibition bouts and singing performances. This was the first time the multi-talented Thai headliner has visited the United States but it will not be his last. Samart plans to return to the States to open a muay Thai training gym with long-time friend and fellow muay Thai great Soekson Janjira, and American muay Thai champion Walter "Sleeper" Michalowski. It is said that learning muay Thai from Samart is the equivalent of learning basketball from Michael Jordan.

Known as the Muhammed Ali of Thailand for his clever and elusive fighting style, Samart has an unparalleled string of muay Thai and Western boxing accomplishments including four Lumpinee Stadium crowns, a WBC boxing championship, and several European kickboxing titles. In addition to his fighting prowess, which he honed and developed through years of hard work in muay Thai camps around his Thailand hometown of Pattaya, Samart has starred in many Thai television shows and feature films and is also a well-known and popular singer in his native land.

Muay Thai Great
SAMART PAYAKAROON

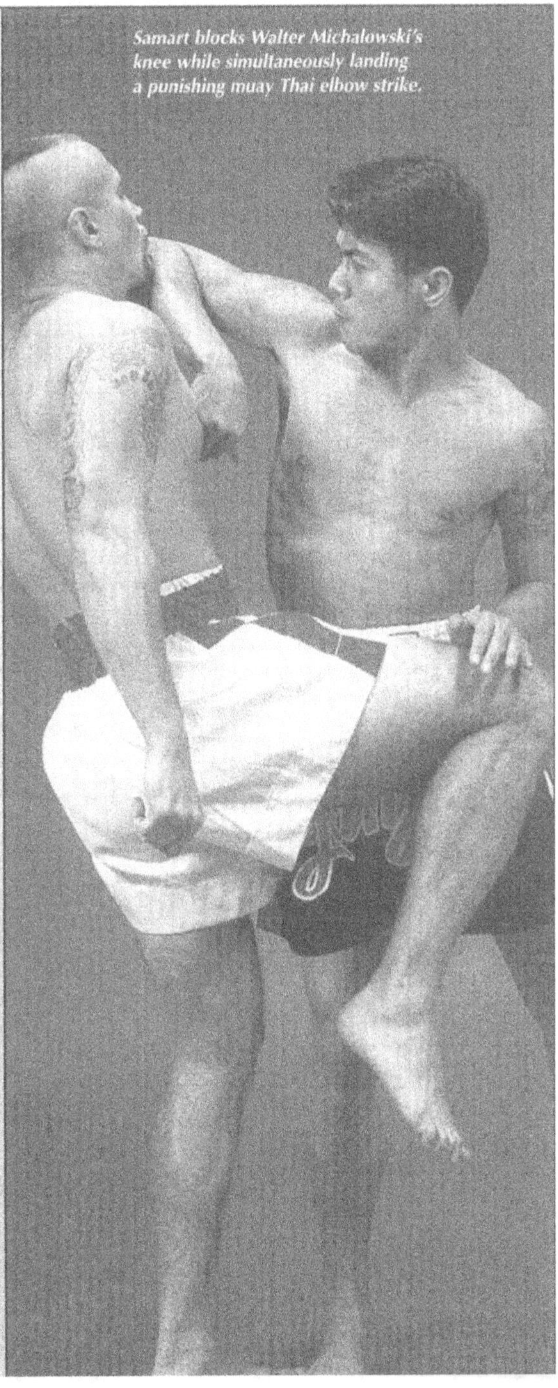

Samart blocks Walter Michalowski's knee while simultaneously landing a punishing muay Thai elbow strike.

Saekson Janjira (left) with Samart Payakaroon

governor who had just died. Khunying Mook and her sister, Khunying Chan, rallied the women to dress like men to fool the invaders as all of the men were off fighting in other wars on the mainland. The army led by the two women was successful in repelling the Burmese and today a statue in their honor stands guard over the island on a roundabout on the airport road.

The locals believe that the sprits of the two sisters are still watching over them and when passing the Two Heroines Monument, they will offer joss sticks, flowers and prayers to the women who saved their island so many years ago.

Another place where history has been turned into theater is at the Phuket Orchid Garden & Thai Village. A colorful stage show pays honor to the women who fought off the invading Burmese soldiers. A nicely choreographed Muay Thai demonstration and colorful presentation of native customs and dances compliment the kicks and sword play.

Verea Nitsak is 35 years old and has been training in the fighting arts of Thailand since the age of 6. He is a master of sword fighting known as Mai San. He works tirelessly with the performers to make sure that their moves are precise and accurate. During the show one of the "warriors" uses a weapon that looks similar to a Japanese tonfa. However this weapon is mostly for defense, unlike the Tonfa which can be used for blocking and striking. "We use it like a shield," explained Nitsak. "The weapon can be used use it to strike but it is used mostly to block a sword attack."

While the Japanese weapon allows the user to spin and twirl it freely, the Thailand weapon has an extra peg that is strapped to the arm of the user, thus making it a stationary weapon. The Thai warriors would block the sword attack with the extremely thick wooden device then counter with a muay Thai kick or sword thrust. In addition to their stage performance, the Phuket Orchid Garden & Thai Village has an elephant show that is sure to delight young and old alike.

Another spot on Phuket for some great muay Thai action is the Vegas Beer Bar. Located in the center of Patong Beach, this giant open air bar seats more than 500 visitors and there is never a cover charge to sit and watch the action. Every night from 8pm till 2am Vegas features non-stop muay Thai fights.

While in Patong I was a nightly visitor to Vegas. Each night I would stop in for a few hours to watch the show. After spending a week training in a muay Thai gym I felt a kind of comradeship with the combatants in the ring. However, something was different about these fighters. At first I wasn't

able to put my finger on it, then one night it dawned on me that these guys were acting. What I was watching was the WWF of muay Thai.

Once I realized that the fights were basically choreographed all my questions were answered. For example, I noticed that it was always the same handful of fighters performing each night, and they never threw any kicks to their opponent's legs, which is a favorite muay Thai target. I also noticed that they were not turning their hips into the many high kicks thrown to their opponent's head. Instead, the Thai fighters were "snapping" the kick back like a karate technique. I'd just spent a week trying to break myself of that habit so I knew it wasn't something that muay Thai fighters did when fighting for real.

The reason they didn't kick to the legs was because of the damage such a blow would result in when being struck night-after-night. The fighters go about their task with great energy and speed. They fight at a controlled, but furious pace and there was no way they could throw leg kicks without making contact and still make it look real. The high "snap" kicks afforded them the ability to smack their opponent while controlling the amount of force with which the blow was landed.

Muay Thai warriors defend their land against evil invaders (left), and beautiful women perform traditional dances (below) in Phuket Island's wonderfully- staged shows at the Palace of the Elephants.

These guys do this for tips. After the "show" they walk around the audience shaking hands and accepting "tips" from grateful spectators. The muay Thai fights at Vegas look like the real deal to the untrained eye and are a lot of fun to watch. Like their show biz counterparts in the States, these fighters also have an "on stage" personality. However, unlike the extreme behavior of our TV wrestling heroes and villains, the muay Thai fighters are more subtle. Two of my favorite fighters were in what I called the David and Goliath match. One giant muay Thai fighter was pitted against a much smaller fighter. The David and Goliath show was a real hoot. The big man knocks the smaller man down with a series of spinning backfists (another technique that is not often used in a real muay Thai bout) then the little man bounces up and, with a flurry of kicks to the head, sends his larger adversary to the canvas. The excitement generated from the packed house adds to the thrill of the moment as each fight takes on a personality of it's own.

When you visit Phuket don't miss an evening at the Vegas Beer Bar, and be sure to tip the fighters a hundred bahts (that's about $3.00 U.S.). They've earned it! These guys are top-notch athletes who afford the visitor a unique perspective to Thailand's national sport. Check it out and be sure to have a camera at the ready because there are many Kodak moments to be captured as the fighters do their best to show off the art of muay Thai.

Ryoki Abe

Turning Dreams Into Reality

Sue McGlynn

If you meet Ryoki Abe on the street, you'll see a normal-looking man with a quiet, pleasant personality. If you meet him in the dojo, you will see an exceptionally skilled, highly focused, passionate, master of karate. If you meet him in competition, you will see one of the most fierce and powerful karate champions of modern times.

From his quiet beginnings in Miyagi Province, Japan, he began training karate at ten years of age. The movies of Bruce Lee had just come to Japan and started a wildfire of interest in the martial arts. Abe found himself becoming inspired to follow Bruce Lee and become a champion. He went to high school and college, eventually becoming a chiropractor. He even opened a chiropractic business next to his karate dojo. During the time he was in school, however, he spent every spare moment training karate. When people around him went to movies, parties, or on vacation, Abe spent time in the dojo. Abe always focused on his dreams and goals about what he wanted to accomplish in karate, and dedicated his training to accomplish his goals. These two things, more than anything else, have made his championship dreams come true.

Sensei Abe has a special feeling for the study of kata. In his opinion, it is the true test of the quality of a person's karate training. A student cannot cheat with kata. If their training is poor, their kata will be poor. If, however, the training is focused, constant, and fueled by passion, then their kata will be extraordinary. As a child, Abe dreamed of becoming a kata champion. He trained like a champion and worked his way up from small, local tournaments to the most highly-respected competitions in the world. Now he is arguably the world's top kata champion with a list of unequalled accomplishments.

Kokumin Tai Iku Taikai (Japanese Olympics): 6-time champion
All Japan Championships: 7-time champion
Asia Karate Championships (PUKO): 5-time champion
Asian Olympics: 2-time champion
World Games; 2-time champion
World Karate Federation World Championships, Brazil

Q: When did you start training karate?

A: When I was about ten years old, I started becoming interested in karate. At about that time, Bruce Lee movies, and other kinds of karate films, were becoming very popular with everybody in Japan. Like everyone else, I saw those movies and wanted to do the things I saw Bruce Lee doing. The more

Applying techniques from the kata on the facing page, Abe faces his opponent (1), blocks the kick (2), and deflects the punch (3). Countering with a neck strike (4), he knees the stomach (5), elbows the head (6), and smashes a backfist to the face (7).

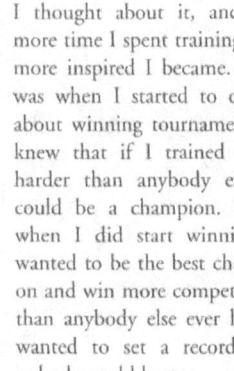

I thought about it, and the more time I spent training, the more inspired I became. That was when I started to dream about winning tournaments. I knew that if I trained hard, harder than anybody else, I could be a champion. Later, when I did start winning, I wanted to be the best champion and win more competitions than anybody else ever had. I wanted to set a record that nobody could beat.

Q: What do you think of the idea of karate becoming part of the Olympics?

A: I am very interested in this. I am sure that if karate were to become an Olympic sport that it would inspire karate students all over the world to train hard and dream of becoming an Olympic champion. I have this dream for myself also. I know that if karate was part of the Olympics, it would get more respect from people and organizations, especially here in Japan. Right now, there is also a lot of attention paid to KI, a knockoutstyle fighting competition. Many karate competitors focus on that competition, and it is receiving a lot of respect right now. However, I believe that if karate becomes an Olympic sport it will receive more respect than any other type of karate competition, including KI. I have won almost every top competition and I want very much to compete in the Olympics. It is the next challenge—the next dream for me.

Q: What is the future of karate?

A: Most karate today has a sport focus that emphasizes rigorous competition. This is fine for most students in the 10 to 30 age group,

Standing in a beginning kata stance (1), Abe brings his hands up parallel (2), steps forward (3), executes a front snap kick (4), followed by an elbow (5), and a backfist (6).

Abe demonstrates a kata (right, A-E), then shows an application of it against an opponent (left, 1-8).

and for exceptional students younger and older than that. However, not everybody can compete this way. Karate needs to be for everybody—for people of all ages. Many of the students in my dojo are over 40. I always recommend that, as part of their training, my students learn *taiso*, which is a form of exercise that focuses on controlled movements and breathing, similar to tai chi. I believe that it is very important to give every person a chance to be involved in and benefit from karate.

Q: What has karate meant to you?
A: Karate has always been, and will always continue to be, a very important part of my life. It has helped me learn many important lessons. I have learned that if you work hard in life the rewards you receive will have value. If you receive rewards but haven't worked hard for them, they will have no value. Don't worry about winning and don't expect to lose, just work hard. The greatest reward you receive is not the winning; it is the trying itself—it is the value that will be seen in you by others because of the person you are. One of the most important things people should remember about karate is to always keep training. A powerful lesson I learned early is from Nana-korobi Yaoki, "Seven times fall down, eight times get up." That is the essence of karate—hang on and don't give up!

Wai Hong's Words of Wisdom

When fu-jow pai grandmaster Wai Hong speaks, everyone listens. And that's just what happened when he came out of retirement for a seminar in Florida.

Julian K. Duran

"Jng Mon," a term not often heard or associated with modern-day kung-fu, means owner or founder of a particular system. Grandmaster Wai Hong is such a man. The grandmaster began his training in the fu-jow pai, tiger claw system of kung-fu in the early 1950s under the late, venerable, Wong Moon Toy. The late grandmaster was the sole successor to this ancient system.

The style was renamed to fu-jow pai of Hoy Hong Temple, Canton from the hark fu moon or black tiger style of the Shaolin Temple, Honan. The fu-jow pai was passed on to Wai Hong by Wong Moon Toy in 1960. This act made Wai Hong grandmaster of the art.

Grandmaster Wai Hong had become Jong Mon of the fu-jow pai by organizing the Fu-jow Pai Federation and reorganizing the art of fu-jow pai in 1968. He made the art available to the public for the first time.

The Jong Mon adjusts the methodology of the relative art to meet the socioeconomic requirements of the new organization and its constituents. Grandmaster Wai Hong has reworked the approach to training in the ancient fu-jow pai to make the art more easily understood and attainable to the general public. This reworking of the original format resulted in the present-day

Grandmaster Wai Hong performs the "tiger coming out of the cave" movement from the fu-jow pai system.

The reworking of the system in no way reduces its effectiveness; rather it enhances the practitioner's absorption of material by diminishing the disparity associated with cultural readjustments. The art has become something other than an austere practice behind temple walls and clandestine training in the mountains.

The system has been reformatted so that the knowledge can be more easily digested and myster-

Grandmaster Wai Hong exhibits effortless technique in demonstrating tiger claw application on student George Litz of The Kung Fu Conservatory.

ies can be dispelled. The system becomes an endeavor for all that try to meet its standards, rather than solely for Chinese monks or lifetime devotees of lineal descent.

Grandmaster Wai Hong has been in semi-retirement as an instructing master since the mid-1980s. He has come out of retirement periodically to hold seminars for those who wish to enhance their knowledge and to give new knowledge to the students and sifu of the fu-jow pai.

The grandmaster is known for opening the doors of Chinese kung-fu to the outside word on many levels. It is in this vein that he now offers instruction, once reserved for students of the fu-jow pai, to the outside world.

The Method

Fu-jow pai is a system which utilizes the characteristic movements of a fighting tiger as the basis for its many strategies. The tiger claw system is designed to epitomize the human potential for dynamic power.

The true nature of fu-jow pai is greatly misunderstood by many, even though some aspects can be found in most martial arts styles. Tiger claw techniques can be found in almost every kung-fu system, but correct execution is rarely achieved. The common misconception is that the tiger claw is stiff, rigid and ballistic in

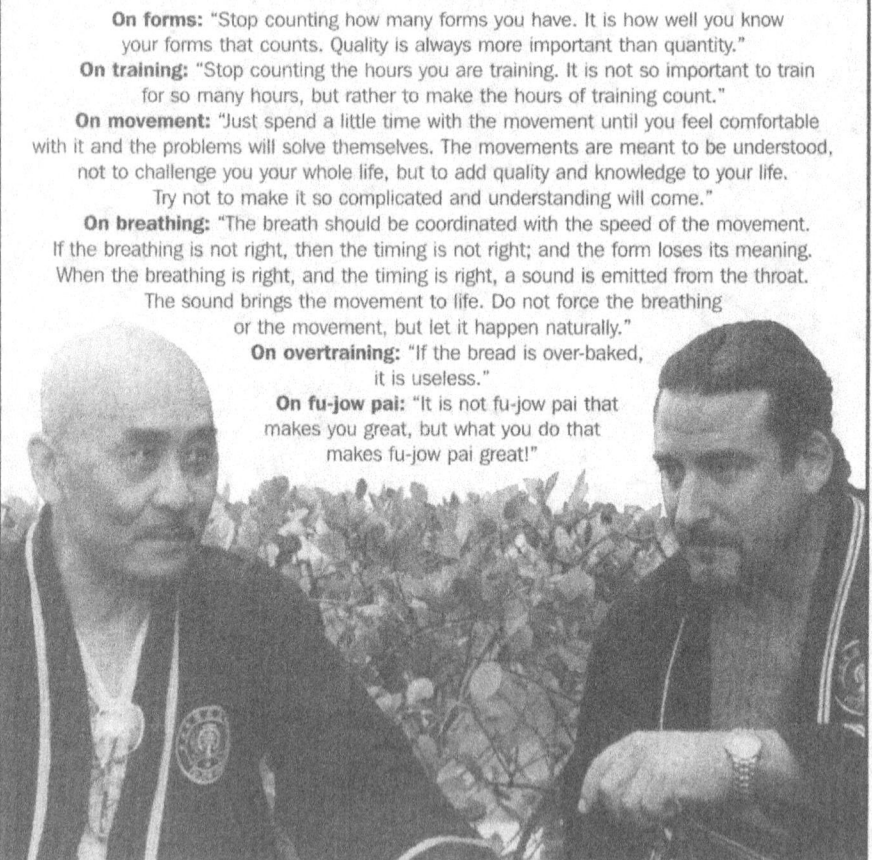

On forms: "Stop counting how many forms you have. It is how well you know your forms that counts. Quality is always more important than quantity."
On training: "Stop counting the hours you are training. It is not so important to train for so many hours, but rather to make the hours of training count."
On movement: "Just spend a little time with the movement until you feel comfortable with it and the problems will solve themselves. The movements are meant to be understood, not to challenge you your whole life, but to add quality and knowledge to your life. Try not to make it so complicated and understanding will come."
On breathing: "The breath should be coordinated with the speed of the movement. If the breathing is not right, then the timing is not right; and the form loses its meaning. When the breathing is right, and the timing is right, a sound is emitted from the throat. The sound brings the movement to life. Do not force the breathing or the movement, but let it happen naturally."
On overtraining: "If the bread is over-baked, it is useless."
On fu-jow pai: "It is not fu-jow pai that makes you great, but what you do that makes fu-jow pai great!"

Grandmaster Wai Hong intercepts (1) and then redirects the straight punch, which reduces its power. The grandmaster then slides (2) his foot back into an "X" stance and traps the straight punch with a single tiger claw, forcing Litz to commit further into the grandmaster's zone. The grandmaster continues to pull Litz into his zone (3), which causes him to lose his foundation in footing. The grandmaster prepares to close the technique with the assisting tiger claw of the left hand. He finishes by striking with his elbow (4) against Litz' forward momentum. The unseen left hand controls the attacker's hand, since it is "cradled" in the tiger claw.

ments are swift, decisive, relentless, courageous, tenacious, agile, dexterous, balanced, domineering, territorial, extremely powerful and fluid.

One of the reasons practitioners have trouble with achieving fluid application of the tiger claw is that the claw requires the use and articulation of every finger in an extended and hooked position. This places a great deal of stress on the muscles and tendons in the hand and forearm, which in turn causes tension. This tension in the extremities of the arm causes cessation of the flow of intrinsic energies, greatly diminishing the dynamic force of the movement. The result is stiffness, tightness and an unnatural jerkiness referred to as the "incorrect way."

It is common knowledge among fu-jow pai practitioners and others who have the patience and insight to pursue mastery of the claw that these problems should be transcended by working through them. This is an arduous task that requires! many years to achieve. However, excellent results can be gained with tenacity and proper guidance.

Another common misconception is that the tiger claw style is solely a short-hand system. This is merely an oversight by those with relatively little experience. All systems of kung-fu rely upon knowledge of the long, medium and short bridge to acquire proficiency.

A principal component of fu-jow pai is claw development and dynamic application of this technique. The tiger claw is of utmost importance as a tool in executing the myriad techniques found in this system. Prerequisite to claw training is knowledge of yin and yang, or cooperative palms and enhanced power as translated through the waist.

Wai Hong, Tai Yim Join Forces

By Herb Borkland

NEW YORK CITY—East Coast dragons are joining forces.

Fu jow pai grandmaster Wai Hong Ng's New York-based United Kung-Fu Federation of North America (USKFFNA) will merge with hung fut grandmaster Tai Yim's Maryland-based North American Chinese Martial Arts Federation (NACMAF).

At a ceremony and news conference held in this city's Chinatown, NACMAF notables including sifu Yim, eagle claw grandmaster Lily Lau, and U.S. jow ga founder Hoy Lee officially acknowledged their endorsement of the merger between NACMAF and USKFFNA.

The new organization, as yet untitled, will be the largest-ever U.S. alliance of traditionalist Chinese martial artists, boasting "over 100 regional, national and international organization memberships, representing a vast array of kung-fu styles."

Sifu Wai Hong expressed his satisfaction at the coming alliance saying, "We have over 20 years of friendships and many cooperative ventures in the past... We have the same vision and seek the same goal, to unite all martial artists, and to promote mutual respect and cooperation among different styles and schools. This (unification) is a natural step for us to do."

Sifu Tai also cited the two Federations' long-standing social and martial arts community ties. "We share mutual friends, a basic respect and our traditionalist backgrounds," he observed.

Another famous East Coast grandmaster, Florida's Wah Lum mantis boxing sifu Pui Chan, is credited with first broaching the idea of a union between the New York and Maryland organizations. Serious talks were initiated in 1996.

It is expected that sifu Chan will also play a prominent role in the new federation, whose name and initial officials will be formally announced at a special inaugural celebration June 30 at the USKFFNA's 5th General Assembly/Convention in Orlando, Fla. This occasion will coincide with sifu Chan's 2nd International Open Kung Fu Championship, Tournament 2000, July 1-2 at the University of Central Florida Arena.

The Seminar

Grandmaster Wai Hong was once again ready to teach and inspire those who would strive to meet the standards of the time-honored tiger claw system. He arrived at The Kung Fu Conservatory in Boca Raton, Fla., and was greeted with great anticipation by students of many disciplines. The reality of his presence brought new energy to the kwoon.

The focus of the seminar was fu-jow yat choun, the first tiger claw fist form. The grandmaster related the movements of the tiger claw form to universal principles found in all martial arts. He spent time speaking about the utilization of the waist in coordinating the arm movements with the movement of stances for enhanced power; utilizing the body's natural levers. "In this way," he said, "it is almost like doing nothing."

The students listened and observed as the grandmaster showed how to translate the movement through the hips to attain fluidity. Although his movements appeared to be effortless, and although he was stressing the simplicity involved for proper execution, the students knew they had their work cut out for them. Practice sessions, under the grandmaster's guidance followed each point in the lecture.

The grandmaster spoke of appropriate breathing patterns and how to harness the proper energy for powerful execution of technique.

"The breath should be coordinated with the speed of the movement," he related. "If the breathing is not right, then the timing is not right; and the form loses its meaning. When the breathing is right, and the timing is right, a sound is emitted from the throat. The sound brings the movement to life. Do not force the breathing or the movement, but let it happen naturally."

Balance in motion was stressed in transferring the weight from one stance to the other. The grandmaster seemed merely to be walking through the most challenging movements. He showed, by example and lecture, that simple understanding of the intended goal will charge the movement with energy. He cautioned the class not to overdo it for fear of proceeding in the wrong direction, away from the design of the exercise and/or form. "If the bread is over-baked, it is useless."

As the students progressed to the main body of the form, the grandmaster turned his attention to the simplest of principles. As always, when it is exposed, the simple becomes profound. The grandmaster said, "Think about the path of the elbow." Lecture and demonstration of correct alignment followed this moment of head nodding and coalescing.

From left: Tony Lau, Andrew Lee, Wai Hong Ng, Tai Yim, Lily Lau and Hoy Lee.

fu-jow pai alike. At The Kung Fu Conservatory both styles are **Double tiger claw with execution** taught with equal vigor. The tai chi stylists came prepared to **unique to fu-jow pai.** experience something different in the way of the tiger. They were not disappointed. The grandmaster took them through the claw movements as if they were fu-jow students. The students who train in fu-jow pursued this refinement of their skills with appreci-

ation and regard for the newly imparted insights. Everyone experienced the energetic and invigorating execution of the tiger claw under the hand of grandmaster Wai Hong.

The students listened attentively as their kung-fu grandfather imparted words of wisdom concerning their well-being in the martial arts. "It is not fu-jow pai that makes you great, but what you do that makes fu-jow pai great!"

These words reminded fu-jow pai students of their duty to represent the system with humility and humanitarian concern, and that the body of the system is actually governed by the heart and mind.

Noticing there were a few students wearing ranking sashes denoting accomplishment, the grandmaster noted that it is the student who gives the rank credence, not the other way around.

"Stop counting how many forms you have," he insisted. "It is how well you know your forms that counts. Quality is always more important than quantity. Stop counting the hours you are training. It is not so important to train for so many hours, but rather to make the hours of training count."

Proficiency in the more intricate movements seemed to be out of reach for some students. Upon seeing this, the grandmaster simply said, "Just spend a little time with the movement until you feel comfortable with it and the problems will solve themselves. The movements are meant to be understood, not to challenge you your whole life, but to add quality and knowledge to your life. Try not to make it so complicated and understanding will come."

The tiger claw first fist form contains signature movements of the system. These are derived from the 18 hands of the tiger claw. Proficiency in these extraordinary training tools transforms the hand into a claw that may ultimately be used for splitting tendon and muscle and removing them from the bone, dislocating and breaking joints and bones, attacking nerve centers, ripping the flesh and permanently removing cartilaginous tissue.

All eyes were glued to grandmaster Wai Hong as he demonstrated proper execution of the signature movements. One can only assume what the variety of expressions held for each individual. The grandmaster's gentle and expressive hands were transformed to claws shredding the air before him. He became the thing he is known for but is rarely seen to do. His eyes pierced space like daggers, his countenance that of a fighting tiger with one thing on its mind: "I am the top of the food chain!"

This spectacle had a tremendous effect on the seminars' aspirants. They were not mesmerized or frozen with admiration. The time had come to cull from the source those qualities that define the art of fu-jow pai. The students were becoming more of themselves. They were going where they had never been. They were moving into another realm of understanding, focusing on that which would transform them into better martial artists. They were following in the footsteps of the Jong Mon. ®

Julian K. Duran has trained in Ju-jow pai since 1974 and is personally commissioned by grandmaster Wai Hong. Siju Duran also teaches Yang style tai chi, hung gar, mu chung I, law horn, Gh'an, Taoist meditation and iron hands. He is master at The Kung Fu Conservatory in Boca Raton, Florida.

The Art of the Flow

Encompassing knife fighting, jiu-jitsu, karate, and kendo, Ernesto Presas' Filipino Kombatan system might just be the ultimate combat art

Jose G. Paman

Born in 1945 in the fishing village of Hinigaran, Negros Occidental in the Philippines, Ernesto Amador Presas Sr. was introduced to martial arts at an early age. In grade school he received lessons in traditional amis from his father Jose, a renowned teacher. Young Presas mastered his lessons well and soon expanded his studies to include karate, ju-jitsu, judo, kendo, and Okinawan weaponry.

The year 1970 was a turning point in Presas' life. Together with a group of other Filipino martial artists, he was invited to perform at the Osaka Trade Fair in Japan. The presentation by Presas' group was enthusiastically received by the Japanese spectators, many of whom were experienced martial artists in their own right, and were thus uncompromising in their view of the combative arts. Later that year Presas relocated to Manila and opened the Arjuken Karate Association in Quiapo, in the heart of Manila's downtown area.

"In real-life combat, the individual must be able to flow from one range to another, from grappling to striking and kicking, and from barehanded conflict to armed fighting."

The beginning of the Arjuken (a combination of the names amis, ju-jitsu and kendo) Karate Association was tough for Presas and his early followers. Because 1970 was the beginning of the golden age of the Manila martial arts scene, opposing schools and organizations jockeyed for power and influence. Stylistic pride ran high and rivalries sprang among the differing factions. Challenge matches between schools became a harsh reality, sometimes with injurious results.

Presas persevered through these difficult times and devoted his energy to the development of his martial arts methods. A thinker and innovator, Presas observed that the practice of amis, as handed down by past generations, largely consisted of the undisciplined and disorganized swinging of the rattan canes (sticks). Injuries were commonplace as the haphazardly directed canes made hard contact with unprotected fingers, wrists, elbows, and faces.

In order to become acceptable for modern, widespread instructional purposes, Presas concluded, training had to be modified. First, he introduced basic striking, blocking, and countering patterns,

and devised effective footwork. He organized the training procedures into a regimented structure not unlike karate training sessions. Presas designed a distinctive uniform for his organization—amis exponents up to that point wore attire ranging from khaki pants and white t-shirts, to karate and judo gis, to sweat pants. Finally, he instituted a ranking system.

The innovations made by Presas led to the acceptance of amis as a physical education course in Manila's secondary and collegiate school systems. In 1972 he began teaching the Presas style of amis at the University of Santo Tomas, the University of the Philippines, and the Lyceum in Manila. Teaching assignments at the Far Eastern Military Academy, the Philippine National Police Academy, the General Headquarters Military Police Academy, and the Officer's Schools for the Philippine Army and Air Force soon followed. A dynamic organizer, Presas also formed the Modern Amis Association of the Philippines, and the Philippine Kendo Association (the first to teach that Japanese fencing art in the islands).

Attracted by Presas' curriculum, numerous practitioners from other systems began joining the Arjuken. Presas also drew the attention of foreign martial artists who were visiting the Philippines and had the opportunity to sample his training. In 1977, Presas was invited to teach at a seminar in California, and his international seminar circuit was officially launched. He founded the International

Philippine Martial Arts Federation shortly afterwards as a monitoring and promotional organization, linking his followers the world over.

The Art of the Flow

According to Presas, "Kombatan is a complete system of armed and unarmed fighting." Effectiveness in total combat, as the name denotes, is the art's ultimate goal. Included in its armed techniques are applications employing the *dulo dulo* (a double-tipped short stick), staff, the *yantok,* and various bladed weapons. The unarmed techniques encompass striking, kicking, throwing, and grappling.

Presas emphasizes that while some arts distinctly separate weapons training from unarmed training, Kombatan blends both. The practitioner of the art can readily switch from bare hands to blade to stick, and back. Application techniques are a trademark of the system, as is the ability to adapt to the ever-changing nuances of a violent encounter. "In real-life combat," states Presas," the individual must be able to flow from one range to another, from grappling to striking and kicking, and from barehanded conflict to armed fighting."

The Flow is a constant theme of the dynamic grandmasters teachings. "All techniques in Kombatan emanate from the Flow," Presas asserts. When pressed to define the Flow, he says that it is the phenomenon of one movement leading naturally to another, and then to another—endlessly. In Kombatan sequences, counters, follow-ups, and variations automatically spring from the basic, initial movements. "Kombatan is not stagnant—it is a living art," Presas continues. Aware that counters to existing techniques are constantly being devised, his combat methods undergo a constant process of refinement and modification. "We are in the business of making counters to the counters," Presas says.

Given the lofty explanation of the Kombatan system, one might wonder fundamental techniques are based on classical arnis. The student is first taught the 12 strikes with the cane. This principal sequence consists of seven strikes and five thrusting techniques that form the core of Presas' method. In the sequence, the practitioner executes a forehand strike to the opponent's left temple, a backhand strike to the opposite temple, a forehand strike to the left shoulder tip, a backhand strike to the right shoulder tip, a penetrating thrust to the abdomen, a thrust to the left pectoral area, a reverse thrust to the right pectoral area, a downward strike to the right knee, a downward strike to the left knee, a thrust to the left eye, a reverse thrust to the right eye, and a descending, heavy strike to the crown. Each technique, delivered fullforce, is potentially disabling.

The student then learns the six blocks,

Presas delivers a forearm slash (1, 2) against an attack by Lito Concepcion. Checking Concepcion's wrist, Presas thrusts (3, 4) to the solar plexus, executes a takedown with the butt of his blade (5), and poises his weapon to prevent further attacks (6).

also with the cane, as counters to the 12 strikes. These consist of the outside block, inside block, downward block, reverse block, rising block, and the vertical block. Stances and footwork patterns are next taught, with an emphasis on developing the ability to maneuver and switch positions to gain a tactical advantage in combat. Also a part of the beginner's training are the block-and-counter drills where the student blocks his partner's attack, controls the partner's cane, and delivers a counterstrike.

Block and Counter

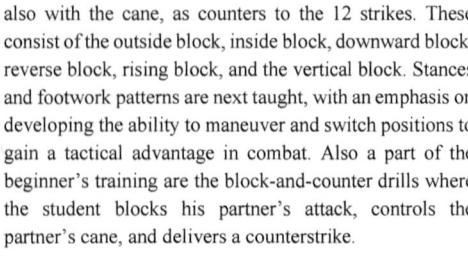

The 12 strikes, six blocks, footwork and block-and-counter drills serve as the basis for Kombatan training and are repeated many times by the student. When the student demonstrates these skills adequately, the cane disarms and releases are taught next. Incorporated into these are empty-hand blows, kicks, takedowns, and joint locks.

Other cane striking patterns are likewise taught the student, including the distinct *sungkiti* (or *salag- tusok}* thrusting techniques, *ocho ocho* figure-eight maneuvers, *pinayong* umbrella blocks and sweeps, and the *abanico* fanning strikes. Skills in specialized two-

Presas meets Paman's attack (1, 2) with an inside strike. He delivers a counter to the ribs (3), then executes a twisting take down (4,5) and controls Paman on the ground.

hand weapons usage in the form of the double-cane *sinawali* weaving patterns and the *es/ ada y daga* (sword and dagger) methods are also imparted.

Further along, the student begins practicing the more dangerous, bladed variation cf the basic techniques. Swords and machetes of various configurations, such as the wavy-bladed *kris;* the twintipped *kampilan;* the *itak*, a common farm implement in the Philippines; and the *binakoko* named after the bakoko fish, are standard weapons. Later still, barehanded defenses (considered a desperate, last-ditch but nonetheless essential measure) are learned against blade attacks.

Does the seemingly endless curriculum overwhelm the students? "Not at all," replies Presas. "All of the techniques, be they with a cane, blade or empty hand, follow the same planes of movement that are learned early in basic training." The various skill categories are not regarded as single, isolated methods but as crucial, interrelated facets of the natural continuum comprising the totality of combat.

"A man can defend against a punch in a hundred ways," Presas states, "but can he deal adequately with a knife attack?" Kombatan training, Presas points out, prepares the individual for the realities of modern-day combat. In this day, when many people carry some form of club or bladed weapon in their vehicle or on their person, the observation seems particularly valid.

Spreading the Word
Ernesto Presas has written a number of books highlighting his system. In 1979, he published his first volume entitled *The Art of Amis*. This was followed bydnwi, *Presas Style and Balisong 'm* 1988. In the three consecutive years of 1996, 1997 and 1998, Presas published, respectively, *Modern Mino Mano, Philippine Armas de Mano,* and *Filipino Knife Fighting*. In 1999, he produced a comprehensive series of videotapes on the Kombatan method, revealing his diverse training techniques. The m altitude of techniques, Presas repeats, instills in the student a deep understanding of the vital concept of the Flow.

Master of the armed and unarmed aspects of personal combat, Ernesto Presas confidently carries on the centuries-old traditions of his warrior forefathers. Through his tireless efforts the ait of Kombatan is ensured

A first-generation student of Ernesto Presas, author Jose G. Paman joined the Arjuken Karate Association in Manila in 1971. He currently holds the rank of lakan apat (fourth degree expert) in Kombatan.

Wing Chun Trapping
The Key To Unlocking Chi Sau

Alan Lamb

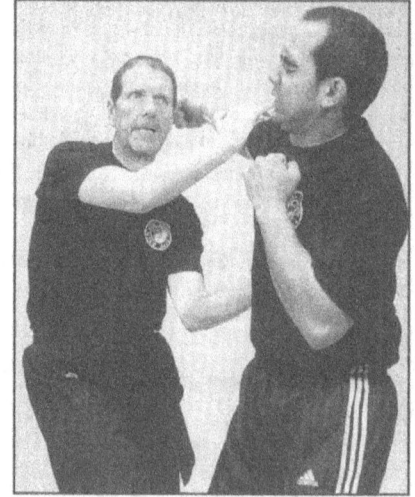

Trapping is the key to unlocking wing chun's fighting strategies, which are mastered through chi sau (sticking hands) practice. Why? Because those who master trapping must develop effective in-fighting positions which are crucial for close-quarter fighting—the hallmark of wing chun. Although sticking hands requires a highly developed level of skill and sensitivity in order to be functional in combat, trapping drills are fairly easy to learn and will train one in the art of counterfighting, of which trapping and sticking are extremely important. For those who are not familiar with wing chun, sticking is a means of maintaining contact with your opponent's arms so that you can stay in control and anticipate what he is going to do with his hands. Trapping drills prepare you for chi sau, which in turn prepares you for real combat. Good trapping ability allows you to suppress and control your sition into other fighting techniques and ranges. Therefore, trapping drills are important for all combatants and martial artists who are serious about developing a fighting strategy.

Wing chun students often have trouble "sticking," especially when it comes to dealing with the fast snapping blows of karate or other hard styles. Indeed, without knowledge of trapping, it is very difficult to apply sticking or push hands techniques because trapping helps to develop the strong forward energy needed to make your chi sau effective. Sitting in a back stance and just hoping to pick-off fast attacks is not a very sound fighting strategy. In fact, without any forward pressure or adhesion it is only a matter of time before a determined attacker will break through your defenses. Remember, if you are just blocking, you are playing catch-up. To win a fight you must be pro-active and take the fight to your attacker. Again, the wing chun method of doing this is through trapping combined with good sticking-hand strategy.

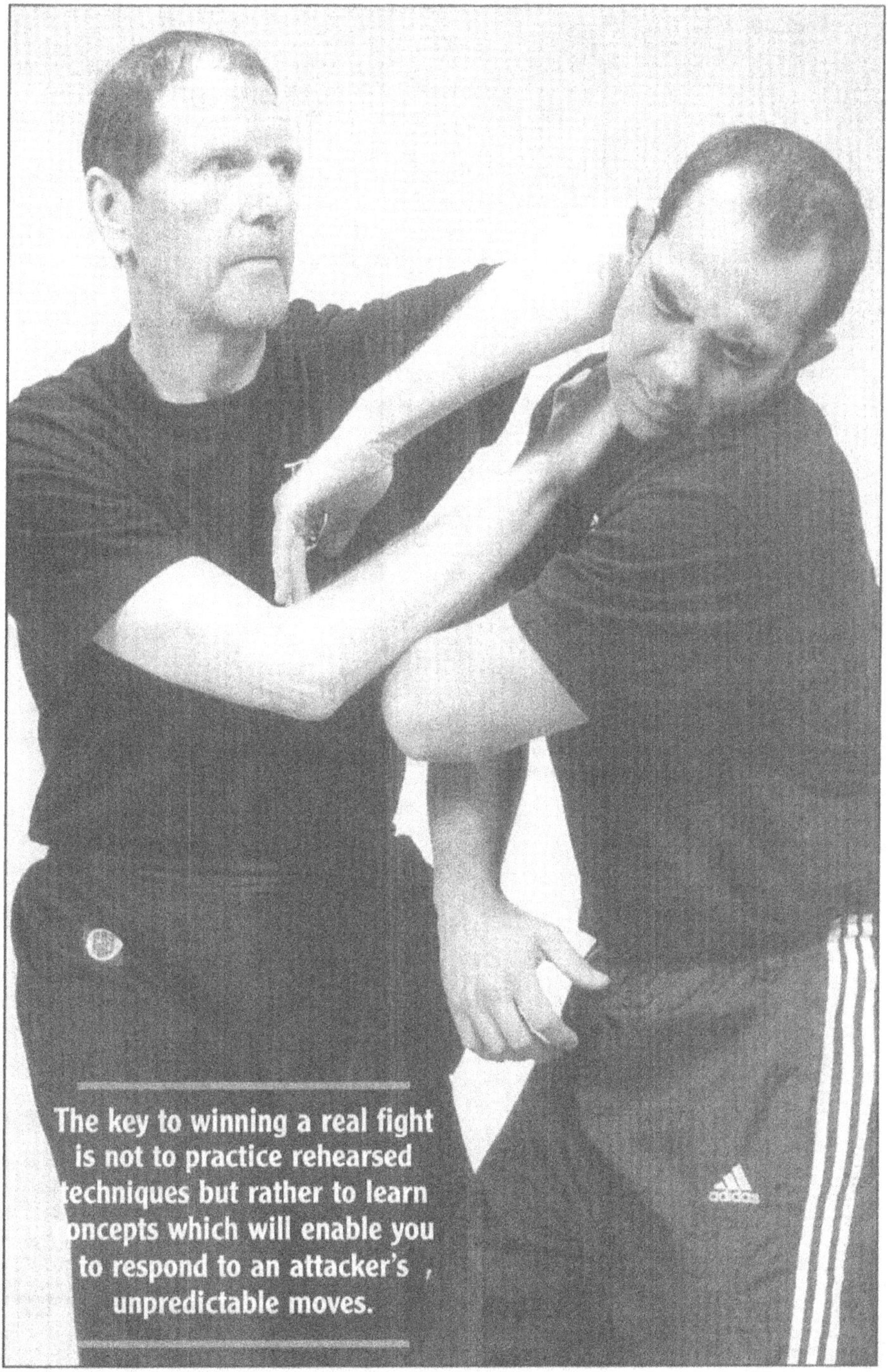

> The key to winning a real fight is not to practice rehearsed techniques but rather to learn concepts which will enable you to respond to an attacker's unpredictable moves.

Four Ranges of Combat

In combat, there are four basic fighting ranges: kicking, striking, trapping, and grappling. Trapping range is being close enough to your opponent to control both his hands. Remember, even if you are a grappler you must pass through trapping range before you can take someone to the ground. Therefore, good trapping ability can be of benefit to students of all styles.

At its most basic level, trapping involves pinning or trapping your opponent's arms or legs as you move into a position which allows you to keep control as you continue to attack. This greatly reduces your opponent's ability to counterfight. Good trapping skills will permit you to transition into other traps, strikes, or throws. Ideally, a good trap should allow you to attack, but should severely inhibit your opponent's ability to protect and counterfight.

There are many ways of effecting traps. However, two of the most basic traps involve the use of the wing chun *lap sau* (grabbing block) and *pak sau* (slapping block). Photo 7 demonstrates a classic wing chun combination: the inside lap sau straight punch. This leads into photo 8, which demonstrates the pak sau pin, and punch. Here, the forearm and elbows are used to trap and suppress the attacker's arms. Also, the distance has been closed, which allows for the attacker's lead leg to be pinned. Both photos 7 and 8 show the correct range for effective trapping. Once you are in effective trapping range, it is important to pin your opponent's lead leg with your forward knee. This further reduces his ability to fight back and keeps his kicks under control, thereby allowing you to focus on your hand techniques which are wing chun's fighting forte.

Pre-fighting positions (1). Alan Lamb uses pak sau *(slap block) to deflect right lead punch (2). Due to lack of forward pressure, attacker repositions and throws another lead punch (3 & 4). Then Lamb uses* pak sau, *but keeps the pressure on by attacking with the right hand (5). This causes the attacker to protect himself with his own* pak sau *block (6). Now Lamb can use that block to his advantage by pulling down with a* lap sau *(grabbing hand block) and striking his left punch, keeping his elbow down to pin his attacker's right arm (7).* Pak sau *follow up (8), trapping arms and elbow strike (9).*

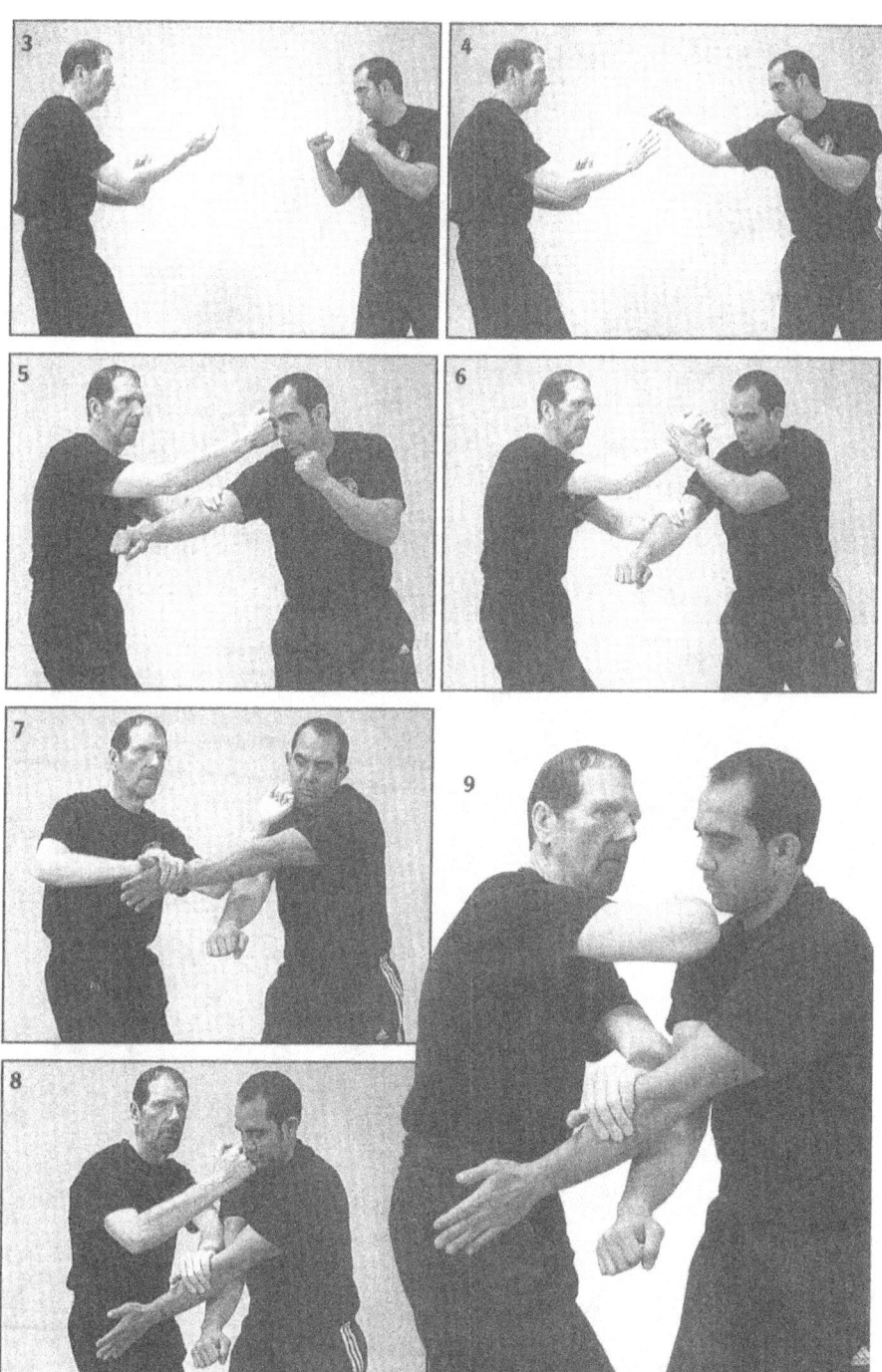

"Good trapping ability allows you to suppress and control your opponent. Additionally, trapping allows you to transition into other fighting techniques and ranges."

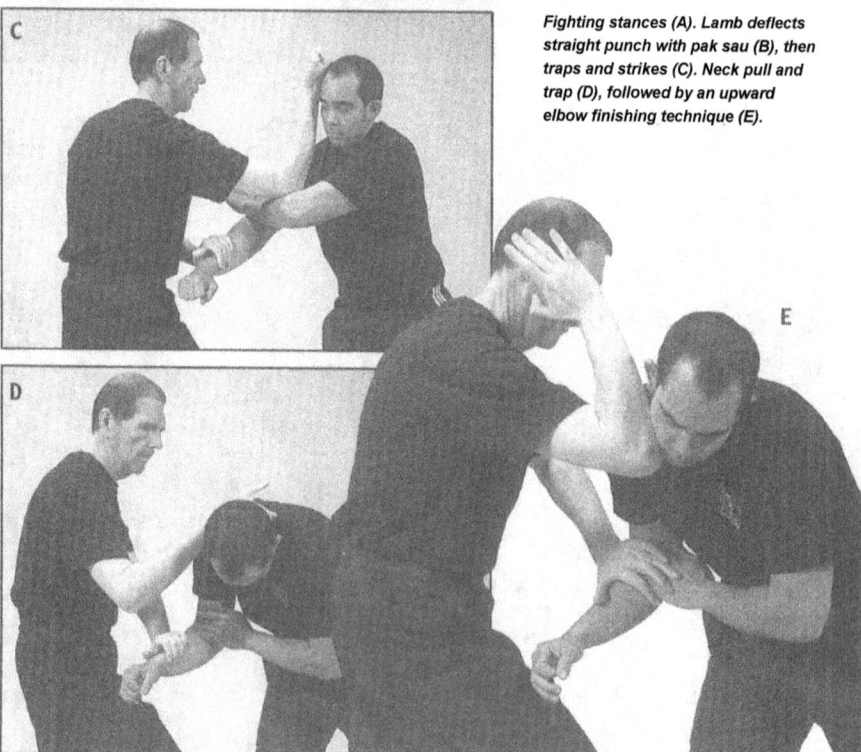

Fighting stances (A). Lamb deflects straight punch with pak sau (B), then traps and strikes (C). Neck pull and trap (D), followed by an upward elbow finishing technique (E).

Conversely, photos 1 and 2 show the danger of being too defensive and not positioning oneself in the correct fighting range. Photos 1 and 2 show a pak sau defense—a slap block without any forward energy—against a straight punch. As illustrated in the photos, unless you close the distance to trapping range, as shown in photo 5, you are still open to a variety of striking techniques. Getting your opponent on the defensive and forcing him to block will give you his hands. Once you have contact you can continue to strike, trap, or use your big guns—elbows and knees—to finish him off.

Trapping drills allow you to become conversational with your hands by developing hand speed, technique, and coordination. You must be able to act and react naturally and be able to exploit any weakness in an attacker's defenses. Wing chun must be in your bones, and you can only attain that level of skill through practicing sticking hands drills. No other exercise gets your arms to respond to attacks as well as trapping and chi sau training. You must be able to stick, and the easiest way to learn how to do this is through the trapping drills.

Sticking allows you to form a bridge with your opponent. In a nutshell, trapping drills consist of creating a bridge—which forces you to learn sticking—and breaking the bridge. In wing chun, a bridge is a point where you and your attacker's limbs make contact, as in photo 6, which illustrates a crossing point or a bridge. To maintain your bridge you must sustain forward pressure. Allowing an attacker to back off or break contact destroys the bridge and you puts you back into striking range where your attacker has the advantage.

Once you have created a bridge, the next phase is breaking it. Bridge breaking allows you to deflect an attacker's forward energy and create a trap, as shown in photos 6 and 7. Therefore, basic attacks or entries in chi sau training are sometimes called "breaks" because they involve some kind of deflection or trap combined with a simultaneous attack. Functionally, bridge breaking teaches you how to neutralize and escape from locks and holds. Also, once you have broken the bridge and attacked, the only logical way for an attacker to protect himself is by blocking your attack with his hands. Once he does that you have created a situation similar to chi sau where you can continue to trap and attack, and thereby control the centerline. Should an attacker try to circle his arms to the outside and redirect in an effort to counter punch, you should still have the advantage, providing you keep the forward pressure on and continue to trap.

Remember though that wing chun is not a "fixed" system, you are dealing with concepts not hard and fast techniques. Real combat involves constantly changing circumstances and you must be able to adapt to those changes. Trapping, sticking, and chi sau training are all excellent methods for getting started on the road to becoming a thinking martial artist. ®

World-renowned wing chun kung-fu master Alan Lamb is available for classes or seminars by calling 818-841-4430. His videotape series Combat Wing Chun *is available through Unique Publications Video at 800-332-3330.*

The Makiwara

The Abandoned Tool of Karate

Michael J. Lorden

The *makiwara* is a wooden post approximately six feet tall. A bundle of rope, wrapped straw, or canvas-covered rubber is affixed on top for the purpose of toughening the skin of the hands and feet of a karate student through repeated striking. This is the basic concept of makiwara construction and purpose; however, it is a narrow definition and not entirely correct. Actually, makiwara can be of various sizes and configurations, and there are many beneficial skills and techniques that students can acquire through training with the makiwara.

There is a misconception that the sole purpose of makiwara training is to toughen the skin of the hands or feet. Training on a makiwara will toughen the skin, but it will also strengthen muscles, improve power, and help develop focus in technique. However, there are very few karate schools that still use the makiwara in their training regimen. Why is this valuable training tool becoming extinct?

The abandonment of this traditional training apparatus can be attributed to a number of factors. Some karate instructors do not see a need to toughen the skin of the hands and feet. School owners worry that students may injure themselves or feel the training is too hard and leave. There are also some instructors who believe that the makiwara is an antiquated device that has outlived its usefulness. Since many schools train students for sport fighting, the instructors see no use for makiwara training. Although some of the concerns and worries are justified, instructor care and competence can reduce and/or completely eliminate student injuries. As for the makiwara being outdated and obsolete, nothing could be farther from the truth.

If students are not properly instructed and monitored on the use of the makiwara, injury is a possibility. While the toughening of the skin of the knuckles, hands and feet is to be expected, this is also true of many other activities. Going barefoot in the karate school will harden the bottoms of the feet—as will manual labor, planting a garden, or participating in baseball, football, and gymnastics. All of these activities can cause the skin of various body parts to harden, crack, and callous. However, we do not see these activities being eliminated. We also do not see participation is baseball, football, soccer, or any other sporting activity dwindling.

On any weekend visit the local playground or athletic field and witness the masses of children playing organized sports. You will see children as young as four and five years of age wearing football helmets, shoulder pads, jerseys, and pants, tackling each other. The number of young people participating in baseball, soccer, gymnastics, and other sports is growing. So are the number of injuries associated with these sports. However, a child has more risk of receiving an injury from one of these activities than from striking a makiwara in a karate school.

Appropriate instruction and guidance is essential in team sports. It reduces the risk of injuries and allows the participants to mature while improving their individual skills. Appropriate instruction and guidance is just as important in karate and provides the same benefits. This is true in every facet of karate training, including the use of the makiwara.

Makiwara come in many shapes and forms. They can be made from a 4x4 wooden plank that is bolted to the floor, or buried or secured into the ground. Makiwara can be hung on walls or suspended from ceilings. They can also be affixed to wooden platforms, free-standing frames, or centered in concrete surrounded by an automobile tire. The striking surface can be the traditional style consisting of a bundle of straw, wrapped manila rope, or the commercially manufactured makiwara surface, now available, which consists of a piece of canvas-covered rubber bonded to a piece of plywood. You can also make your own striking surface using readily available materials such as discarded phone books, duct tape, empty rice bags, or carpet scraps—the possibilities are limitless. With a little imagination and ingenuity you can fashion any number of practical devices that will serve the purpose of a makiwara.

Knifehand strike to makiwara made with traditional straw striking surface (above).

The striking surface of the makiwara should be at the approximate level of your solar-plexus for hand and arm techniques. Although you can deliver kicks at this level, a second striking surface can be attached at a lower level for low kicks. When struck, the tension of the makiwara should be such that it yields only slightly then rebounds. This shock-absorbing action reduces the risk of injury. Care should be given for proper makiwara tension during construction. All legitimate karate techniques can and should be practiced on a makiwara.

Training on a makiwara is very similar to that of *kihons* (basic techniques in a karate school) and particular attention must be given to detail. Corrections and adjustments, no matter how small, need to be done immediately. Failure to correct small mistakes at the beginning can turn small problems into bigger, more-difficult-to-correct mistakes later down the road and lead to sure injury. Just as balance, breath-control, rhythm, muscle tension, correct form, and repetition are essential elements of kihon training in karate, all of these same elements are just as important during makiwara training.

Before training commences on the makiwara the student should be fairly comfortable executing the basic techniques. The delivery of the techniques should be in such a rhythm that they coordinate with the breathing. The stances should be stable with a strong display of balance. An overall increase in muscular strength and endurance compared to when the student first began training should be noticeable. In other words, the student should have advanced measurably from that of a beginner. Then and only then is the student ready to begin training on the makiwara.

The various karate techniques can be delivered to the makiwara from any stance. First-time users of a makiwara should select a stance that is strong, stable, and offers the highest degree of balance. The *sanchin* (hourglass), *kiba* (straddle or horse) and *zenkutsu* (forward) stances are best suited for beginning makiwara users.

Select the appropriate stance and face the makiwara. Center yourself so the makiwara post forms a parallel line with the vertical centerline of your body. Make a fist with both hands and extend your arms to the front with the fists touching each other and also touching the center of the makiwara. Retract the right fist to a chamber position under your armpit. You are now ready to begin striking the makiwara with the *seiken* (forefist).

"Before training commences on the makiwara the student should be fairly comfortable executing the basic techniques."

Knifehand strike (top), fore-fist (seiken) above and low roundhouse kick (gedan mawashi geri) to tree wrapped with belt (obi) right.

Makiwara with leather striking pad (left).

Strengthening arms for blocking using a split makiwara.

Students training on various types of makiwa.

Concentrate on hitting with the knuckles of the index and middle fingers. Focus on a spot on the makiwara that is in-line with your solar-plexus and attempt to land your strikes to the same spot each time. Until your hands, arms, and shoulders strengthen and become accustomed to striking the makiwara, use only light, bouncing blows—this could take several months depending on how frequent you utilize the makiwara. Execute a right *seiken* to the makiwara as you retract the left hand to the chamber position. Now execute a left seiken to the makiwara as you retract the right hand. You should try to acquire a steady and slow rhythm in the delivery of your techniques. Do not attempt to strike too fast or too hard. Remember, you want to develop power and focus in your techniques. Going too fast and too hard in the beginning stages of training will cause your techniques to be sloppy and inac-

The wooden makiwara shown in this article were specially built by master craftsman Les Parker of Colorado Springs, Colorado to withstand stress. They are constructed of laminated oak for strength and durability, and all mounting holes were drilled and planed. This is the same process used in building wooden airplanes. Planing the holes makes for a stronger joint. Sanding drilled holes tears the wood fibers and weakens the structure. The bases are welded steel with drilled holes for mounting. Contact Les Parker at (719) 599-3114 or lesparker@user-enchilada.com for purchase information.

curate. You also risk injury by going too hard and fast. Continue to alternate between right and left strikes until you complete the number of repetitions you have selected for your first time on the makiwara. You can alternate between various stances and also change the angle which you face the makiwara at. This change in stance and angle allows you to utilize the various strikes of your style against the makiwara.

After several months of regular training on the makiwara you should notice an increase in the strength and accuracy of your strikes. You can then modify your stances as well as the force and delivery of your techniques. Now, instead of using bouncing type blows, try to penetrate the makiwara with each technique. Push hard against the floor with your feet as though you were trying to push the floor out from under yourself. This will generate energy from the legs and lower torso. Attempt to go through the makiwara with each strike. Do not bounce your techniques or stop them upon impact—let the makiwara stop your momentum. Maintain a steady rhythm in the delivery of your strikes. Continue in this fashion every time you train on the makiwara. In time, you will develop techniques that generate penetrating energy known as *kime*, into an aggressor. You will find out, as karate masters of old found out, that focus and power can be enhanced through the use of a near extinct karate tool—the makiwara. $

The Karambit: The Curved Blade of West Java

A martial implement of great spiritual and physical might, the karambit is

Steve Tarani

Blade designs of Indonesia were heavily influenced by the migrating Hindus of the early 6th century AD. For example, the curves of the *kris* blade took the shape of fire. This was very symbolic to the early Hindus since fire was a symbol of life and death—quoted from the ancient Vedic prose "from ashes to ashes." In those days a kris was created by a swordsmith to exactly match the spirit of the fighter for which it was designed. If the fighter was aggressive then the blade was made to be aggressive. If the fighter was passive (or a counter-fighter) then the blade was made passive. The smith's design was based upon the *prana* or life/spiritual energy of the combatant. Thus, the warriors of that age claimed that the kris had a certain power. This is why many old tales of the blade spoke of a "magic" of the kris whereas it seemed to move magically in one fighter's hand but when wielded by another of equal skill, it seemed like dead weight.

Centuries ago, prior to AD 1289, most of West Java was part of the indigenous Pajajaran kingdom. The Badui tribe of West Java, the aboriginal people of Sunda, considered to be the ethnic group of the Pajajaran, lived relatively peacefully until the coming of the Majapahit empire in AD 1351. At that time the Badui tribe quickly migrated to the mountainous regions, brought their weapons with them, and remained self-governed. Thus, the word *Badui* literally translates as "the people who won't follow the rules."

The kings of the ancient Sundanese kingdom were considered very powerful. When a king died, it was believed that his spirit went into the jungles and became the spirit of the tiger. There are two terms for the tiger. One is *harimau* which is the generic Bahasay Indonesian word for tiger and the other is *pak macan* (pronounced pah-mah-chan and sometimes anglicized and spelled *pamacan*),

"The karambit is unique from any other blade as it can be used for both a medium and close fighting-ranges without changing the distance of the striking arm."

which loosely translates as "great tiger." It is this exact reason the great tiger is very much revered by the Sundanese. So awed were the ancient Sunda peoples by the power and ferocity of the pamacan, that the common blade of the people was patterned after the shape of the claw of pamacan. This blade was known as *kuku macan* or "claw of pamacan." Literally translated as "tiger claw" the kuku macan was revered symbolically as well as practically employed.

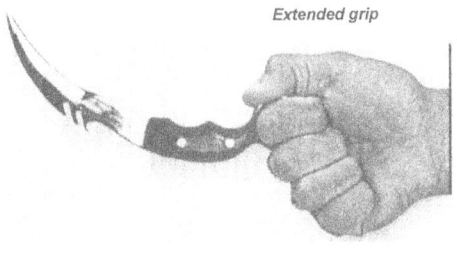

Extended grip

Originally wielded in battle, the oversized kuku macan was a bit cumbersome to manipulate so it was scaled down to smaller sizes which augmented maneuverability. Various permutations of the kuku macan were developed based upon practical usage—the saying goes "necessity is the mother of invention." The blade design came in smaller sizes and eventually found itself in the smallest size—the very personalized *karambit*.

The karambit can be traced from Sumatra to Malaysia and Java. The karambit of Lombok, (the

island between Bali and Sumbawa), is traditionally a larger or battlefield-sized karambit and is much larger than its more personal-sized Javanese cousin. There is also another variation of the karambit which comes from Madura Island (located Northeast of Java) which is more curved and known as the *clurit*. There are also many different shapes and designs of the karambit such as *rajawali* (bird-head shape) and others which include protruding spurs used for tearing flesh in the heat of battle.

The karambit is also referred to as the *kuku Bima* (literally "the claw of Bima"). Pre-12th century influence as a result of Hindus settling in the Indonesian archipelago brought the *Mahabharata* and the

1) Change elevation by dropping below eye level. 2) Deflect with outside hand while stepping to his back. 3) Secure his weapon arm with outside hand and position karambit. 4) Change elevation again and follow through while maintaining a secure grip.

Ramayana, (two major epics of India, valued for both high literary merit and religious inspiration) to Java. Contained within the Mahabharata is the *Bagavadgita* (The Lord's Song) which is the single most important religious text of Hinduism. Bima is a character from the Mahabrapta.

Also known as *kuku Hanuman* ("the claw of Hanuman," a character from the Ramayana), the karambit, the magical claw which protrudes from between the center of the hands of Bima and Hanuman, has become the weapon of the traditional art of the Indonesian archipelago called pencak silat. The combination of the original design of the tiger's claw combined with the hand weapons of the ancient characters of the Mahabharata and the Ramayana has evolved into the karambit. It is now recognized internationally as a traditional weapon of Indonesian pencak silat.

Normally, in ancient times, when a fighter unsheathed a battlefield karambit, the cutting edge was almost always smeared with some type of deadly poison which acted almost instantly upon entry

1) Change elevation by dropping below eye level. 2) Pass outside weapon hand with your karambit and use your body weight. 3) Secure weapon arm as you drop to a three- point stance. 4) Continue dropping to low seated harimau stance and extend karambit for groin strike upward.

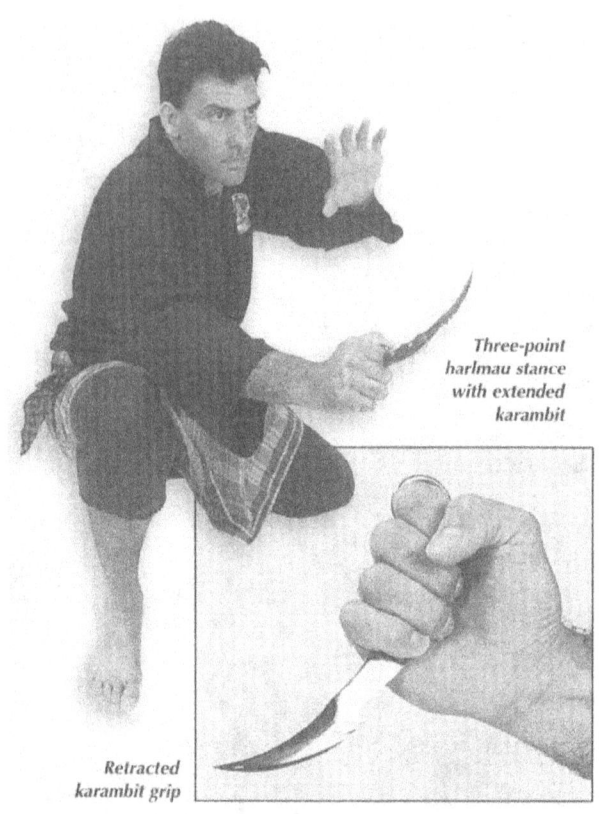

Three-point harImau stance with extended karambit

Retracted karambit grip

into the bloodstream via laceration of the flesh. Even the smallest cut was good enough to get the poison into the bloodstream. Knowledge and usage of poisons derived from various species of poisonous frogs, snakes, scorpions, and spiders were considered an essential element of a warrior's arsenal of close-quarter combative skills. These poisons rapidly accelerated death and were most feared for their near-instantaneous killing power. This is another reason why pencak silat techniques and systems such as Sabetan and Rhikasan focus on the immobilization of the hands at close quarters.

The personal karambit (a smaller version of the battlefield karambit) was primarily designed for targeting the nerves and joints. As a result of such a small cutting surface, most cuts cannot be made deep enough to kill someone. That is why the karambit is considered a personal self-defense weapon. In contrast, the blade of the *karambit besar* (larger battlefield version of the karambit) is longer and thus permits deeper cuts. According to the ancients, the battlefield karambit was preferred not only for it's superior length but for the fact that you could, as a result of the lengthy cutting edge, "spill the entrails of your enemies onto the ground."

The personal karambit targets include eyes, testicles, the Achilles tendon, carotid artery, biceps, forearm, and wrist. A particularly nasty target of ancient times was the clavicle (collarbone). Executed perfectly, the karambit would catch the collarbone (tip pointed-down) and then quickly turn-up from palm-down position to palm-up position which, using your body weight, would snap the bone thus rendering your enemy's weapon arm useless.

Specifically designed as a close quarter self-defense weapon, the karambit is additionally quite difficult to see in the hand due to its method of deployment and covering of the fingers. Doubly menacing is the fact that it cannot be disarmed as a result of its forefinger grip design. It is unique from any other blade as it can be used for both a medium and close fighting-ranges without changing the distance of the striking arm. It is also the only blade that can cut twice with a single arm stroke. All other blades need one motion for one cut. The karambit is unique because it cannot be easily seen, it cannot be easily disarmed, it can change ranges without body movement, and it can deliver two cuts in a single motion.

Seated harimau with retracted karambit

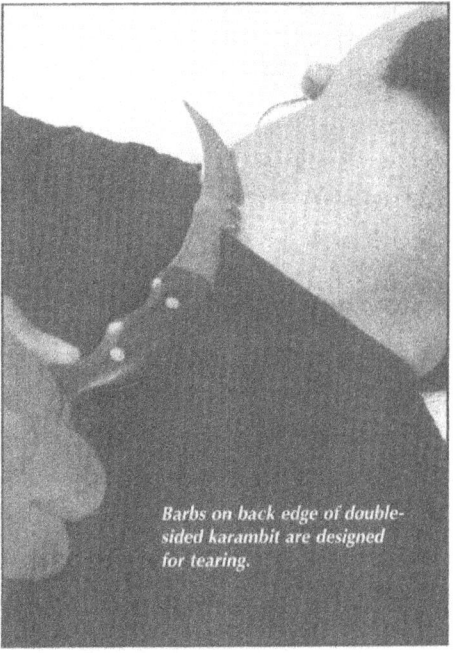

Barbs on back edge of double-sided karambit are designed for tearing.

Although quite a remarkable weapon, and as fierce as it looks, it's primary application is self-defense. Its small tip and blade length are not conducive to delivery of lethal blows and the karambit cannot be used for thrusting and thus cannot be considered a dagger. However, when used correctly it can deliver a nasty and menacing payload to any threatening extended limb. Originally used for personal backup, there were specific styles and systems of training which employed the karambit as an "add on." For example, the Cikalong and Rhikasan systems of mande muda pencak silat, are the base systems of hand immobilization and close-quarter technique. Once you became proficient in these systems in empty-hand application, you could then easily "add on" the karambit to your technique. This would be like attaching nuclear warheads to your conventional missiles.

The karambit is, therefore, a tool of personal protection and represents, skill, maturity, honor, and wisdom. Those who are well-versed in its usage have a greater advantage over those who do not. An ancient code of ethics reminds the warrior that his weapon should not be unsheathed without good reason nor draw blood without honor. ®

The Unstoppable Richard Norton

From zen-do kai karate innovator, to celebrity bodyguard, to martial-arts movie star, Richard Norton has risen to the top of a dog-eat-dog world without sacrificing friendship for personal gain.

Todd Hester

He's more Australian than Crocodile Dundee, more macho than Rambo, and more deadly than the American Ninja. He's been the on-tour guardian angel for The Rolling Stones, Joe Cocker, David Bowie, Linda Ronstadt, Fleetwood Mack, John Belushi, and James Taylor. He's appeared and starred in over 60 movies, fought Jackie Chan on-screen three times, been directed three times by Sarno Hung, battled Chuck Norris in *The Octagon* as the villainous Kyo (one of the top movie fights of all time), made eight appearances on *Walker: Texas Ranger,* and appeared in more Hong Kong movies than a pair of chopsticks. Yet despite the Hollywood hype, if you were in a knockdown-dragout brawl, Norton might be the one person you'd want guarding your back.

Five minutes after meeting the down-to-earth Norton you forget who he is, start swapping jokes and stories, and end up wanting to go out to a local pub and hoist a few—just don't get too boisterous. This 4th dan zen-do kai expert is the real deal who bounced in some of Melbourne's most notorious nightspots and helped popularize karate in Australia the hard way—by standing up to any doubters who walked into his zen-do kai schools and tried to start trouble.

Yet the easy-going and casual Norton is a very old-fashioned martial artist who has taken a very progressive approach to martial arts training. He's a star and a fan, a leader and a follower, and a traditionalist and a modernist. He doesn't talk trash, is fiercely loyal, and his most treasured possessions are his friends and family. Richard Norton's unofficial motto might be "I get by with a little help with my friends—and a little karate doesn't hurt either!"

The Early Years

Born in Elwood, Australia, he moved to Croydon when he was a year old. His interest began with comic books and the back page ads where he would read about judo. As Norton recalls, "It was really the only martial art available to us back in those days. As a 1 0-year-old kid, the thought of doing some martial art like judo, which had a mystical Far Eastern lure to it, was very appealing. The prime reason for me learning the martial arts was not just to learn how to fight. There were a lot of reasons, many of which probably weren't obvious to me at the time."

Norton finally got his chance to turn his dreams into reality when, at age 12, a door opened up into the world of martial arts. Little did he know at the time that it would be the start of a life-long odyssey. "The people who lived opposite me in Croydon sold their house and a new family moved in," Norton recalls. "They had a teenaged son who I started hanging out with. I noticed that he was disappearing two nights a week, so I asked where he was going and he told me judo school in Nunawading. That pricked my ears up and that's how I decided to visit the club."

Norton trained in judo for two years until another friend who was training informed him that a karate school had opened up closer to his home. That was all the incentive young Richard needed. "At that time karate was virtually unknown to us," Norton says, "except for the odd book which I would stumble across. So I went to the club in Baywater, three miles from where I lived, and the instructor was Tino Ceberano and the style was goju kai. Tino had only been in Australia for a year and had been teaching in the headquarters in Canterbury. On this night he brought out some lower belts to do some demos for those of us who had come to check out the school. What they did was an h-pattern kata, and I just fell in love with it and knew that was what I wanted to be doing. You see, I was very skinny and small at the time and with judo I felt like one of those cartoon characters who gets thrown from one end of the room to the other by the big guy. Karate was more of an art where

Richard Norton Timeline

- **1962:** Started judo with John Burge in Melbourne, Australia
- **1964:** Earned judo brown belt
- **1965:** Started goju-kai with Tino Ceberano
- **1967:** First bouncer job
- **1969:** Earned goju black belt
- **1970:** Helped develop zen-do kai (best of everything) with Bob Jones, eventually becoming Chief Instructor of over 500 schools.
- **1973:** Bodyguard for The Rolling Stones. For the next 12 years worked with Joe Cocker, Abba, Fleetwood Mac, Linda Ronstadt, James Taylor, David Bowie, John Belushi, and others.
- **1976:** Met Chuck Norris.
- **1979:** Moved to the U.S. and did The Octagon as ninja assassin Kyo. Started studying with Fumio Demura, Tadashi Yamashita, and Peter Cunningham, and training with Bill Wallace and Benny Urquidez among many others.

size wasn't such a big consideration—and that was the catalyst for me getting into karate."

A Different Direction

Norton trained with Ceberano for several years, and during this time he developed a friendship with fellow goju kai student Bob Jones. This friendship was to have a ripple effect that would change his life forever. "Bob was an innovator and an idea man," Norton says. "I see now, more than I did then, just how true that was. He'd traveled to America and looked for ways to do things differently. He wasn't content to do things the same as everyone else. That's what led him to breakaway from goju kai and help form zen-do kai, which basically means "the best of everything in progression." "When I started working with him," Norton says, "we adopted an approach that made us freer in our ideas as to what martial arts moves we would incorporate into the zen-do kai system. Being with Bob meant that we were running the zen-do kai schools and we were training six days a week. What we lacked in technique and finesse we

Richard working with his coach, Pete Cunningham of House of Champions, Van Nuys, CA.

1981: After numerous supporting roles, landed lead role in *Force 5* with Joe Lewis, Bong Soo Han, and Benny Urquidez.
1990: Started studying Machado Jiu-Jitsu. Introduced Bob Wall and Chuck Norris to the Machados. Helped Machados open school.
1992: Machado blue belt
1993: Married Judy Green (the Vanna White of Australia) in L.A.'s Bel Air Hotel. Chuck Norris best man.
1997: After numerous movies roles accepted part in T.V. series *Robin Hood*.
2000: In development to produce and star in *The Sam Hill Chronicles*

1978 Linda Ronstadt

made up for in hard work, sweat, and blood—literally. We had these young guys testing us in every class, getting better and better, thereby prompting us to get better. That made me very hungry for knowledge. I had to keep searching. I read books, I bought tapes, I went to look at other schools and I went to other tournaments always with the idea of what I could learn that would help me instruct the next week, and the next week, and the week after that, and make the classes interesting. It was incredible for my development, the fact that I left goju kai and was now running this school as chief instructor for zen-do kai. I honestly think it helped me grow because I had to think for myself, find my own knowledge and express different ways of teaching the knowledge that I had found. I had to internalize to make it my own."

The Bodyguard
Through his goju and zen-do kai training, his tireless teaching at numerous schools, and his endless fights while working door security at the notoriously tough Aussie bars, Norton became somewhat of an Australian martial arts folk hero. So when the Rolling Stones "rolled" Down Under for a series of concerts Norton and Jones were the obvious choices to run security. As it ended up, he also spent time with Stone frontman Mick Jagger, teaching him karate. "Mick's a real smart guy," Norton says. "Somewhat of a bloody genius, actually. Plus, he keeps himself in great shape and he learns quickly. That was a crazy time."

At Adelaide Stadium, during one of the Stone's rowdiest concerts, Norton got his baptism by fire. "I remember that Mick just built the crowd to a frenzy. Each song was louder, heavier, and stronger and they began to rush the stage to get to him. Only a rickety wood retaining fence was keeping them back. We could see the fences beginning to bow inward and we knew they wanted to take the stage

over," Norton remembers. "They were hitting cops, each other—they didn't care. There were only five of us on the other side of the fence and we knew we were the last line of defense. So as they started coming over the fence we would take them out and then throw them back over. I was taking on two or three blokes at a time. But we were gradually getting overwhelmed and were to get stampeded. Luckily, the riot police emerged and about brought the crowd under control before anyone was seriously hurt."

After that Norton's and Jones' reputation within the rock scene grew as men who could get things done and who, more importantly, would put themselves on the line for their clients. Soon, whenever any major rock act came to Australia they would call on Norton and Jones.

Bright Lights, Big City

As big as Australia is, though, it would soon prove too small to contain the talents of the "Thunder from Down Under." In 1976, Norton and zen-do kai partner Bob Jones decided to bring Chuck Norris to Australia to do demonstrations at some of their tournaments. "We all knew about Chuck in Australia, of course," Norton says, "because of the martial arts magazines. All of the magazines in those days were always about the duels between Joe Lewis and Chuck Norris. So when Chuck arrived in Australia we got on like a house on fire, we really got on well. And Chuck said if I ever got to California to drop in and we could do some training. I didn't think much of it at the time, but then in 1979 I was offered a job doing security on a U.S. tour with Linda Ronstadt as her personal bodyguard and trainer. So I went out to Southern California. I told everybody in Australia I'd be back in a month and 20 years later I'm still here."

One day, remembering the good times he had shared with Norris in Australia, Norton looked him

1998 "Robin Hood"

up. "I called Chuck and went around to his house, and that's where my film career started for me because we started working out every day. He just happened to be in pre-production for *The Octagon,* and he realized after seeing me in Australia that I could handle Okinawan weapons. I started helping Chuck put the fight scenes together for the film with his brother Aaron. I ended up with a part in *The Octagon* as the hooded ninja assassin Kyo, which was a great role for me and a great start in movies, even though I never showed my face. I actually played four ninjas in that movie and died eight times—I still think that's a record. And away it went. I really owe everything to Chuck Norris. He's an amazing martial artist, a true gentleman, and a great friend."

The photogenic Norton was soon offered roles without a mask—and with each new movie, more offers came in. Some of his most memorable roles to American audiences were in *Rage and Honor* and *China O'Brien* with Cynthia Rothrock, *Under the Gun* with Cathy Long, *The Blood of Heroes* with Rutger Hauer, *Gymkata* with Kurt Thomas, and *Mr. Nice Guy* with Jackie Chan. All told, Norton has done over 60 movies in addition as being the second unit director

1993 Married Judy Green

1994 Steven Segal

1998 "Robin Hood"

1999 "Walker, Texas Ranger" with Frank Shamrock

1997 with Rigan Machado

1997 "Mr. Nice Guy" with Jackie Chan, directed by Sammo Hung (above).

1998 "Robin Hood" with Montel Williams

2000 "The Sam Hill Chronicles"

and stunt coordinator on the syndicated TV series *The New Adventures of Robin Hood*, since 1998.

Norton is very complimentary to actors he's worked with over the years, and two of his favorites has been Jackie Chan and Sammo Hung. "Jackie and Sammo are great. I've got all the respect in the world for them. They're so incredibly creative, more so than anybody I've worked with in the United States. I worked with them in my first Hong Kong movie called *Twinkle, Twinkle, Lucky Stars* which Sammo Hung directed. Sammo is like the Steven Spielberg of Hong Kong action movies. It was my first Hong Kong movie and I didn't really know what to expect. What an eye-opener. I was shooting around the clock. You'd only get an hour, hour-and-a-half sleep on the set, and that went on for three weeks. I lost 18 pounds and was an absolute wreck. I was in a studio that was never under 115 degrees with no air conditioning—and man did you have to fight hard. My fight in that movie with Sammo took three weeks to shoot and involved full body contact. And don't let the body fool you, Sammo can really fight. I gained a lot of respect for Jackie and Sammo after that, just seeing what they went through, day in and day out, for year after year."

Partial Filmography

(COMPILED BY STEVEN FELDMAN)

American Ninja (1985), *Black Thunder* (1999), *The Blood of Heroes* (1988), *China O'Brien* (1990), *China O'Brien II* (1991), *City Hunter* (1992), *Cybertracker* (1994), *Direct Hit* (1994), *Fugitive X: Innocent Target* (1996), *The Deadliest Art: Best of the Martial Arts Films* (1990), *Deathfight* (1994), *Equalizer 2000* (1986), *Eyes of the Dragon* (1992), *Forced Vengeance* (1982), *Force Five* (1981), *Future Hunters* (1986), *Gymkata* (1985), *Hawkeye* (1988), *Ironheart* (1992), *Jungle Heat* (1988), *The Kick Fighter* (1994), *Lady Dragon* (1991), *License to Kill* (1998), *The Magic Crystal* (1986), *Millionaire's Express* (1986), *Mr. Nice Guy* (1997), *Nautilus* (1999), *Robin Hood* (1988-), *The Octagon* (1980), *Overseer, The Adventures of Tex Murphy* (1998), *Rage and Honor* (1992), *Rage and Honor II*

But Norton is not one to dwell on his past and is continually looking to the future. "The rapids ahead are much more exciting to me than the water under the bridge," he says. "I'm very excited about a new TV series that it's in development right now that I'll be producing as well as starring in. It's called the *Sam Hill Chronicles,* and it's basically a turn-of-the-century *X Files.* Sam Hill was actually a real person who investigated paranormal events in the early 20th century. He's the reason that people started saying 'What in the Sam Hill?' when they saw anything strange. We've got great scripts ready and the whole thing is set to start filming in September of this year. I think it's going to be a huge hit around the world."

Norton continues to apply his forward-looking philosophy to martial arts as well as acting, having just received his brown belt in Brazilian jiu-jitsu from Jean Jacques Machado. "To learn is to grow—dare to participate and make mistakes," says Norton. "Many people are too afraid to be found out for what they don't know. As Benny Urquidez has always said, 'Knowledge is power.'" Norton, along with Chuck Norris and Bob Wall, was instrumental in bringing Machado jiu-jitsu to the United States—a fact that he's very proud of. Norton, above all, considers himself a martial artist first and foremost and continues to learn and to grow. A phrase he coined for the Machado school is "Leave your ego at the door," a philosophy that Norton himself has followed for years.

"There's no doubt the reason I got started in movies is because of my martial arts abilities. I've since expanded my acting ability but I haven't forgotten my roots. I love the martial arts and I love the people I've met through them. I don't know where I'd be without my training but I do know that even without the movies, as long as I had martial arts, I'd be happy. Martial arts gives you a sense of family and belonging. Many of the friends I've made through my training have turned out to be just like family to me. Because when you get right down to it—when you really think about it—the only thing that really matters in life is the relationship with your friends and the love of your wife and your family."

Pai Lum Tao's White Crane

The ever-changing movements of white crane keep attackers off balance and confused.

Glenn C. Wilson

Few systems can match the diversity and effectiveness of Pai Lum Tao's way of the white dragon. This revered system was brought to the public eye in the early 1950s by the legendary great grandmaster Daniel Kane Pai. A time-tested combative art, it proved its worth in the tough back streets of Hawaii. Daniel Kane Pai became legendary for his no-nonsense and highly successful form of fighting which he called, "fighting to survive."

Pai would formulate the teachings of his grandfather's dragon movements, his aunt's white crane style with his kodokan judo, white lotus kenpo, chuan fa and tai chi to give birth to an awesome system of modern Pai Lum Tao. Within these teachings are three disciplines: pai te lung chuan kung-fu; bok leen pai kenpo; and pai yung tai chi chuan.

The Key To Success

Understanding the depth and zones of attack are keys to the combative success of Pai Lum Tao. Depth of short- and long-hand boxing becomes the basic categories of study within the system. To know which to use and when becomes the science of the warrior.

Lhe devastating long-hand techniques of Pai Lum Tao teach one to strike like a whip. The body is kept relaxed and supple while the hand emulates a metal ball. This allows the practitioner to move in the "nei," soft and smooth, and strike in the "wei," hard and powerful. Maximum range is the goal of the "long wing" movements. The muscle, tendons and sinew are worked continuously to assure their flexibility at the time of execution. Exercises such as swing arm, horizontal whips and extended wings are practiced daily. Arms become extremely strong yet supple; this ensures good "chi" flow when the technique reaches its destination. The short-hand techniques slice, pierce and crush in circular, vertical, horizontal and figure-eight patterns. These moves are kept close to the body and require countless hours of speed drills to assure the "lightning-fast" snapping motion. Such drills as pecking beak, crane's head and spearing the enemy assure pinpoint targetry. These drills are practiced solo for speed and technique and with a partner for timing and targetry. They move quickly in close range and are accentuated by powerful waist whipping. The attacker who runs into the short-range combative techniques will quickly fall or yield back into the long-range zones.

Encompassing both long hand and short hand, a variety of hand and arm arsenals are practiced diligently. Basic hand strikes such as spear, leopard, sun, ram, uppercut, backfist, heel palm, willow

Grandmaster Glenn C. Wilson delivers a pecking crane's beak from the Pai Lum Tao white crane series.

anything in its path. Arm strikes begin with white crane's wing, white ape, on-guard, searching rod, and bear. These techniques serve as a battering ram to offset, dislodge and disrupt the attacker's flow.

Back To Basics

Before the Pai Lum Tao practitioner can hope to master his arsenal he will spend countless hours working the basic disciplines of stance, posture, and technique. Then he must understand the principles of distance and depth. This will determine the warrior's "plan of action"——which technique to use with the long-hand sets and which to use with the short-hand series.

Once the mind has sent the signal, the techniques must be reactionary. With this reactionary response Pai Lum Tao's white crane theories evolve around a speedy, powerful execution of technique. This is a formula that cannot be successful without the ingredients of both lightning and thunder; speed

techniques must be spontaneous in nature. One may not have the luxury of time to think of a response to an attack. Speed drills must be practiced on a daily basis. The key to speed is relaxation. The pupil is taught to move in the "nei" soft-smooth movements. Such exercises as picking the fruit, thunder and lightning and elusive wind are practiced diligently to insure that one develops and maintains the lightning speed for which Pai Lum Tao has become known.

Power must be built from the ground up. Stance is the root of the movement. A weak stance may prove disastrous for the practitioner. The three-step formula of "stance, posture, then technique" becomes a "checkpoint" for the student to gauge his success in preparation. The student is trained to understand the full effectiveness of "waist whipping" of the dragon. The waist whipping can triple the power of a punch when executed correctly. With a smooth, fluid motion the waist will preceed the punch then recoil to its "set" position. With this immense power the punch will then be able to penetrate with a magnified result.

Physical and mental training play a most important role in the success of the outcome

Rich Wilson and Bob Earl assume the on-guard position (1). Rich attacks with a ram's head punch while Bob counters with an inside wing (2). Bob strikes with a shortrange slapping wing and a long-range heel palm strike (3). Bob then pierces with a spearhand technique (4).

of a conflict. Physical training can be complex and dangerous if not instructed by the proper tutor. Iron body training is part of the practitioners carefully practiced formula. The conditioning of the body to not feel pain when the punch or kick lands is a slow, careful process. Thousands of carefully placed strikes by a trained partner will become routine. Herbal medicine, such as dragon dit da jow, will be essential for protection of external and internal bruises that may occur during rigorous training. With this in mind, partner training such as "seven star," becomes common place.

Finding The Perfect Balance

Balance is just as important as speed and power. The very essence of white crane training evolves around balance. Balance encompasses stance, posture, technique, execution, timing and breathing.

Balance training begins with the cat stance (low and high) and works toward the sleeping crane—on one leg for 15 minutes. This is slow, yet direct training designed to reach the level desired by the students. Mastery of balance is key for any student who wants to become proficient in his art.

Pinpoint striking is a well-known characteristic of the white crane. Knowing where to strike can make the difference between success and failure. The technique will be partially determined by the practitioner based on his target area. Pai Lum Tao's white crane teaches fingers to pierce; blade of hand to slice; palm of hand to stun; and fist hand to crush.

They say that "timing is everything." But as most martial artists know, perfecting "timing" is one of the most difficult training aspects to conquer. Students will practice a cat-and-mouse type of training with a partner. The offensive partner attempts to tag his defensive partner's extended palms with a variety of crane strikes while the palms are moving. The moving palms will be purposely deceptive and evasive to the attack. This teaches one to relax and explode spontaneously with pinpoint accuracy.

Off Balance And Confused

The crane teaches us the epitome of patience. While practicing white crane, a student practices patience as he moves about the floor in a smooth, fluid motion. Once his opponent obligates himself, and ultimately compromises his guard, the white crane explodes with a beautiful flurry of techniques which

Caimano and Sindy begin in the on-guard position (1). Jeff attacks with claws while Ron strikes with crane's beak (2). Ron drives in with double willow palm strikes (3). Ron finishes off his attacker with a scooping monk's spade kick (4).

render the attacker helpless. Such development in one's patience is a time-tested discipline which separates the winners and losers.

The ever-changing movements of white crane keep its attacker off balance and confused. There is a continuous linking of movements in a systematic array of strikes. The Pai Lum Tao practitioners goal is to develop spontaneous reaction. Movements link into one another with a rhythm of energy release. One will not only begin to read

Hilda Wilson and Ron Caimano assume the on-guard position (1). Ron attacks with a backfist punch while Hilda cuts with an inside wing (2). Hilda drops into a long bow stance while executing an outside wing (3). Hilda then whips back and drives an uppercut into the target (4).

his attackers moves, but he will actually predetermine them by his own movement.

Pai Lum Tao puts a great emphasis on the combined development of mind, body, and spirit. The practitioner learns that the mind triggers the body, the body awakens the spirit, and the spirit creates the mind. The natural blending of the three creates a true harmony. This is never more evident than in Pai Lum Tao's white crane. $

Glenn C. Wilsons videotape series on the Pai Lum Tao system are available through Unique Publications/Video.

Pai Lum Tao's White Crane

STRIKES	KICKS	STANCES
Ram's Head	Front Heel	Square Horse
Hooking Hand	Stomp	Side Horse
Willow Palm	Side Heel	Cat
Crane's Beak	Monk's Spade	Single Leg
Crane's Head	Front Broom	Long Bow
Lifting Hand	Back Broom	Short Bow
Outside Wing	Inside Crescent	Twisting Horse
Inside Wing	Outside Crescent	Hidden Stance
Uppercut	Tornado	
Noni Slap	Back	
Crane Grab	Knife Edge	
Backfist		

Sindy and Wilson open in the on-guard position (1). Sindy delivers a front kick and Wilson counters with an inside crescent scoop (2). Wilson explodes with a palm slap then hooking hand wing (3). Wilson then twists in and delivers a long-range spearhand (4).

The Legacy of Professor Vee

Professor Florendo Visitacion, professor Vee to his legion of admirers, remained a true martial arts visionary to the end.

Robert Dreeben

One thing in life is certain: as soon as we think we have all the answers, we stop asking questions. And that usually means we stop learning. Professor Florendo Visitacion never wasted a day, never stopped learning or studying his beloved martial art until the day he died.

Supreme grandmaster Florendo Visitacion died last year in New York City at the age of 89. He left behind a rich legacy spanning more than five decades. With thousands of students, professor Vee, as he was affectionately known, produced many masters and even grandmasters who today share their own interpretation of the theory, concepts and application of professor Vee's system.

According to Roberto Torres, "Professor Vee was into cross-training before cross-training was popular. He would study any martial art that was available to him, along with other subjects such as physical fitness and philosophy. He loved books and had an extensive library on a broad range of subjects."

Professor Vee, professor Wally fay and Roberto Torres.

The Beginning

Florendo Visitacion was born in the Philippines in 1910. In 1920 he began his martial arts training. His first teachers were his brother and his uncle who taught an indigenous family art complete with empty hand, knives and sticks. When he was 16 he left the Philippines and moved to Hawaii, where he lived for many years before moving to California to work in the famous wine vineyards.

"Filipinos were known to work in those labor camps," Torres relates. "He told me that the ones who were running the labor camps and the ones who were respected were the martial artists, especially if you were known for the use of a blade. He said people would come to them for advice and that they would practice all kinds of different martial arts with the blade and empty hand."

During World War II he enlisted in the service. When the war was over, he was invited by an exArmy buddy to visit New York in the early 1950s. He was there for the remainder of his life, where he continued to study various martial arts. In fact, professor Vee was one of the few instructors in this country certified in "vermani," an East Indian martial art.

"It was through his collaboration with Wally Jay that Vee's art became known as Vee-jitsu," Torres explains. "He became a member of the American Judo-Jiu-jitsu Federation. It was here that professor Vee presented his art.

"Many people called him professor "Vee" because they had a hard time pronouncing his name," Torres adds. "The name of his art when he presented it to the Federation in 1968 was called Vee-jitsu, which simply meant the art of Vee. From what professor explained to me it was never classified as Vee-jitsu jiu-jitsu. Other people on their own added that later on.

"Professor also achieved a master's degree in danzan ryu jiu-jitsu, which is professor Okazaki's system. In creating his art, professor Okazaki combined jiu-jitsu with kung-fu, lua, Philippine martial arts and knifefighting."

The American Judo-Jiujitsu Federation recognized professor Vee's art in 1968 and named him a 10th dan.

"At one point professor Vee was actually my classmate," Torres remembers. "That's how we met. He was studying amis with master (Mat P.) Marinas, Sr., who was my teacher and I was shocked when they said professor Vee will be here soon."

Torres already had an extensive martial arts background, having studied and earned degrees in kung-fu, silat, and kali as well as being an amateur boxer.

Many people were surprised at the sight of a well-respected master like professor Vee wanting to study another martial art. This was just another example of how professor Vee's quest for knowledge and how his humble attitude prevented his ego from getting in the way of his training.

"It was amazing to watch him move," Torres says with reflection. "I remember him showing me some stick movements. I then became his student."

Beyond Jiu-Jitsu

Even today many practitioners of professor Vee's system call it a style of jitsu. As Torres explains, "We cannot say that professor Vee's martial art was jiu-jitsu. A lot of people wanted to classify Vee's art under that but to professor Vee terminology was not that important. He could use a Filipino term as he could an Indonesian term or a Japanese term. It was a matter of the relationship to the technique he was teaching you."

Torres shares another story: "There is a well-known New York jiu-jitsu grandmaster who teaches in the Bronx, who received his black belt from professor Vee. He was one of professor Vee's first black belts. This instructor then went to Japan to further his jiu-jitsu studies he learned from professor. He came back and never spoke to professor again because when the Japanese saw his art they said, 'that's not jiu-jitsu'."

While many practitioners argue about the terminology of the professor's system, one thing they all agree on is the brutal effectiveness of Vee-jitsu in combat application. Professor's locking technique resembles sophisticated kung-fu chin na rather than standard jiu-jitsu holds.

"Professor Vee's system fell very much into the southern Chinese martial art, the kun tao, the silat," Torres notes. "If you watch tapes of him you'll see a lot of Fukien influence with the front toes turned in."

Against a knife slash, professor Vee angles his body and cuts down (1). Flowing, he then cuts up while checking the arm (2) to a straight thrust (3). Vee then disarms the attacker (4).

"I was very young then," Torres adds. "In 1988 I was 27 years old and (professor Vee's) telling me he's going to leave me the system. When he named me as his heir, back then, it created a lot of controversy among his students, a lot of jealousy. In fact, one Filipino individual who was a friend of mine felt that the art should not be left to a non-Filipino."

Because professor Vee had different sides to his martial art and shared unique relationships with all his students, Visitacion named three other heirs. In 1992 he named Frank Edwards Sr. and his son Frank Edwards Jr. as heir to Vee-jitsu 75. Also in 1992 he named David James as the heir to Vee-arms jitsu.

When Torres inherited the system it was called Vee-jitsu te, later changed by professor to Visitacion kun tao. Among the heirs only Torres had the right to use the name "kun tao" when referring to his version of professor Vee's art.

"When professor named me the heir to his art in 1988, I felt a huge responsibility because the torch is being passed on to me," Torres says. "However, I was doing other martial arts that I was not about to let go of and so it created a struggle for me. My other concern was there were other teachers here in New York who were using the name 'Vee' even though they had nothing to do with professor. I didn't want my teacher's name to be marred. So, the professor and I came up with the idea of changing the name of his art to 'kalasag kali kun tao' system because I was also teaching kail as well."

Professor Vee did not expect Torres to give up his other martial arts. On the contrary; it may have been the professor recognizing Torres as a young and gifted student eager to learn the best every fighting art had to offer.

Professor Vee's Art Today

Torres talks about the development of Visitacion kun tao: "Professor was constantly developing his art. I used to make modifications to the art," he relates. "Professor presented a certificate to me because of my further development. So he realized that I was going to take the art to another area. Not that I was going to make it better than my teacher but that I was going to carry it on and further develop it."

Following professor Vee's quest for study and research, Torres met Willem de Thouars, who passed on the art of tjimande. After studying with Willem de Thouras, Torres put together the pencak silat perisai setia.

Torres also integrates boxing into his system because, "All my teachers—professor Vee, Willem de Thouars, Edgar Sulite, Chris Sayoc, and grandmaster Illustrisimo—have felt that my boxing was a great influence on what I do and it brings the art alive."

Although Torres teaches his own system, he does have a four-tape series on the kun tao available from Unique Publications/Video.

Conclusion

Today, many students of other arts whose instructors may have cross-trained with professor Vee or one of his instructors have been influenced by Visitacion concepts. Professor Vee's teaching was not about the tradition of purity. Quite the opposite. He encouraged individuality of expression through concept. To know that professor's art is being passed on, regardless of the package, has brought a happy conclusion to professor Vee's legacy. $

Robert Dreeben is Inside Kung-Fu's *2000 "Writer of the Year."*

A Quarter-Century of Capoeira

Capoeira Master Jelon Vieira celebrates 25 years since he introduced the Afro-Brazilian martial art form to the United States

Sergey Gordeev

Jelon Vieira is comfortably seated at a hip café in downtown Manhattan, ordering a healthy lunch and sharing the fascinating tale of a pioneer in every sense of the word. A master capoeirista, founder and Artistic Director of his world-renowned dance troupe, master teacher, serious scholar, philosopher and ultimately a true gentleman, Mestre Jelon remembers when he first arrived in the U.S. from the Brazilian state of Bahia with a mission to introduce to America the Afro-Brazilian art form of capoeira.

"When I just came to New York in 1975 with the late Loremil Machado, I found a completely unexplored cultural terrain in terms of African influence on Brazilian culture. Nobody knew anything about Afro-Brazilian dance, and the only image that came to peoples mind when Brazilian dance was mentioned was the image of Carmen Miranda with fruit on top of her head. Of course, people knew about Bossa Nova and Samba, but that was all. There was very little and limited understanding. That's when I decided to stay in New York and introduce the African aspect of Brazilian dance and culture."

Very soon, a chance to do that availed itself when the late Louisa Roberts—then a director of the Clark Center for the Performing Arts in New York City—invited Jelon to participate in a Clark Center Dance Festival in 1977. Jelon and Loremil gathered a group of Brazilian dancers, and their two performances were completely sold out. Encouraged by the success, Jelon decided to keep the company, giving birth to the very first Brazilian dance company in the U.S.— *The Capoeiras of Bahia*.

The Capoeiras of Bahia—as is evident from the name itself—dedicated themselves to a dual purpose: to promote and introduce to American audiences the Brazilian art form of capoeira, as well as introduce the African influence on the Brazilian culture as a whole. Needless to say, education was as needed then as it is now. Developed in the 16th century by Africans who were brought to Brazil as slaves

as a form of self-defense performed under the guise of dance, capoeira has always been an object of both fascination and fear—which is evident from the mere fact that Brazilian government has banned capoeira twice in the past. The first ban came when the Portuguese colonists found out what capoeira really meant for the enslaved Africans in Brazil. The abolition of slavery in 1888 briefly allowed capoeira to emerge into the open, only to be forbidden again once the government realized that it could be lethal. Often manipulatively used for exploitative purposes such as breaking strikes or controlling crowds, capoeira sustained quite a negative reputation—to the point where anyone found practicing capoeira could have either been severely punished or sometimes even killed. Still, it was secretly practiced in capoeira *rodas* ("circles") and homes until the 1930s, when the attitude towards the art form slowly began to change. The change came after Mestre Bimba performed capoeira for the president of Brazil, Getulio Vargas, who then announced that capoeira deserved to be considered an important part of Brazilian history and should be taught as a national sport of Brazil. It is perhaps from then on that people started referring to the interaction between men in capoeira rodas as "playing" rather than "fighting" or "combating."

Jelon was formally introduced to the art form when he was 9, although he says he had always felt he was a capoeirista—even before he realized what capoeira was. "Capoeira is not the muscle

"Capoeira has always been an object of both fascination and fear—which is evident from the mere fact that Brazilian government has banned capoeira twice in the past."

power, it's the power of the mind," he explains. "It is an art form that manifests itself through a human being." The young Jelon could not study with Mestre Amerito, who was a great berimbau player and the first capoeira master he encountered, because his house was too close to where the boy's family lived—and "mother didn't even want to hear the word capoeira." So he trained under someone else, but soon found out that this person's heart was not in the art form. In 1963, going to a soccer game, he ran into Mestre Bobo, who was a well-known capoeira angola master, and ended up studying with him for seven years.

"Mestre Bobo taught me a lot about capoeira Angola and its traditions. He paid particular attention to the correct composition of all the instruments involved in capoeira, which include the *berimbau* (a traditional instrument consisting of a wooden stick, a gourd, and a steel string to form a bow shape), *pandeiro* (a tambourine with a head and flat jingles), *agogo* (two iron bells), *reco-reco* (a bamboo scrapper) and *atabaque* (tall barrel style hand drum). I feel very fortunate to have met Mestre Bobo and to have had the honor of being his student. He taught me how to be a 'gentle warrior.'"

Having firmly grounded himself in the traditional "capoeira Angola" which Jelon calls "the mother of all capoeira," he encountered "capoeira regional"—a completely new style of capoeira developed in Bahia by Mestre Bimba. His style impressed Jelon with its relaxed coolness—Mestre Bimba's students had always played with a smile, no matter how tough the situation. Jelon studied at Mestre Bimba's school until the master moved away and passed his school on to Mestre Vermelho and Mestre Eziquiel, under whose tutelage Jelon continued his education in capoeira. "Mestre Eziquiel taught me respect for life," says Jelon, "which was, perhaps, one of the most important lessons for me."

It was not until the 1980s, after doing capoeira for many years, that Jelon Vieira himself received the title of "Mestre"—an honor which indicates both the mastery of the various capoeira techniques and a very high level of maturity and sophistication in the understanding of capoeira as a life philosophy. Mestre Jelon's initiation ritual was performed by his latest teacher, Mestre Eziquiel, in Bahia. "Lots of people call themselves masters," says Jelon, "but many of them aren't. It takes a lot of time, studying, self-discipline and growth to become a Mestre."

His very focused, crystal-clear understanding of this important part of Afro-Brazilian culture has expanded Mestre Jelon's renown as a teacher and master of capoeira far beyond his native state of Bahia. His students range from hundreds of underprivileged children in Bahia to university students in the United States to the soccer great Pele and American movie star Wesley Snipes. In Bahia, Mestre Jelon's year-round outreach activities to underprivileged children are designed to help them make a transition into the educational system and the mainstream society by using capoeira to build self-esteem and self-discipline. He conducts these activities under the auspices of Grupo Capoeira Brasil, and dreams of one day opening a center specifically for underprivileged children. He has taught in master classes and workshops all over the world, and has been a guest instructor at major American universities, including Yale, Stanford, Princeton, Columbia, Duke, Oberlin College, and the University of Nebraska. He currently teaches as the Bacardi Distinguished Visiting Scholar at the University of Florida in Gainesville. His teaching legacy is also passed on through his students, who teach in San Antonio, Houston, Denver, St. Louis, Atlanta, Gainesville and Anchorage.

Mestre Jelon recalls the first lessons he gave to Snipes. "Wesley started taking classes with me in the late 1970s. He studied with me for four years—until 1984. Then he emerged as a serious martial artist. In 1988, he instituted an award to recognize the 20 most important masters who have contributed to the martial arts in this country in the 20th century. There were awards given to Chuck Norris, Bruce Lee, David Carradine, Jackie Chan, and Jean Claude van Damme—but I was the only capoeirista chosen to receive this award."

Mestre Jelon has received many other awards in recognition of his achievements

as both a capoeira and a dance artist. He has received fellowships from the National Endowment for the Arts, New York State Council on the Arts, and New York Foundation for the Arts, and had been recognized with awards from the city of Cleveland and from Marcelo Alencar, Mayor of Rio de Janeiro, Brazil. A former panelist of the NEA, Dance Critics! Association, and the Massachusetts Cultural Council on Arts, he has also served on the Board of Trustees of DanceUSA. In

1990, he was inducted into the International Hall of Fame of Martial Arts and last year in New York City's Hall of Fame for his cultural contributions.

When asked about the relationship between capoeira and dance in his life, Mestre Jelon smiles and pauses before he answers. "Capoeira and dance are naturally intertwined. When you do capoeira, you are also a natural dancer, because what else is dance but movement to a certain rhythm? Capoeira is inherently connected to the Afro-Brazilian folkloric heritage, which includes dance, and it has many aspects. It is a martial art, a performing art, a form of discipline, and also a way of life. I know how to separate them very well. With DanceBrazil, I explore the performance aspect of capoeira, whereas as a teacher, I treat capoeira as a discipline and a life philosophy."

Jelon Vieiras story as artistic director of a dance company is just as impressive as that of a master capoeirista. After forming his group, The Capoeiras of Bahia, in 1977, he decided to form a non-profit organization, which he called The Capoeira Foundation. The Capoeiras of Bahia was soon renamed "DanceBrazil," becoming a program of the Foundation, and so the umbrella organization with the aim to present and promote Brazilian culture was born. By that time, Jelon's mission was much larger than merely to promote capoeira and Afro-Brazilian culture through the activities of a single dance company. His goal became to cultivate a Brazilian community in the United States by providing a supportive structure for Brazilian performers to grow and develop themselves.

With the growing reputation and recognition of DanceBrazil's cultural significance came Jelon's realization that there needed to be more than the home base in New York City to support his activities in Bahia and in the U.S. In 1993, "Yle Bahia"—the "Home of Bahia"—was born as an umbrella organization for DanceBrazil's performances and outreach programs in San Antonio. That same year, "Artes Connection International" was founded in Salvador, Bahia to provide DanceBrazil's dancers with the opportunity to spend more time in the country whose culture they represent all over the world.

Since then, Jelon has guided the company through breathtaking performances of capoeira and Afro-Brazilian dance before audiences in Europe, Asia and Brazil, as well as at Spoleto USA, the Kennedy Center and Lincoln Center in the United States. The company has been featured on the PBS program *Alive From Off Center* and has been a part of PBS' 12-part documentary series called, *Egg: The Arts Show*, which aired nationally on February 24, 2000. It was not a surprise when for *Times Square 2000*—a momentous, globally televised 24-hour dance marathon on a specially constructed stage in New York City—Jelon was chosen to create and direct the only Brazilian performance to represent the advent of the Millennium in Brazil.

Now approaching the 30th Anniversary of DanceBrazil and the Capoeira Foundation of America, Mestre Jelon notes with satisfaction all the work that he has done to promote the art form and Brazilian culture in the U.S. He points out that even when funds were scarce, he was always ready to help his fellow Brazilian artists by giving them opportunities to perform and choreograph for his company and the events he produced with his organization. "Our purpose as dance and capoeira artists is to help Brazilian culture grow by working together, rather than compete for the already limited audiences," says Mestre Jelon, continuing to prove this statement by his actions again and again.

it's Shanghai Noon for Jackie Chan

For Jackie Chan, his new movie is not just his third U.S. action comedy, it's the culmination of a career-long dream.

Ric Meyers

"Say that again." Jackie Chan had just pulled over his Golden Harvest Studio associate, David Chan (no relation) to have me repeat what I had just told him. It was during our first meeting in 1984 Hong Kong. I dutifully did so, having just found out that James Glickenhaus was to direct *The Protector*, Jackie's third attempt at finding stateside success (after the abortive *Big Brawl* and the crowded *Cannonball Run)*.

"No one knows, and can direct, Jackie better than Jackie." You must excuse me, but I had recently seen *Project A,* and was still under its spell.

"See?" the Asian superstar had said triumphantly to his producer. "See?" But it was not to be. Once again, despite my declaration, Jackie was to be mishandled—forced into a Western studio's concept of what constituted a hero. "I make you Clint Eastwood," as Jackie would quote his director. "But that's not me!"

No, it was not him, but *Police Story,* the movie he made in response to the frustration of being unable to make *The Protector* a real Jackie Chan film (despite his reshot, re-edited Hong Kong version featuring Sally Yeh), was. It revolutionized the modern Asian action movie, much as *Project A* had transformed the period kung-fu film.

Casting A Spell

I was under its spell as well when I was the last writer ushered into Chan's suite at New York City's Helmsley Towers just hours away from *Police Story's* triumphant screening at the 1986 New York Film Festival. It had been several long years since we met, and a very long day for Jackie—trying to explain to Manhattan reporters who only knew Arnold Schwarzenegger what it was that Chan did.

"Nobody knows who I am," he said, remembering the days of promoting *The Big Brawl.* "Everyday I go to different city, and they say, 'Where are you from?' I say, 'Hong Kong.' They say, 'Is that in Japan?'"

Shanghai Noon

The Wild West meets the Far East in Jackie Chan's newest adventure comedy, Shanghai Noon. Jackie plays Chinese Imperial Guard Chon Wang who comes to America to rescue beautiful princess Pei Pei who has been kidnapped from The Forbidden City.

With the help of a partner he doesn't trust, a wife he didn't expect, a horse with a personality all its own and unbelievable martial arts moves, Chon finds himself facing the meanest gunslingers in the West.

When the lovely princess Pei Pei, played by Lucy Liu of "Ally McBeal" is kidnapped from China, the Emperor dispatches three of his fiercest and noblest Imperial Guards to deliver the ransom in gold to her keepers in America's Wild, Wild West. Chon Wang, however, isn't among the chosen. But he manages to tag along anyway by offering to carry the luggage for his uncle, the Interpreter.

Heading through Nevada by train, the Imperial entourage is hijacked by a motly crew of would-be train robbers. This gives Jackie a chance right from the beginning to show his action acumen and prove his worth to the guards. He also gets to ride a horse, which initially provided cause for concern.

"I was afraid of horses before Shanghai Noon," he admits. "I would pet them but not ride them because I was always afraid I would be thrown off the horse. But after about ten days of lessons, I knew that I could control the horse and wanted to find out how to get the horse up on its back legs like The Lone Ranger."

According to director Tom Dey, one of the intriguing elements of the Old West was that people came from all over the world to reinvent themselves.

"It was a place in which cultures collided," he explains. "For Shanghai Noon, I wanted to give the audience the exciting feeling that they were going on a journey."

On working with Jackie Chan, Dey notes, "Jackie was incredibly generous and gracious. He never once refused to try something, even if he knew it probably wasn't the best thing. He's a man who's done 45 movies and directed many of them himself, and was very generous to a first director, when he didn't have to be. I feel very fortunate to have been able to work with such a big star who was so open to my suggestions. He's extremely hard working and disciplined."

That, however, was not an issue with me. Within minutes, Jackie was back to his trademark self, practically bouncing around the room to describe how he choreographed fight scenes, reliving sequences from all his films, and imagining what it would be like to make "A Jackie Chan Production" in America.

"I'll make a movie with all Caucasians," he said. "Just one or two Chinese. Me, maybe a female co-star. Then they'll see...."

But it wasn't until we were in the elevator, heading down to the lobby

where his limo waited to whisk him over to Lincoln Center for the screening, that one of his producer's told me the hard truth. "American theater owners have told us...they will never show a movie with an all-Chinese cast...."

"What about Bruce Lee?" I countered.

The producer smiled sardonically. "Oh, Bruce Lee...! They tell us, 'He's the exception...!'"

He's The Exception

Jackie was not yet, it seemed, the new exception—despite the success of *Police Story* at the Festival, as well as a short subsequent run on video as *Jackie Chans Police Force*. As always happened when he couldn't crack the American market, Jackie returned to one film feat after another in Hong Kong. Despite scoring his highest grossing film to date, *Armor of God* (and nearly dying in the process) and gaining credibility as a producer of both award-winning dramas *{Rouge}* and crowd-pleasing comedies *{The Inspector Wears Skirts}*, the door west was still closed to him.

Something had to be done...which is when Britain's Channel 4 came calling. I had convinced them to do an episode of its "Incredibly Strange Film Show" on Jackie (it wasn't hard...all they needed to see were a few scenes from his Asian blockbusters).

"Normally," host Jonathan Ross said in the episode's introduction, "we concentrate on the 'strange,' but this week we'll meet a man who can, quite honestly, be called 'incredible'...."

This time we were at the Shaw Brothers Studio, on the rambling, several-acre set of *Miracles* (aka *Mr. Canton and Lady Rose),* again talking to Jackie about his dreams, which had been battened down a notch or two by the reality of Hollywood and his near career-ending injury making *Armor of God.*

"If I can gain the Western market with my own films, then okay. If not, I'm happy to stay in the Asian market. I'd rather be a king in Asia than be a small potato in America."

Time Line

1954—Born Chan Kong Sang in Hong Kong	**1971**—Played his first hero in the movie, *Little Tiger from Canton*.
1954—Family was so poor almost sold at birth for $26	**1972**—Doubles for Mr. Suzuki and is kicked through a window by Bruce Lee in *The Chinese Connection*.
1961—Family moves to Australia without Jackie.	**1976**—William C.K. Chan (Jackie's current manager) brings Jackie to the attention of producer Lo Wei.
1961—He is boarded in the Peking Opera School.	**1977**—Lo Wei promptly changes Jackie's name to "Cheng Long" or "Sing Lung" in Cantonese. It means "one becoming a dragon."
1964—Began doing dramatic parts in films.	
1964—Under the stage name "Yuan Lou," named one of the "Seven Little Fortunes" along with Sammo Hung, Yuen Baio, Corey Yuen and Mang Hoi.	

created over a 17-hour period...then had to film twice. And, happily, he let us touch the piece of plastic covering the hole in his skull, courtesy of the "Armor" accident, which vibrated when he hummed.

Star of Stars

But, despite what he said, he still had great hopes for the film he had talked about in New York—the "little" movie with a mostly Caucasian cast. By then American filmmakers knew what many American moviegoers didn't—that Jackie was a unique talent. Directors and actors like Oliver Stone and Sylvester Stallone made pilgrimages to his sets. Stallone and Paul Verhoeven were lifting moves and ideas from his films.

And there were meetings...lots and lots of meetings. Some of them even resulted in newspaper articles, like the one which reported that Jackie would be working with Francis Ford Coppola on a film about a Chinese kung-fu master finding adventure in the Wild, Wild West. But that project, like so many others, never saw a camera.

Instead, Jackie was exhausted by the arduous two-year production of *Operation Condor*—that "small film" with the mostly Caucasian cast—little knowing what the cinematic fates had in store for him ... that the British TV special on him would be shown repeatedly in America ... that film festivals and cable stations would play his Hong Kong classics over and over ... and that a new generation would ignore the theater owners' fears and declare Chan a worldwide superstar.

How else could another truly "little film with a mostly Caucasian cast," *Rumble in the Bronx*—made in the wake of his kung-fu masterpiece *Drunken Master II*—be such a surprise hit in the U.S.? Finally, American reporters knew him, and he basked in his well-deserved success at *Rumbles* American premiere. But he wasn't fooled ... not after all his previous near misses in the U.S.

"In Asia, I'm *Jurassic Park*, I'm *E. T.*," he admitted. "But here...?"

And, sure enough, the step forward of "Rumble" was tempered by the seeming backsteps of several hastily redubbed, re-released movies from Jackie's past—most of which weren't even directed by him. It was deja vu all over again, as Jackie's American progress was slowed by his being unable to produce his own American movies.

"What Have They Done?"

He had great hopes when we saw him at the premiere of *Supercop*, but the frustration finally boiled over when we again met at the New York premiere of *Operation Condor*. "Movie guy," he called me in mock anguish, "what have they done to my movie?!"

But then came *Rush Hour*. Suddenly Jackie was not the $30-million man, which had been *Rumbles* gross, but the $150 million man, which is what *Rush Hour* made in the U.S. alone. Finally, there were executives at the studios who knew his work from the television special, books, and film festivals. Finally, they were willing to let Jackie choreograph the action and produce his own American film.

Only one problem; by then someone else had made an "Eastern Western." *Once Upon a Time in China VI: The Lion Goes West,* starring Jet Li and directed by Sammo Hung, seemed to not only steal Jackies thunder but, apparently, what had been his subtitle as well. But Chan was not going to let anything as pesky as another movie on the same subject slow him down. Anyone who loved his work already knew he worked brilliantly in reaction to a challenge.

His experiences on *The Big Brawl* resulted in *Project A*. Likewise his frustrations on *The Protector* begat *Police Story*. Now, *Once Upon a Time in China VI* was all he needed to inspire him to make *Shanghai Noon,* the culmination of a career-long dream. He had *Lethal Weapon 4* screenwriters Alfred Gough and Miles Millar. He had first-time movie director Tom Dey. He had Lucy Liu (of "Ally McBeal" fame) and Owen Wilson (a superstar waiting to happen) in his cast.

He even had his good friend and fellow Peking Opera school graduate Yuen Baio by his side to help choreograph the action.

But, perhaps, more importantly, he had the full creative backing of Touchstone Pictures and Spyglass Entertainment (the company that also shepherded *The Sixth Sense* to the screen). Now he could finally make the movie he wanted—a film created by him specifically for his own unique skills, and one that would not attempt to fashion him in the mold of an American star.

It was also one, since it was set in the past, where he could not fall back on car stunts to carry the climax, as he had in many of his latter-day Hong Kong films *(Rumble in the Bronx, First Strike, Air. Nice Guy)*. The kung-fu he had eschewed, in deference to American studio sensibilities, was now back in style, thanks to his fans. The result so impressed the studio that the film's premiere was moved to Memorial Day, 2000—ironically putting it in direct competition with *Mission: Impossible-2,* helmed by fellow Asian immigrant John Woo...the man who had directed him in *Hand of Death* (aka *Countdown in Kung-fu)* way back in 1975.

"One day," he told us back on the set of the aptly named *Miracles,* "I hope that I'll be remembered. In the books of film history, they have all the names: Charlie Chaplin, John Wayne, Steven Spielberg, etc. If there's even just a small note ... Jackie Chan ... then that's enough. I'm happy."

With *Shanghai Noon* capping an already miraculous career, it is fairly safe to say that the name Jackie Chan will be far more than a small footnote in the history of cinema. He will be, fittingly, the exception that makes the rule and the man who brought Asia to America for good. $

Ric Meyers is a contributing editor o/Inside Kung-Fu.

Mande Muda: The JKD of Pencak Silat

Up to the day he died pendekar Herman Suwanda tried to make this unique Indonesian offshoot part of the American martial arts landscape.

Mike Young

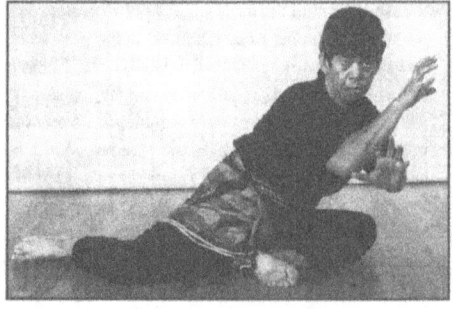

Although the Indonesian martial art of pencak silat has been around for hundreds of years, many throughout the world are just beginning to discover it effectiveness. Of prime importance in today's violent society is pencak silat's combat effectiveness against street attacks.

One effective and deadly pencak silat system making its way into America is mande muda, which was taught by the late pendekar Herman Suwanda (see accompanying story).

The style is so effective that even the legendary Dan Inosanto regularly scheduled pendekar Suwanda to teach at his academy so he could learn more about this fascinating Indonesian martial art.

A Style Of Plenty

Mande muda originally combined 18 different pencak silat systems. Today, the system draws from 26 different silat styles. Like JKD, the founder of the system, Uyun Suwanda (Herman Suwanda's father), studied many different silat systems and took the best movements and techniques from 18 different silat systems he considered most useful and blended the techniques into a formal martial art/pencak silat system. Today, we call this system mande muda.

His son, Herman Suwanda, added the best from eight more pencak silat styles. The root of the style is based on the cimande system, one of the more dangerous forms of pencak silat. In this system the cimande expert will "hunt for the arm," meaning he will first attack the opponent's arm and try to disable him. An attack to the arm means breaking anything from his fingers to his shoulders.

Developing the arms requires years of practice in cimande's complex two-man hand drills along with an application of a secret herbal treatment called balur to toughen the arms.

Mande muda is based on many styles. One of the most important is the cikalong style, which emphasizes avoiding punches and kicks. A cikalong practitioner tries to move to the outside of his opponent so he doesn't have to worry about the opponents other hand or foot attacking him. To prac-

tice these movements, the cikalong practitioner works many two-man drills called "buah." This helps him work the outside.

Mande muda utilizes three of the cikalong forms to help develop the proper footwork. The forms feature unusual knee, elbow and shoulder strikes. On special occasions these forms are often performed with special silat live music.

One of the most dynamic systems of mande muda comes from the harimau or ground tiger system of West Central Sumatra. The movement of the harimau system resembles a tiger fighting with his four limbs touching the ground. The theory in the harimau style is to hunt or break the opponents leg, which is called "patahkan tulang." They also hunt other joints and bones, however the legs are the nearest once they go to the ground.

The Harimau Trap

A harimau stylist will always go to the ground to bring his opponent with him. From there, he will dip into his arsenal of leg, arm and joint breaks to disable an opponent. Although free-style sparring is a harimau favorite, it is done in only the most controlled environments because the techniques can be deadly. According to pendekar Suwanda, a harimau practitioner was killed in Bandung, Indonesia, in 1988 during a hard free-sparring match.

Another style associated with mande muda is called syahbandar.

The theory in this predominantly hand style is to attack an opponent from the center, going first

Pendekar Suwanda waits for his opponent to strike (1). As his opponent strikes, pendekar Suwanda jumps to the side (2) and catches his opponent's arm with his feet and one hand. Pendekar Suwanda then applies an armlock and begins to take the opponent down (3). Once the opponent is on the ground, pendekar Suwanda applies a finishing arm break with his feet (4).

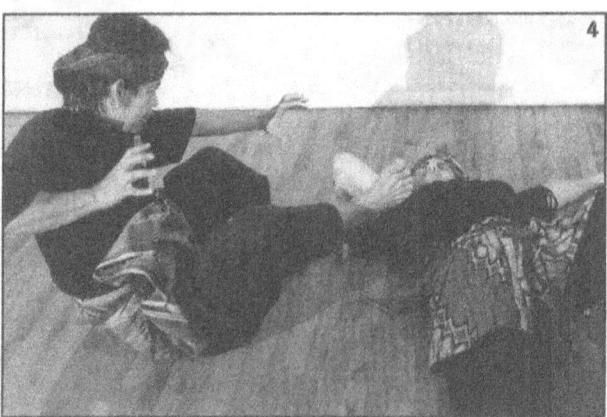

for his arm and then his face. Many of the two-man syahbandar drills resemble wing chun pak sao and lap sao drills, but movements are done from a fighting application unlike chi sao. Mande muda takes the direct application of syahbandar fighting drills and blends the movement into their system.

The kari pencak silat style is also incorporated in the mande muda system. In the kari system, the practitioners utilize a unique close-in fighting system making primary use of a scissors hand technique. This helps the kari practitioner respond quickly and effectively to an opponents attack. Kari practitioners are known for their instantaneous block and counter.

The madi system of pencak silat stresses jumping onto an opponent, pulling him off balance and striking with either hands or feet. The nucleus of this system lies in the madi stylist pulling or jerking his opponent off balance while simultaneously striking him into submission.

Mande muda also draws techniques from the cipecut system. Cipecut comes from cikalong silat and means a whip in Indonesian. But the principles of this system apply to any flexible weapon. A favorite cipecut weapon is the Indonesian sarong. A sarong is a common Indonesian garment. The cipecut system developed the sarong into a deadly weapon, which utilizes complex chokes, locks, takedowns, breaks and devastating strikes. A towel, scarf, belt or whip can also be used when executing cipecut techniques, but the favorite weapon of choice is the sarong.

Bone-Wrenching Techniques

In the cipecut system, the practitioner applies the cikalong system theory to evade punches or kicks and to move to the outside, so he doesn't have to deal with the opponent's opposite hand. Cipecut stylists also apply bone-wrench-

Suwanda Remembered
By Mike Young

This is a tribute to Herman Suwanda and his wife Shannon, who died in a car accident last March 22 in Germany while enroute to a mande muda silat seminar.

Herman was a dedicated martial artist who strived to constantly learn and develop new techniques to improve his ever-changing silat style of mande muda. I can remember in 1992 Indonesia when Herman's system consisted of 18 different silat styles. In the latter part of 1999 (during the interview for the accompanying article), the silat styles Herman incorporated into his system had now reached 26.

Herman Suwanda, 45, was not only the pendekar of a unique and deadly martial art system, he had a warm, friendly, giving, humble and respectful nature you rarely find in martial art instructors today. Herman's willingness to unselfishly share his knowledge with others was unparalleled.

ing, wrist, arm and leglocks from the rikesan silat system to enhance the effectiveness of their style.

To become proficient in the cipecut system, the practitioner must work on over 1,000 sarong techniques under the watchful eye of an experienced instructor. The sarong techniques cover kicks and punches from any angle and from any stance until it becomes second nature. There are no forms, sets or pre-arranged sparring—only constant practice of specific techniques.

Another system found in mande muda is timbangan silat. Timbangan translates as "scale" in Indonesian, but in martial art terminology it refers to the balance of the energy flow between practitioner and opponent. The timbangan stylist redirects his opponents energy and causes him to trip or fall in a manner similar to the principles of aikido.

Since there are also no strikes in this system, distancing and timing are crucial to the art's effectiveness. To develop this timing the timbangan stylist practices on complex two-man drills to learn how to read and redirect his opponent's energy. When practitioners become comfortable with their technique, they engage in light sparring under the strict supervision of a timbangan instructor.

To protect the body from receiving serious internal or external damage during combat, mande muda also incorporates the nampon style of silat. In the nampon style, deep

Pendekar Suwanda waits (1) for his opponent to throw a punch (notice that the sarong is chambered to strike). As the opponent strikes, pendekar Suwanda strikes his opponent in the head as he blocks the incoming strike (2). Using the momentum of the downward sarong strike, pendekar Suwanda quickly strikes his opponent in the groin with the sarong (3). As the opponent is stunned by the groin strike (4), the sarong is quickly wrapped around his opponent's neck and a sarong choke is applied (5).

Dan Inosanto practices a silat form at a Suwanda seminar.

breathing exercises are coordinated with specific body movements to strengthen and invigorate sections of the body. A well-trained nampon stylist can withstand a violent physical assault to any part of his body.

Hands-On Training
Training in this system involves practicing 20 hand motions, which are coordinated with specific breathing patterns. Next, footwork is added to make sure you can apply the breathing techniques in motion. Dynamic tension and relaxed body movement are applied during the breathing exercise to strengthen specific muscles not normally exercised by conventional methods. After three-to-six months of regular practice of nampon, the body becomes strong enough to withstand a heavy and prolonged physical attack.

Mande muda also draws elements from the sera system. Mande muda incorporates six jurus (prearranged movements) from the system to improve footwork and hand techniques. Even when attacking, a sera stylist uses angles to strike without fear of being hit. Mande muda utilizes the exact angles of sera to enhance the effectiveness of its own style.

One of the most painful aspects of the silat system—rikesan silat—is also incorporated into the mande muda style. Literally translated as "breaking" in Indonesian, rikesan incorporates techniques aimed at breaking bones. A rikesan practitioner will wait for an attack, then apply a jointlock that renders the limb useless. The rikesan stylist must slowly and carefully practice jointlocks on a training partner because many of the locks and throws can permanently disable the training partner. Speed and force are increased when skill level gets better. A skilled rikesan practitioner can grab an opponent anywhere and bring him down by applying a disabling lock.

A silat system called tanjakan also is utilized in mande muda. Meaning "hill" in Indonesian, tan-jakan is sometimes referred to as mountain silat. Because the system was developed in the mountains, the uneven terrain led to unusual ground techniques. In the tanjakan system, the practitioner likes to pull an opponent off balance while kicking him at the same time. Varying his stance from high to low makes the tanjakan stylist a more difficult target and allows him to add power to his punch.

Herman Suwanda (bottom right) teaching the L.A. Sheriff's Dept. SWAT Team.

There are no forms or sparring in this style, so to develop the proper application of the technique, two-man drills are constantly practiced under a qualified instructor.

Mande muda also incorporates ulinapas silat. This style utilizes a series of breathing exercises to help the practitioner control his emotions during a fight. Relaxation and breath control are keys to this system. The practitioner is directed to first control his breathing patterns while laying down, then sitting and finally standing.

There are many 99 "forms" or kata in mande muda. One form, paleredan, is rich in movement and takes the student through advanced movement of classical silat.

The classic "depok" posture, found primarily in silat systems, develops a student's ability to attack and retreat from the seated position.

"Married" To The Form

Once the 200-movement form is memorized—the practitioner is then "married" into the form and repeats it over and over to a designated number. The number of times the form is repeated is determined by Sudanese numerology system. The number is determined through a complex formula, which figures in his birthdate, the day he was born, and the hour and year in which he was born. The form can be as little as 20 or more than 100. "Marrying" into the form comes as part of a ceremony that includes a band of Indonesian musicians.

Ulan bade silat is an extreme, combat-based form of silat incorporated into the mande muda system. In this system, the practitioner goes directly at his opponent; footwork and specific angles of attack are secondary. The primary goal of this system is to take the opponent out as quickly as possible. Basic linear hand and foot techniques are taught in a no-nonsense manner and are practiced in two-man sets called "bialys." The Ulan bade practitioner primarily makes his opponent's throat his primary target.

Mande muda also has an array of weapons systems that deal with everything from the Gaelic knife, which measures 18 inches in length, to a 32-inch rattan stick. But this is an article unto itself.

The last system of silat that has been added to the mande muda system is called benjang silat, more commonly referred to as Sudanese wrestling.

> "The madi system of pencak silat stresses jumping onto an opponent, pulling him off balance and striking with either the hands or feet."

enjang silat is a rough art which is commonly played out in the dirt. Because of the harsh rules and tough environment in which the art is practiced a benjang practitioner risks death everytime he steps onto

Choking, armlocks, wristlocks and throws all encompass the benjang system. Because there is no "tapping out," broken bones and serious injury are not uncommon.

Many of the mande muda techniques are so simple, yet so effective the Los Angeles Sheriff's Department Special Enforcement Bureau (SWAT) utilizes many empty-hand techniques from the style in their advanced SWAT school.

As you can see, the founder of this silat system put a lot of time and thought into creating a well-rounded fighting discipline. The style has everything—punches and kicks, takedowns, armlocks, leglocks, weaponry, groundfighting, pressure point control, and breath control and mind control. This system has all the elements of a dynamic ever-evolving fighting art and has earned the right to be called the JKD of silat. $

Mike Young is a Southern California-based author and martial artist.

Choy Lee Fut's Steel Fan

Called the Dr. Jekyll and Mr. Hyde of kung-fu weapons, choy lee fut's steel fan is as innocent as it is deadly.

Howard Choy

The Chinese have a saying regarding weapons: "The shorter it is, the more dangerous. The more ordinary looking, the deadlier it is." This saying is also perfectly appropriate for the steel fan. The Chinese often turn ordinary household implements, like a pair of chopsticks, a wooden stool, a rice bowl and even a pair of sandals, into a deadly weapon. It is considered a short weapon, about 14 inches long, very innocent looking and not that much different from an everyday paper fan, except the ribs are made of stainless steel instead of bamboo strips, and the paper is replaced by toughened silk. When you carry one unopened no one can tell it is a weapon. Even when you open it to fan yourself it looks quite ordinary and harmless. However, in the hands of an expert, the innocent-looking fan can be a lethal weapon.

One such expert was monk Jou Yud of the Shaolin Temple. He lived during the Qing dynasty (1644-1911) and raised the art of the steel fan to a new height. His legacy was passed down onto Chan Heung, the founder of choy lee fut kung-fu through monk Choy Fook. Chan Heungs grandson, Chan Yiu-Chi, also adopted the fan as his favorite everyday weapon. He was often seen carrying the fan as he taught kung-fu and as he went to Yum-cha with his students. Chan Yui-Chi's grandson, our teacher, Chen Yong-Fa, inherited the art through his family.

Fair-Weather Friend

The steel fan is a handy weapon because it is easy to carry and highly inconspicuous. When the weather is warm, you can use the fan to cool yourself and chase the flies away. When you are in danger, you can use the steel fan as an effective weapon for self-defense.

Because the ribs are made of steel, you can use it to block and deflect much larger weapons by wrapping the fan against your forearm and turning it into an "iron bridge hand." You can use it for

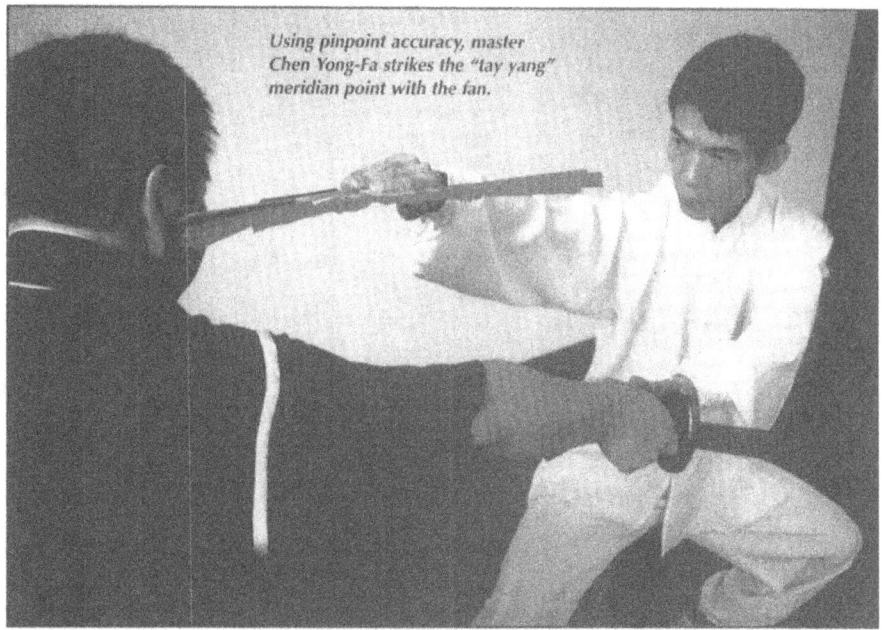

Using pinpoint accuracy, master Chen Yong-Fa strikes the "tay yang" meridian point with the fan.

chin na (grappling) and you can use it for dim mak (acupressure point striking). When folded, the fan can be used like a short dagger—to cut, jab and slash. When unfolded, the fan is like a spring-loaded knife for stabbing, slicing and spearing your opponent.

Combining it with your body movement and footwork, you can turn the short fan into a long weapon by launching yourself at your opponent while throwing it open. This turns a soft implement into a hard weapon with the flick of your wrist.

You can also flick open the steel fan as a fake. The action makes a loud noise that will distract your opponent's attention while you kick or throw a punch elsewhere. The open fan can work like a saw to slice with the tips of the ribs opened into a semi-circle. While the fan is open you can use the broad surface like a backhand slap against the face of your opponent.

When folded, you can throw the fan like a Bowie knife at your opponent from a distance. It is a versatile "secret" weapon, favored by gentlemen scholar/martial artists of China.

Inside The Fan

The choy lee fut steel fan has either 18, 24, or 36 ribs. Sometimes, the tips of the ribs are tapped to a point to increase its effectiveness. The two outer ribs are often sharpened to make them behave like the sharp edge of a sword for cutting or slicing.

Often, a beautiful landscape scene with Chinese calligraphy is painted onto the toughened silk fabric to conceal its deadliness. It has a Jekyll and Hyde split personality, characteristic of all "kei mun" (ingenious and unusual) weaponry.

Since it takes a high level of kung-fu to use the fan, it is classified as a tertiary-level weapon in the choy lee fut system. The fan is considered an "internal" weapon, because it uses the "soft" to overcome the "hard" and the short to overcome the long.

For the choy lee fut student, there are three steel fan forms to master. They are called seu seou sin (the breaking hands fan), gum loong sin (the golden dragon fan and fei loong sin (the flying dragon

The fast and sharp action of the fan combines well with the "cat stance" or "dil gerk ma" of choy lee fut (1). Stepping to the side to avoid attack, Davenport opens the steel ribs of the fan on the arteries of the neck of his opponent (2). ▶

◀ When blocking, the open fan not only distracts and obscures, but also increases the blocking area (1). The double-handed block (2) efficiently protects the practitioner while slicing the foot of the opponent. Following through, sifu Craig Davenport uses the ribs of the open fan to block the opponent's view and strike him in the neck (3).

▼ With both hands helping to block, Davenport opens the fan to distract his opponent and obscure his vision (1). With a quick flick of the wrist, Daven-port is inside the guard with his fan and in t position to slice the arteries of the neck (2).

Using a simple "parry, punch," Davenport attempts to use the fan as an extension of his hand in a stabbing action (1). Seeing the simple frontal attack, sifu Darryl Choy steps his left foot back and delivers a "jow chui" or the choy lee fut haymaker with his right hand. Davenport quickly changes directions, turns and strikes low to the groin (2).

Master Chen demonstrates the inside "sart sin" in a fast and nimble cat stance.

fan). In sen seou sin, the fan is used mainly like a hard weapon; in gum loong sin, the fan is used mainly like a soft and flexible weapon; and in the fei loong sin it is used mainly for dim mak (acupressure point striking).

Dummy Training

At a higher level of training, the steel fan is used with a copper-man dummy to improve a student's acupressure point striking techniques. The copper-man dummy is constructed in such a way that when the correct acupressure point is hit, it makes a distinct clicking noise. The idea is to strike as many points as accurately as possible in the shortest time. The student has to strike points with force and accuracy for the clicking sound to be heard.

Our teacher often said, "It is easy to strike the points but difficult to locate the points." To perform dim mak, the student has to study the meridian charts, know its locations by heart and understand the damage each one causes. The surface area of an acupressure point is very small—two-to-three millimeters at the most—so accuracy is important, especially when you try to hit a fast- moving target.

The trick is to deliver the strike with ging (penetrating force), while maintaining speed and accuracy. In the choy lee fut manual for steel fan dim mak it is stated that when using the fan, "The mind must be coupled with the heart, the heart with the strength, the strength with the qi, the qi with the fan, the fan with the eyes, and skill with dexterity." ®

Thai Boxing in JKD

Thai boxing has a wealth of "hard-core" techniques that JKD practitioners, and martial artists of all styles, can absorb and incorporate to increase their intensity and effectiveness.

Paul Vunak

In order to understand where Thai boxing fits into the puzzle that is known as jeet kune do, we must first understand a little about the process by which JKD evolved. The operative word here is "process." To quote Dan Inosanto, "JKD is not about the product, but about the process." When Bruce Lee first came to America, he quickly observed how much larger and stronger the average American was compared to the average Chinese. This was the original impetus that caused Lee to start the process of modifying his mother art of wing chun. Between 1964 and 1973 Lee, with the assistance of Dan Inosanto, dissected every fighting art that the two could discover and selected elements that formed the foundation of what would eventually be called jeet kune do. Not every aspect of every art was included, of course.

In certain cases, only training methods or combat theory were extracted. This is the case with Western foil fencing, which lent its concept of the "stop hit" (or interception) to JKD's combat philosophy and, indeed, to JKD's very name (Way of the Intercepting Fist). All systems of martial art have their strong and weak points. Bruce Lee observed that, "There is a range in which Western boxing will counter any kicking art; there is a range in which wing chun will counter boxing; there is a range where tai chi will counter wing chun; and there is a range where grappling will counter tai chi." In short, Lee chose elements from the selected arts to give his students an integrated framework that would prepare them to fight any opponent at any range.

Those who witnessed Lee at any of his closed-door sparring sessions saw this principle in action. Limited by the vocabulary of their time, these witnesses were never able to find a label for Lee. Sometimes he would dance and shuffle at long range—boxing with his lead foot and hitting the opponent at previously unknown angles, like an experienced savate man. But if the opponent countered, Lee

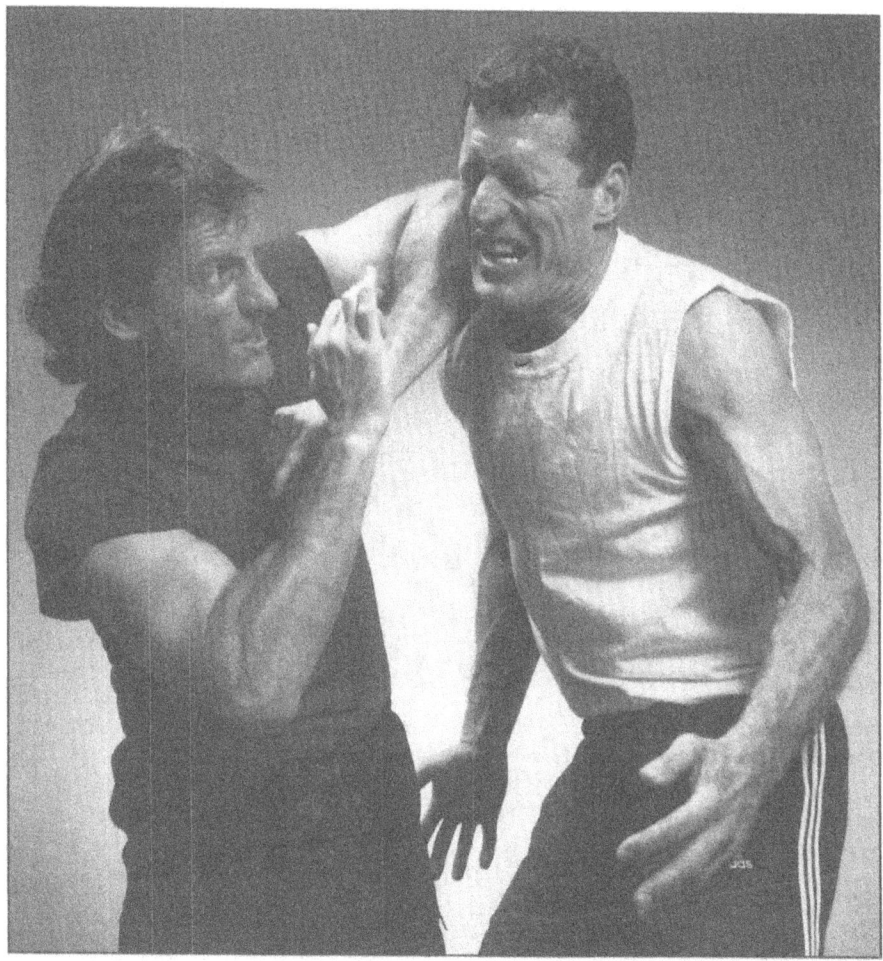

would bob and weave and throw body shots like a professional boxer. Upon being blocked by the opponent, he would shift into wing chun's *chun choy* (straight blast), trapping any obstruction, pum- meling with a flurry of elbows, knees, or head butts, and ending the encounter with a foot sweep or throw. All of these difficult elements would appear in a "match" that lasted just ten seconds!

Before his death, Lee, along with Inosanto, had been investigating muay Thai extensively. After Lee's death, Dan continued the research with the help of Chai Sirisute. We currently find three elements of Thai boxing to be most useful in JKD.

The Thigh Kick

The thigh kick used by Thai boxers is perhaps the most formidable kick on the planet. Thai boxers rely on their thigh kick much like a Western boxer relies on his jab. One might say that this kick is the hub of their wheel.

Back in the late '60s and early '70s, low stances were very common—martial artists of the time

strongly favored stability over agility. This facilitated Bruce Lee's use of the *jeet tek* (sidekick) to the knee to intercept his opponent. Nowadays, we see boxing footwork more often than low stances. This makes the knee a much more difficult target to hit with a side kick. Therefore, many modern JKD practitioners also use the thigh kick as a tool to intercept.

As we look at 90 percent of todays no-holds-barred contests, we see that the thigh kick is predominant among winning fighters. For example, one of the most highly acclaimed fights in the Ultimate Fighting Championship's history was the bout between Maurice Smith and Mark Coleman. Maurice Smith literally controlled the fight using the thigh kick. Another example of the use of the thigh kick was the fight between Marco Ruas and Paul "Polar Bear" Varelans. Again, the thigh kick was the pivotal weapon, allowing Ruas to control the distance and cadence of the entire match.

These are just two examples (of many) of how potent this weapon really is. To truly appreciate the power of the muay Thai thigh kick, you simply must be on the receiving end of one! Many good Thai boxers double up their kicks, executing two in a row. Landing multiple thigh kicks in quick succession on the same area of the body is nauseatingly painful. In short, if you have not already incorporated this kick into your arsenal, start now!

The Thai Boxing Mindset

When I think of a Thai boxer, one thing comes to mind immediately: hard core! These are some of the toughest people on Earth. Bruce Lee incorporated the very same mentality into his trapping. Any martial artist can take any aspect of his or her art and use the Thai boxer's mindset to "hardcore" their particular art. For example, anyone can put on a set of boxing gloves, poke shots at a partner, and call that boxing. But if one truly wanted to "hardcore" his punches, he would find a boxing gym and get in with an actual pro. The training regimen of a pro (i.e. stamina, heavy-bag workouts, weight training, and sparring sessions) is completely different from that of an amateur boxer.

It's one thing to roll around on the mat and practice arm locks, triangles, and chokes. However, if you were to go to Brazil and train for the Pan Am Games, then you'd be able to experience the hardcore side of jiu-jitsu and appreciate it at an entirely different level!

Many people like to practice various trapping techniques working from reference points only (or training exclusively on the wooden dummy). If these very same people go to a professional boxing gym and recruit a pro boxer, put a motorcycle helmet on him, and then spar full-contact while they try to apply their trapping techniques, this would be an example of a wing chun person applying the muay Thai hardcore mentality.

"One of the most highly acclaimed fights in the Ultimate Fighting Championship's history was the bout between Maurice Smith and Mark Coleman. Maurice literally controlled the fight using the thigh kick."

In the world of stick fighting, many people train themselves only—singly doing various drills and disarms. These people could use the Thai boxing mentality to "hardcore" their training by incorporating the use of lead pipes or heavy sticks in their drills, and by sparring full contact.

To a jeet kune do practitioner, the Thai boxing mindset provides a way to inject realism into his or her training. It is not enough to simply practice the same drills day-after-day. When a martial artist knows that he can go all out, take some punishment, and keep going, it does a lot for his survival mentality.

Anyone can benefit immensely from watching a good Thai boxing match; however, this mentality is one attribute that is best learned by experience. There are many great Thai boxers in the world— I highly recommend investing the time, money, and courage to go and actually train at one of the many Thai camps. If you think boot camp was tough, try a Thai camp!

The Clinch

Being on the receiving end of a flurry of savate kicks is a very intimidating prospect. Having a barrage of punches thrown at you by a professional boxer is equally intimidating. Being stuck on the ground, in the guard of a black belt Brazilian jiu-jitsu stylist, knowing that you are seconds away from being put into an arm lock, triangle choke, or sweep, is downright humiliating. However, being in the grasp of a professional Thai boxer in clinch position is nothing less than sickening! You can't go forward, you can't go backward, you have no balance or base; and to make matters worse, you are being assaulted by two of the most barbaric tools on Earth—elbows and knees. For the truly

Facing an opponent (1), Vunak knee-blocks an attempted muay Thai kick (2), straight blasts to the head (3-5), launches a knee to the groin (6), and finishes with a muay Thai elbow (7).

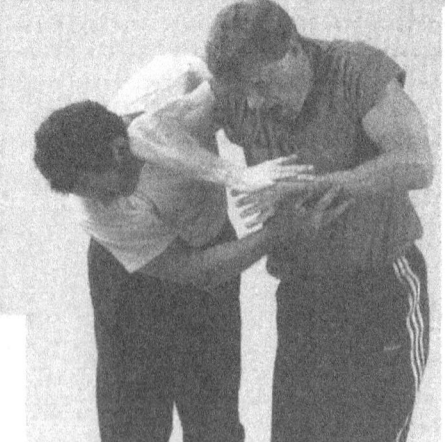

masochistic martial artist, this is the *coup de grace*. It is not recommended for the faint of heart! For a JKD stylist, the Thai boxing clinch is the most natural position to end up in following the infamous straight blast. From the clinch, he can execute tactics such as elbows, head butts, and knees, or take an opponent to the ground if desired.

In closing, as we look back some 30 years, it is obvious that Bruce Lee and Dan Inosanto were the pioneers of modern martial arts. They understood then, what the world is seeing now—no one art, theology, or philosophy has it all. No race or culture has a monopoly on the truth. We can truly see that today's martial artists are harvesting knowledge from seeds that were planted by Bruce Lee and Dan Inosanto. As each year passes, people are becoming more open-minded and more eclectic; more willing to live by the concept of "Absorb what is useful, reject what is useless, and add what is specifically your own." In following this adage, it's quite apparent that Thai boxing offers a wealth of techniques both for JKD stylists, and martial artists of all systems, to absorb and benefit from. $

Paul Vunak is a certified Full Instructor ofJeet Kune Do and the Filipino Martial Arts under Dan Inosanto and is the president and head instructor ofiProgressive Fighting Systems.

Chang Tung Sheng's Training Secrets

Arguably the greatest Chinese-style fighter of the 20th century, shuai chiao legend Chang Tung Sheng was unbeaten in 88 consecutive matches. Now for the first time, his grandson tells you what kind of training went on behind closed doors.

Mark Miller

Chang Tung Sheng, the legendary shuai chiao heavyweight champion of Mainland China, died in 1986 and left the world with many unanswered questions about his life and the unusual traditional training methods his teacher used to create this undefeated champion. Wanting to separate fact from fiction, shuai chiao stylist Mark Miller went straight to the source—the Central Police College in Taipei, Taiwan, where Chang Tung Sheng had taught for 30 years and produced some of the most famous shuai chiao practitioners in the world. At the Central Police College he found Changs grandson, David Chang carrying on the family's martial arts tradition. Here's what he had to say.

INSIDE KUNG-FU: Perhaps you can introduce your grandfather, Chang Tung Sheng, to those readers not familiar with him.

DAVID CHANG: My grandfather was born in 1908, the Chinese lunar year of the monkey, in Hebei province of Mainland China. From the time he was quite young he was already well-known for his shuai chiao skills. In Bao-Ding County of Hebei province, he was the undefeated shuai chiao champion. He went on to compete in two all-China national tournaments and won both. The first tournament was the 5th National Kuo Shu Tournament in 1933 before he joined the army. There were over 1,000 participants of all martial arts styles from all over China and he won the heavyweight division. The second was in 1948 when he entered the 7th National Athletic Meet representing the army. At 40 years of age, he again

Fne *results of traditional training: an intimidaljng changat2s years ofage (far left).*

At age 75 Chang displays great power and flexibility while demonstrating one of his famous shuai chiao sweeps (left).

the Central Police College for 30 years. He was the chief official for the national shuai chiao tournaments in Taiwan, and also traveled to the United States to preside over several national-level shuai chiao tournaments there.

IKF: What did his family do? I have heard that only wealthy families can afford to have their children study martial arts rather than work.

DC: Actually, that was the system in ancient China before the Qing dynasty (1644-1911). During Chang Tung Sheng's life it was already the beginning of the Republic of China so everything had changed. The Chang family had a business selling roast chicken.

IKF: Who was Chang Tung Sheng's shuai chiao teacher?

DC: His teacher was Zhang Feng Yan. Zhang Feng Yan and his teacher, Ping Jin Yi, were famous in northern China for their shuai chiao.

IKF: Was Zhang Feng Yan a shuai chiao champion as well?

DC: At that time there were no organized tournaments, but my grandfather had said that somewhere in the first three-to-five years of the Republic of China the army had a major conference. At the conference, Zhang Feng Yan defeated the top hsing-I chuan practitioner Li Quan-Yi so everyone recognized him as a champion.

IKF: Was Chang Tung Sheng's teacher Zhang Feng Yan a professional martial artist?

DC: No, he was actually a very successful businessman. Zhang Feng Yan was already quite wealthy from

Jin-Yi, was also a businessman who had a business selling bao-zi (steamed buns).

IKF: How did Chang Tung Sheng meet his teacher and begin studying shuai chiao?

DC: Zhang Feng Yan was a neighbor who was in the business of making special foods such as bean paste, soy sauce, marinated vegetables, etc., which were a vital part of Hebei cuisine. He lived only a few streets away from Chang Tung Sheng—just a short walk. Chang Tung Sheng's family used the sauces produced by Zhang Feng Yan for their roast chicken business. Zhang Feng Yan had a big yard with a large garden in which he grew the beans and vegetables for the business. In the yard there were many large clay pots used to make his sauces. Kids from the neighborhood loved to go there to get something to eat and play hide and seek among the clay pots. Because the business was quite large Zhang Feng Yan needed help with the chores. He would get the kids from the neighborhood to help him out and at the same time teach them kung-fu. That was the way Chang Tung Sheng started to learn shuai chiao.

IKF: How did Zhang Feng Yan teach him?

DC: Zhang Feng Yan had regular workers at his business but he had the kids who were studying kung-fu do special chores that would help to train their strength and durability.

IKF: What do you mean by "special chores"?

DC: For example, when you make sauces you have to cook the beans before letting them ferment. Zhang Feng Yan's business was quite large and that meant boiling huge pots of beans, which required a very hot fire. To make the fire hot enough they would use huge bellows to blow on the fire. As one of their chores, the kids learning kung-fu would take turns operating the bellows. They would grasp the handles of the bellows in their hands and squeeze them together repeatedly which, in addition to fanning the fire, would build upper body and arm strength.

IKF: What other methods did Zhang Feng Yan use to train the kids through work?

DC: For his business, Zhang Feng Yan had to use huge crocks to ferment vegetables. These crocks full of vegetables had to be stirred or mixed from time to time for the vegetables to ferment uniformly. Zhang Feng Yan required his students to use a special movement to mix the contents. They would grasp the crock at the mouth with their thumbs on the inside, lift it off the ground, and use a sharp lifting and twisting motion to jostle the contents. The crocks were large and, when full, were very heavy. It required substantial strength to perform the movement. The same movement has various applications in shuai chiao to offset an opponent's balance before throwing.

Also, when making certain thick sauces such as miso, cooked beans had to be strained through a cloth. One method commonly used is to put the beans in a cloth and put a large rock or weight on the top to slowly squeeze the water out. However, Zhang Feng Yan had his students accomplish the same thing more quickly by putting the beans into a long, narrow cloth bag and having them repeatedly swing the bag through the air using a powerful twisting movement of the waist. At the end of its trajectory they would snap it to an abrupt stop causing the water to be squeezed out. There were several different movements used to do this corresponding to different shuai chiao techniques. This training method is still used today by modern shuai chiao practitioners except that instead of using cooked bean mash the bags are filled with dried beans or steel ball bearings. The movements are essentially the same, however.

IKF: I have heard that Zhang Feng Yan loved birds and he would train his students by having them catch crickets with their feet to feed his birds.

his students, but not by catching crickets to feed them. It is the custom of many Chinese people to take their birds for a walk in the morning just like Westerners might walk their dogs. The cages are covered with a black cloth and held at arm's length and gently swung forward and backward while walking. This is called "liu niao"—literally "walking the bird."

As you can guess, Zhang Feng Yan had his students walk the birds. He had many birds, which he kept in cages. He would place four-to-six birdcages inside a large basket with specially made shelves. The baskets were made from wood and were quite heavy. The baskets could be grasped at the very top where the pieces of wood came together in a criss-cross pattern by placing the palm of the hand flat on the top and sticking the fingers and thumb downward into the basket between the pieces of wood. Clutching the baskets in this manner, the students would raise them up to shoulder height with their arms extended to the sides and walk while gently swinging the baskets using a twisting motion of the waist and

shoulders. Early in the morning Zhang Feng Yan would walk through his yard while being followed by the procession of students swinging the baskets. This activity helped the students develop shoulder, hand, and forearm strength.

IKF: So, where did the crickets come in?

DC: Catching crickets was for a different purpose. In the old days, wealthy people loved to bet on cricket fights. Two crickets would be placed in a large container and then prodded with a piece of duckweed until they began fighting to the death. Bets were placed and the owner of the winning cricket would receive money. Zhang Feng Yan loved to participate and had many champion crickets. He would have his students catch crickets for him by using a shuai chiao movement known as "leg seizing" or "jian tui" to sweep their feet through the grass and cause crickets to jump. When the crickets jumped the students would have to catch them in their hands without injuring them. This trained the students' leg seizing technique and also eye, hand, and foot coordination. Perhaps some of the crickets

Chang delivers a casual uppercut to the delight of a crowd in Cleveland, Ohio.

San shou action at the 1986 Chang Tung Sheng Memorial Tournament in Columbus, Ohio.

that were poor fighters got fed to the birds, but the main purpose of the students catching the crickets was to support their teachers love of gambling!

IKF: I have heard that Chang Tung Sheng pulled young trees out of the ground by wrapping his leg around them and pulling upward—ripping them out of the ground roots and all. Was that another Zhang Feng Yan training method?

DC: Not only were Zhang Feng Yan and Chang Tung Sheng both Muslims but, as was the custom in those days, Chang Tung Sheng married Zhang Feng Yan's daughter. At that point, Chang Tung Sheng was not only a student but part of the family as well, so Zhang Feng Yan taught him some things that he would not teach anyone else. One of those techniques was "hua tui" or "han tui" known in English as "tangling leg." This was Zhang Feng Yan's personal special technique. Actually, it is not just a single technique but a system of attacks and counters based on the "tangling leg" technique. Chang Tung Sheng was the only student that Zhang Feng Yan taught that technique to and it became Chang Tung Sheng's most famous technique. To practice that technique Chang Tung Sheng used the training method of uprooting young trees with his leg.

IKF: Is it true that Chang Tung Sheng used a rolling pin to condition his shins?

DC: Yes, that was another training method taught to him by Zhang Feng Yan. Shuai chiao uses a lot of sweeps that require a powerful, straight kicking movement making contact with the lower

Chang demonstrates perfect balance while throwing.

Photo by Beth Mattox

shin/upper foot area rather than the insole of the foot. On occasion the impact can be very painful or even cause damage. Chang Tung Sheng would take a rolling pin and roll it up and down on his shins to condition the bone, muscles and skin so that his sweeps were extremely powerful.

IKF: So, he just used a regular rolling pin?

DC: Yes, but a Chinese rolling pin is a little bit different than the Western variety. A Western rolling pin has stationary handles with a central roller that rotates around the shaft. A Chinese rolling pin, on the other hand, is just a cylindrical piece of wood. It is rolled by using the palms of the hands starting at the fingertips and moving forward to the base of the palms and then back again. You can still see these used all over Taiwan by people rolling out dough to make bread, steamed buns, and dumplings.

IKF: I have also heard that Chang Tung Sheng used some kind of training that involved running on hills. Can you explain?

DC: Yes that's true. That was another training method taught to him by Zhang Feng Yan. It is done by running up an inclined surface and then suddenly stopping and spinning around 180 degrees on one foot while coiling the other leg. The coiled leg then sweeps straight back—scraping across the

Chang demonstrates the shuai chiao training stance "dull sickle reaping the rice," which corresponds to the "jian tui" technique.

ground—while the arms and upper body swing forward toward the ground, simulating a throwing movement. You end up balanced on one foot with the sweeping leg pointing up in the air. By running and repeating this exercise over and over again on the same spot the backward sweeping foot will begin to wear away the grass, expose the dirt, and eventually dig a rut in the ground. The purpose is to improve your ability to keep your balance while throwing an opponent. When doing throws in shuai chiao the goal is to maintain your balance and not fall to the ground or on your opponent. Some throws involve balancing on one leg while using the other leg to sweep up and assist in the throw. So, the supporting leg must be very strong and stable. Doing this movement on a flat surface is difficult enough but on an angled surface like a hill it is really difficult.

IKF: Did Chang Tung Sheng have any teachers other than Zhang Feng Yan?

DC: When he was in the army he had to travel to different places so he came in contact with other famous martial artists and learned from them, but according to my grandfather, Zhang Feng Yan was by far his most important teacher.

IKF: What position did Chang Tung Sheng have in the army?

DC: This is very interesting. Actually, he was a secret agent—kind of like a "007." He was in a group of elite paratroopers—the first group of that kind created in the Chinese army—called "hong qiang," which means 'The Red Wall.' Originally, he was just a normal member but went on to become the commander of the unit. ®

Mark Miller, who has been studying shuai chiao for 20 years, learned the art directly from Chang Tung Sheng, received his first- and second-degree black belt certificates directly from Chang Tung Sheng. He is currently studying shuai chiao and kung-fu with David Chang in Taipei. He can be contacted at mjmiller59@hotmail.com.

The Secret Behind Chang's Strength

Chang Tung Sheng, considered the greatest Chinese grappler of all time, attributed his strength to qi gong training.

Mark Miller

In part two of this exclusive series, David Chang talks about his grandfathers tournament dominance, how he incorporated tai chi into his shuai chiao regimen, and what he was like as a teacher.

IKF: What were the tournaments like in the days when Chang Tung Sheng was competing?

DC: The matches were very rough. They consisted of three rounds. You had to win two out of the three rounds to win the match. There were fewer limitations than there are nowadays, less rules. So you could use more dangerous techniques. The fights were very quick and violent. Once you touched someone you had to throw them immediately like in san shou.

IKF: Did Chang Tung Sheng know any kung-fu styles other than shuai chiao?

weapons. But he told me that among all of those styles he loved shuai chiao the most.

IKF: How did Chang Tung Sheng learn tai chi chuan?

DC: He learned tai chi from a gentleman named General Li Chien Lin when he was at the Central Martial Arts School. General Li was vice president of the Institute and famous for his Yang style tai chi and swordsmanship. He was about 15 or 20 years older than Chang Tung Sheng and was quite fond of him. Also, knowing some shuai chiao himself from when he was in Hebei, he respected Chang Tung Sheng's shuai chiao prowess. The two became good friends and one day General Li offered to teach Chang Tung Sheng tai chi. Not wanting to accept the offer and thereby assume the subordinate position of a "student" Chang Tung Sheng politely refused. Eventually, they decided to "exchange" information. General Li taught Chang Tung Sheng tai chi and sword, and Chang taught him shuai chiao in return.

This was a method commonly used in those days rather than fighting challenge matches to determine who was better. If the person were a friend, you would "test" each other's skill in a friendly man-

Chang Tung Sheng demonstrates tai chi in Cleveland.

ner and then exchange information. In Chinese we say "jau huan" which means "teach exchange." In this way, people could exchange information or teach each other on equal terms without either one "losing face" and being the "student." So, although Chang Tung Sheng considered Zhang Feng Yan his only true teacher, he was able to learn skills from other prominent martial artists by "jau huan."

IKF: I would like to ask this next question by first relating a story. When I was in Columbus, Ohio, studying shuai chiao in the early 1980s, I accompanied Chang Tung Sheng, who was then about 75 years old, to Cleveland where he gave an unbelievable shuai chiao demonstration and taught a clinic. The clinic was attended by one particular martial artist who is known for his ability to take a punch. I have personally seen him go to kung-fo tournaments and openly invite anyone there to punch him in the stomach. I have seen some very big, strong people punch him full power but, to his credit, I have never seen anyone rock him. However, it was another story at Changs clinic. This person invited Chang to have a try by motioning to his stomach and saying that he wanted to "feel his power." When the translator related this to Chang he seemed rather startled by the audacity of the request and asked the translator to confirm. When the same request came back again Chang appeared to be rather offended and also uncomfortable about being put on the spot with a group of people looking on. After hesitating momentarily, Chang, in his suit and tie, nonchalantly punched him in the stomach which doubled him over and then followed immediately with an uppercut which landed under the chin (I remember hearing his teeth hit together) and sent him reeling back—to the delight of the crowd. As he recovered his balance Chang stepped forward and casually landed a right forearm to the side of the neck which buckled his knees.

So, even though Chang was most famous for his throws and takedowns he could also hit with tremendous power. My question is this: how did he train his strikes? Did he use a bag, or iron palm training?

Hsing Jing Kick.   Hsing Jing.

Lo Han.

The shuai chiao technique "kwai."

A Shuai Chiao movement.

DC: No, no, he never hit bags or broke bricks or anything like that! You saw his hands—they were very powerful but the skin was soft and smooth. In addition to being a martial artist, he was also a musician and skilled at playing the er-hu (two-stringed Chinese violin) which requires great dexterity.

His power came from his "qi" (as in "qi gong" or "chi kung"). In Chinese, "kung-fu" literally means "time; work; skill, technique." He spent many, many years working very hard at developing his skills so his qi was very strong. He was in excellent physical condition, practiced qi gong, and used Chinese herbs. So even into his 70s he still had great power and speed.

Shuai chiao does have its own version of "bag" training called "tun bao." It is not actually a bag but a large bundle of long reeds that is hung vertically. Rather than just striking it with the fists, however, it is normally used by combining strikes—mostly forearm and elbow—with sweeping movements of the legs to develop explosive throws and takedowns.

IKF: A friend once told Chang Tung Sheng that he practiced sitting meditation every day. Chang advised him to stop immediately and do shuai chiao training stances instead. Why would he advise him to do that if he himself practiced qi gong?

DC: Because, in shuai chiao training stances are combined with qi gong.

IKF: How do you combine shuai chiao training stances with qi gong?

DC: Well, that's a long story! For now, just understand that there are several important points such as breathing, and the way that you transition from the right to the left side in each stance.

IKF: How did Chang Tung Sheng come to Taiwan?

DC: When the Communist Army took over the Mainland he escaped to Taiwan with the Nationalist Army troops in 1948.

IKF: What did he do after arriving in Taiwan?

DC: For the first two years, he lived in Chia-Yi in southern Taiwan with the army. Later, he moved

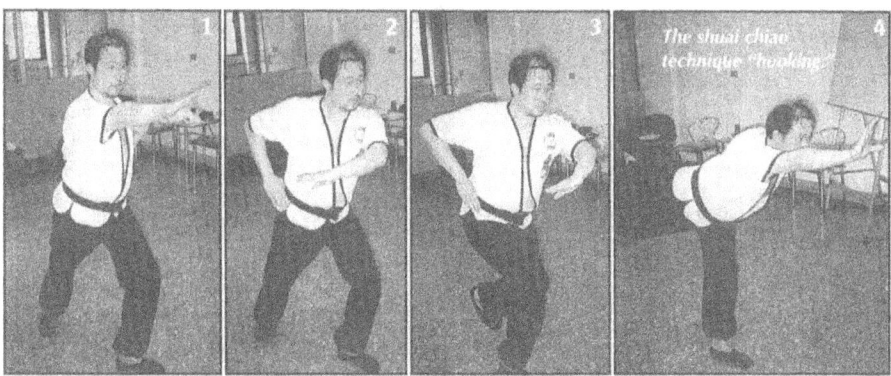

The shuai chiao technique "huoling."

to Taipei where the government provided him with a house. As I mentioned before, he had been working as a kind of secret agent in Mainland China, so one day I was surprised when I came across some family records that listed his job title in Taiwan as the vice president of a government army hospital. At first I couldn't figure it out, but later it dawned on me that this title was probably used to cover up his former position to prevent being executed in the event that the Communists invaded Taiwan.

IKF: How did he become an instructor at the Central Police College?

DC: My grandfather knew some influential people. One was a teacher named Huang Jie, who was the former governor of Taiwan. The other was Bai Chung Xi, who was the Minister of Defense and also a Muslim. They introduced Chang Tung Sheng to the Central Police College where he became an instructor. That is the reason shuai chiao became so popular as fundamental training for the police.

IKF: What was Chang Tung Sheng like as a grandfather?

DC: Because I had an interest in kung-fu, my grandfather was very fond of me. I would follow him around and play with him all the time. As a teacher, he was very strict and harsh to me, but after training he treated me like a friend. I guess that's the way he treated his other students, too. In general, however, his demeanor was rather stern so many people didn't feel comfortable around him. But I did, so I was usually the one who would accompany him to the park, or the opera, or the countryside.

IKF: Did Chang Tung Sheng practice kung-fu at

Grandmaster Chang demonstrates a shuai chiao training stance at the Ohio State University.

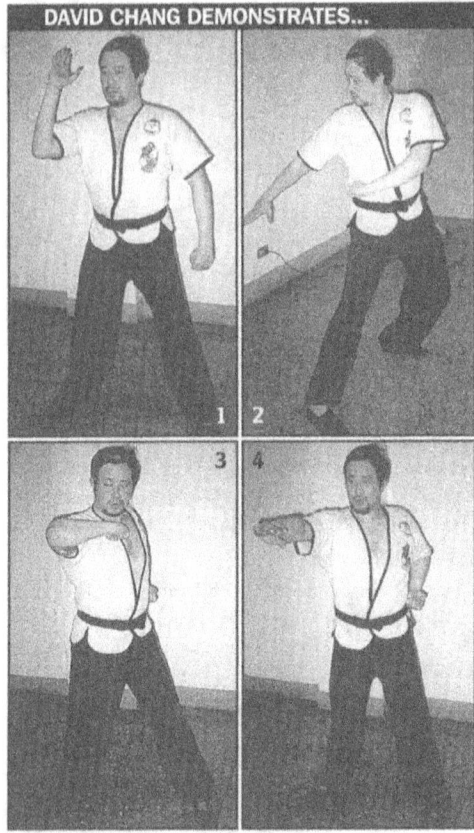

A striking exercise from shuai chiao san shou style.

DAVID CHANG DEMONSTRATES...

DC: He taught shuai chiao at the police college, so at home he usually practiced other forms and weapons. The only time he practiced shuai chiao at home was when he was teaching me. We used to practice shuai chiao in the front and backyards until later on, when I was in high school, we formed a shuai chiao team and got a place to practice with tatami mats (Japanese-style straw mats).

IKF: How did he organize and document his system?

DC: It was already a complete system when Zhang Feng Yan taught it to him so he did not need to arrange anything. Everything was already clear and organized. Training stances, equipment training, falling, jointlocks, strikes and throws were all part of the system since ancient times. As everyone knows, shuai chiao is a very high-level kung-fu that is like a net in which everything is interrelated. The basic movements and forms, training stances, equipment training, and techniques are all related to each other and supplement each other.

He did write his own book covering the basic fundamentals of shuai chiao. He also made his own notes of "secret" techniques.

IKF: What characteristics did Chang Tung Sheng consider important in his students?

DC: He felt that a persons physique really didn't matter so much—fat or thin, tall or short. Also, it didn't matter if they were rich or poor, or what religion they were. First, they had to be well-mannered and polite when they trained. Secondly, they had to have endurance and patience. Sometimes Chang Tung Sheng would test his students to check their patience. Thirdly, they didn't have to be highly intelligent, but had to be able to see things clearly and have good judgment.

IKF: When did he start to teach you kung-fu?

DC: He started to teach me the poem of shuai chiao when I was very young. I couldn't read the characters but he would make me recite them all. I didn't know what they meant but I could say them. By the time I was seven I had the whole poem memorized. Then when I was nine he started to teach me the movements and relate them to the characters in the poem.

IKF: Where did he start to teach you?

DC: Normally, he would teach me at home. He didn't like to teach me in public. But when I got older we would go to the Botanical Gardens in Taipei—arriving early in the morning before 5 a.m. After about two hours of practice we would go out for breakfast. He taught me all the things he learned at Zhang Feng Yan's house when he was a kid. I learned everything except for catching the crickets—unfortunately, there are no crickets there!

differently when he knew his days were numbered?

DC: After he learned he had cancer he didn't really teach me anything new because I had seen most everything already. Rather, he tried to review everything with me to make sure I knew it well. Anytime I ran across a problem and didn't understand something I would ask him and he would explain it to me and we would make notes. He wanted me to understand the entire system very clearly.

IKF: Do you think he took a lot of secrets to the grave with him?

DC: I don't think so—as far as shuai chiao goes. I think I learned all the shuai chiao and fist forms he knew. However, some of the other things he knew—like weapons, for example—I didn't have enough time to learn thoroughly.

IKF: Where are you teaching now?

DC: I am teaching shuai chiao at the Central Police Academy. Other than that, as you know, my grandfather had many special herb tonic recipes and herbal liniments to heal external wounds. I have a piece of land on Ho Lung Mountain in Miaoli hope to make my grandfather's herbal recipes available to the world so that everyone can get the benefit of his knowledge of Chinese herbs.

Chang Tung Sheng performing Using Jing.

IKF: As Chang Tung Sheng's grandson, what is your vision for shuai chiao in the future?

DC: I hope that there can be peace in the shuai chiao world. My grandfather has students all over the world that are very successful. I hope that all his students can set aside their differences and work together to promote Chang Tung Sheng's beloved art of shuai chiao. As we say in Chinese, each person has their own piece of sky above them. I hope that all of them can join their pieces of sky together to become a vast, peaceful shuai chiao universe that will be strong and live forever. $

Mark Miller, who has been studying shuai chiao for 20 years, learned the art directly from Chang Tung Sheng. He can be reached at mjmiller59@hotmail.com

Cary Tagawa, The Martial Artist Athlete

Breathing, centering, resistance against gravity and centrifugal force are the integral parts of Mu Training.

Todd Hester

There's a lot more to Cary Tagawa than meets the eye—and a lot meets the eye. A U.S. Army brat, whose mother was a Japanese actress, Tagawa was born in Tokyo and lived in Ft. Bragg, North Carolina, Ft. Polk, Louisiana, and Ft. Hood, Texas before his family finally settled in Southern California. There, Tagawa began acting in high school and then was an exchange student in Japan while studying at the University of Southern California. Tagawa moved back to Japan after college, but was disappointed when he felt like an cultural outsider, not having lived there for so long. He returned to America, and at the age of 36, began his acting career. He got his first big break when he was cast in Bernardo Bertolucci's feature film *The Last Emperor*. He went on to roles *in Rising Sun, Mortal Kombat,* and *The Phantom,* among many others. He also starred in the CBS series *Nash Bridges.* All told Tagawa has made well over 100 films and television appearances. Continually working, and in constant demand, Tagawa is currently appearing in *The Art of War* with Wesley Snipes, and *Pearl Harbor* with Ben Affleck.

While it may be true that still waters run deep, if Tagawa is any indication, fast waters run even deeper. Constantly in motion, and filled with seemingly boundless energy, Tagawa is a bottomless well of ideas and philosophies. He is currently working on a project that combines two of his deepest passions—martial arts and sports—into an integrated discipline. While the two might seem to only be superficially related, Tagawa has drawn numerous parallels that are not intuitively obvious until they are pointed out—then they seem to be naturally related. Currently working on his first book, *The Martial Artist Athlete,* which will soon be available on-line at his Web site, **www.caryhiroyukitagawa.com,** Tagawa seems poised to revolutionize the world of martial arts and sports by combining the positive elements of both into a complete spiritual and athletic system of "total performance."

Q: What is the current state of martial arts and sports?

A: I think that martial arts and sports have peaked, simply because we've come so far from the original intention of both. Martial arts was always passed as a gift of heaven, really, for the underdogs. However, it came to America as a sport rather than as an art, because of the emphasis of judo and karate tournaments after the World War II by Kano and the Funakoshi. So the budo was lost in the United States, or rather never known, except very indirectly. Traditional values, in general, were never part of the American martial arts culture—martial arts was just another sport.

I think the difference between martial arts and sports, is that in sports you don't necessarily need respect. Sport doesn't necessarily build character. Although they say it does, you don't necessarily have to have character to play sports. So martial arts, when it emphasizes sports, becomes martial sports, rather than martial arts. Sports have also been contaminated. The original Olympics, for example, had very high ideals about sportsmanship. It was about the purity of the body itself and what the body represented. The original Olympians would be horrified to find what we're doing to the body with drugs, and with todays win-at-all-costs attitude. That same attitude, when it got applied to martial arts, was why I got disinterested.

Q: At what point did this happen?

A: I lost interest in martial arts when they became so heavily competition oriented. I was always more focused on the internal aspects and the respect—the traditional things that taught character though actions. You're lucky today if you get any of that in modern martial arts. We've allowed martial arts to become a business, not a way of life. And any time you add business to an art, it's over. So I left martial arts and started developing my own style—*chuu-shin*.

Q: What about sports?

A: I lost interest in sports when NFL football coaches started paying bounties for players to hurt other players. You could see very clearly that it was no longer about the love of the game, or about sportsmanship. It was about business and about how to eliminate the star athletes. The strategies in sports also went downhill in basketball, when coaches stalled in games in order to protect leads against better teams. Where's the honor is winning that way?

So I think we've not only lost honor for the game, but also honor for ourselves as athletes. The samurai aspect of honoring your opponent is gone. Your opponent is not the enemy. This is not war—this is competition. We have such a need to define ourselves as winners and losers that we've lost the sense of respect for ourselves and others. You can't respect other people unless you respect yourself.

Q: So you feel spiritual aspects apply to sports as well as martial arts?

A: Absolutely. The Olympics started as a way for soldiers to stay fit between wars. So it still had a war-oriented purpose. But it was a substitute for war—an outlet for aggression.

Martial arts, on the other hand, trained for war not sport. It's about protecting yourself and, at worse, killing people. There are three different types of martial artists: the martial artist who has trained in the dojo and has traditional respect and honor; the martial artist who is into it for the flash—the Hollywood influence—the trophies—and only goes to tournaments for money; and the martial artists who train in the military and have actually killed people with their hands. I see those three levels as being very distinct and different.

Q: Where did the samurai fit in?

A: Theoretically, the samurai way is based on selflessness—they gave their life for their lord. But it's not truly selfless in that they wanted to die honorably so they didn't bring shame to their family name. The family name actually gains honor from the samurai's death. So there is some self-interest there. And what if their lord was an jerk? They wasted themselves for nothing. That's what actually happened sometimes. A lot of the samurai ended up dying for very little purpose which left only the wimps

That is what makes the nature of the samurai and the ninja very different. The ninja actually started as priests who came from China— mountain priests who eventually degraded into just paid assassins. But at the highest level, when ninjit- su started, the roots are in a mountain warrior called *the yamabushi*. So the ninja were not so much about killing and dying as they were about getting the job done. The highest form of what they did was to get in and get out without anyone knowing they had been there. In that sense, given the difference of dying for a purpose and living for a purpose, I choose living for a purpose. But these principles are very foreign to the Western mentality. Everything in Western society is about displaying your manhood as an identity, rather than just *being* the manhood, which I believe the spiritual Asian energies are based on.

Tagawa shows proper martial arts baseball footwork (1A, IB), as opposed to an incorrect "feet-out" position (2A, 2B).

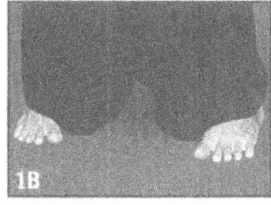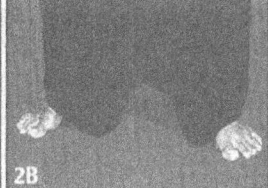

Q: So do you believe there's a way to merge sportive Western thought and Eastern spiritual principles?

A: Yes, which is to go back to that sense of sportsmanship—the respect for your body, and the respect for your opponent. Your opponent is just a person who's perfecting his art just as you're perfecting your art. We're talking about a meeting of two artists, basically. There's no reason to think of him like a dog—to think that he is worthless. Martial arts should work to develop the internal sense that honors the spirit and the heart.

Centering is the key part of any physical activity, whether it be training or actual competition.

Q: Does your training system do this?

A: The whole art of chuu shin was developed without the concepts of competition and fighting. The art, using the staff, is about centering and focusing—concentration without fighting. I've taken martial arts principles of how the physical body works and then worked it into a physical training system for athletes without the fighting.

In sports today, the most used training concepts are aerobics, weight-lifting, and cross-training. Those three levels of training are about to be replaced. I say replaced because actually the system that does this will be called Mu Training and will come from Mu Sports. But Mu Training, which is an evolutionary step even above chu shinn, involves using water as a medium.

Centering is the art of using energy rather than muscle. In the West we train muscles to create power and strength. In martial arts, the true force comes from the breath, or the ki, and involves resistance against gravity through the repetition of forms, and centrifugal force from whipping the hips to create striking power. So this system of chuu-shin, and also Mu Training, is based on three things: breathing, gravity, and centrifugal force. So the body in relation to those three things is going to change the nature of training and change the nature of performance in athletes—physically and spiritually.

Q: How long have you been developing it?

A: Formally, since 1993. I've taken every sport and broken it down by watching their top athletes movements. For example, when I played basketball, we just used to shuffle our feet around and move sideways and go forward and backwards—very linearly. But what is needed is to get moving in a chaotic way, so you don't move in just one direction—in basketball you don't just go in one direction. No one has addressed that kind of physical movement. You don't get that from just lifting weights or running or from an aerobics class. So chaos training applies to basketball, football, hockey, baseball, and soccer. In those sports you're constantly in motion, having to constantly change direction.

Q: Is your training system available now?

A: It exists, and I'm training a few people, but I just haven't put it out. What I say to the people I train is that I could teach you the fighting aspects of martial arts, but I'd much rather teach you the movement principles that relate directly to your sport. How to move like a martial artist in your chosen sport is much more applicable than how to fight, because if you get into a fight on the court you're out of the game. We see that more and more—the fighting—and it's ridiculous. It's simply a result of not having the martial arts concentration and focus without the fighting. Every sport—basketball, baseball, tennis, whatever—has an application of this.

The one major thing that is lacking in sports is breathing—which is a martial arts specialty. The aerobic theory started in the '70s from Major Kubo of the Royal Canadian Air Force. He found that the fittest athletes were the most aerobically positive. So you have to build your body to move the longest, at its most efficient. But aerobic theory focused too much on the heart—the heart is only a pump—the generator that makes the power is actually the lungs. Humans have twenty-five-hundred square feet of lung capacity and only use ten to fifteen percent. An athlete increasing his lung capacity by 85 percent would be capable of astounding performance. When those guarding him are huffing and puffing, he'd just be getting warmed-up.

Breathing is a whole new energy source that Western athletes haven't considered. In a hundred meter race, for example, a sprinter has expended their oxygen by the forty-meter mark. So they have to go sixty meters with no oxygen—no wonder they're cramping. Cramped muscles are a lack of oxygen. If you breathe more you won't cramp, if you don't cramp your muscles will keep going longer. It's the difference between the carbo-loading theory of filling up a fuel tank once, at the beginning of the race, or the chuu-shin theory of constantly adding gas as the race progresses, by breathing. You should actually be running faster at the end of the race than you were at the beginning. But in sports today, it's all about energy declination. So these are all principles that have not been looked at. When I formally implement them they will fundamentally change training and athletic performance. $

Special thanks to Annie James for biographical information. Visit her Cary Tagawa fan site at www.carytagawa.com. *For more information on chuu-shin or* The Martial Artist Athlete, *visit Cary Tagawas personal web site at* www.caryhiroyukitagawa.com

Cary Tagawa Film Timeline

- **2000:** Pearl Harbor
- **2000:** The Art of War
- **2000:** Camp Ninja Ross Kawaii
- **1999:** Snow Falling on Cedars—Zenhichi Miyamoto
- **1999:** Bridge of Dragons—Ruechang
- **1999:** Johnny Tsunami—Johnny Tsunami
- **1999:** Tom Clancy's Netforce—Leong Cheng
- **1998:** Vampires—David Deyo
- **1997:** American Dragons—Matsuyama
- **1997:** Top of the World—Captain Hefter
- **1996:** The Phantom—The Great Kabai Sengh
- **1996:** Nash Bridges—Lt. A. J. Shimamura
- **1996:** Danger Zone—Chang
- **1996:** Provocateur—Captain Jong
- **1996:** White Tiger—Victor Chow
- **1995:** Mortal Kombat—Shang Tsung
- **1995:** Picture Bride—Kanzaki
- **1995:** Soldier Boyz—Vinh Moc
- **1994:** Day of Reckoning—Prakit
- **1994:** The Dangerous—Kon
- **1994:** Natural Causes—Major Somchai
- **1993:** Nemesis—Angie-Liv
- **1993:** Rising Sun—Eddie Sakamura
- **1993:** Space Rangers—Zylyn
- **1992:** American Me—El Japo
- **1992:** Raven: Return of the Black Dragons—Osato
- **1991:** Kickboxer 2: The Road Back—Sanga
- **1991:** Mission of the Shark: The Saga of the U.S.S. Indianapolis—Hashimoto
- **1991:** The Perfect Weapon—Kai
- **1991:** Not of This World
- **1991:** Showdown in Little Tokyo—Yoshida
- **1990:** Vestige of Honor—Thai Major
- **1990:** Murder in Paradise
- **1989:** L.A. Takedown—Hugh Denny
- **1989:** License to Kill—Kwang
- **1989:** The Last Warrior—Imperial Marine
- **1988:** Twins—Oriental Man
- **1988:** Spellbinder—Lt. Lee
- **1987:** The Last Emperor—Chang
- **1987:** Star Trek: The Next Generation - Encounter at Farpoint—Mandarin Bailiff
- **1986:** Armed Response—Toshi
- **1986:** Big Trouble in Little China (uncredited)

Hung Gar's Unbeatable Tiger

Martial arts great Buck Sam Konff shows you how to unleash the ferocious fighting power of hung gar's tiger.

Joseph Plante

student asks sifu Buck Sam Kong about a particular move in a traditional hung / ■ gar set and he replies, "It is a tiger move—it rakes down and across—it looks like a cat—a big cat."

To understand the meaning of the movements contained in animal styles, you must first study the animal in which the movement originates. Within the hung gar system of gung-fu, there are five animals: tiger, crane, dragon, leopard, and snake. The largest and strongest of the five animals is the tiger, known as *panthera tigris*.

An adult male tiger can weigh 600 pounds, stand three feet tall, and measure from seven-to-ten feet head to tail. This heavily muscled carnivore uses force to meet force when overcoming his prey.

For a moment, let us visualize a tiger in action. After many days without eating and many near kills, a hunger-stricken and exhausted tiger waits in the brush. Driven by instinct he stalks another unsuspecting animal. This time he has his eye on a large male deer. Crouched and silent, this graceful orange giant patiently inches into position. Now totally still, he gazes intensely at his prey. Still unnoticed by the grazing buck, the tiger is now less than 25 five feet away.

Suddenly, the tiger jumps from the brush with every muscle fiber in his body committed to the chase. He leaps through the air to pounce on the large buck. Frozen for a moment and shocked by

the unexpected attack, the large buck only has time to turn his head and point his antlers toward the charging tiger.

The tiger seems to stop and change direction in midair, just in time to dodge the spear-like rack of antlers. Now approaching from the backside of the deer, the powerful cat pulls the prey to the ground with both paws. The deer makes one more futile attempt to escape but the tiger counterattacks, using one paw to hold down the deer and the other to go for the throat. Finally, after three days of hunting, the tiger eats.

Gung Gee Fuk Fu Kuen

FORM: From a ready position (1). Move into cat stance (2). Double claw in forward stance (3). Pull claws down as you move back into cat stance (4).

APPLICATION: From a ready position (1), the opponent punches. Now block with the forearm and move into cat (2). Then move into forward stance and strike with claws hook onto the collarbone (3). Pull down as you move into cat (4).

Buck Sam Kong Time Line

- 1940 Buck Sam Kong is born in Hong Kong.
- 1946 Begins taking eagle claw kung-fu lessons from his mother.
- 1948 Begins a lifelong study of hung gar kung-fu with grandmaster Lam Jo.
- 1961 Joined the U.S. Army and was sent to Korea to become hand-to-hand combat instructor.
- 1963 Moved to Hawaii and established his first school that remains operational today.
- 1969 Publishes his first book entitled, *Lau Gar*.
- 1972 Publishes his second book entitled, *Hung Gar Kung Fu*.
- 1976 Moved to the Mainland and established a martial arts school in Southern California.

Strength of the Tiger

Now that we have visualized a tiger in action, we can compare the wild tiger to the hung gar tiger. Like the actual tiger, hung gar's tiger must have exceptional strength. Practitioners execute the powerful movements low to the ground, resembling an actual tiger. The hung gar tigers strength is because of the training precepts taught in the foundational hung gar set named gung gee fuk fu kuen (conquering the tiger form). This set imparts awesome strength to its practitioner. Characterized by powerful ground gripping stances and deceptive techniques, gung gee fuk fu kuen also contains dynamic tension exercises. These dynamic tension exercises condition the back, shoulders, triceps, forearms, wrists, tendons, and fingers.

This set is essential to tiger training in hung gar. Obtaining strength like a tiger is a worthy endeavor for every hung gar practitioner. A weak tiger in the wild cannot hunt effectively and will die from starvation. From the tiger's example, we learn the lesson of using strength in battle.

Breath and Endurance

Even after many days of hunting without success, a tiger in the wild finds the will to endure. Not unlike the wild tiger, a hung gar practitioner must develop mental and physical endurance. And that requires a strong body, a strong mind, and a strong heart. However, before you can obtain any of the proceeding attributes you must first learn to control your breath.

Breath control is fundamental to hung gar mastery. Remember oxygen feeds your muscles and brain. Without oxygen, you will become physically and mentally exhausted. To acquire endurance, sifu Kong recommends you perform each set ten times without resting between sets. If a student practices this way every day, he obtains mental and physical endurance through conditioning.

Sifu Kong stresses that you exhale as you strike or claw to add strength to your attack. If you remember to exhale as you strike, you will naturally inhale as needed. As you execute the form ten times in a row, focus on controlling your breathing. This is how you acquire the endurance of the tiger in hung gar kuen.

A Tiger's Weapons

Tiger weapons combine tiger paws and claws with deceptive movements. Hung gar's tiger claws (fu jow) require secret conditioning techniques to achieve maximum results. Sifu Kong suggests the following method for those wishing to begin tiger claw training.

"To train the claw, begin by picking up a five-pound sandbag with the claw and dropping it, then pick it up again and drop it again," he explains. "Gradually do this until you are able to pick up a 50- pound sandbag with the claw."

1972
- **1980** Opened a hung gar school in Germany.
- **1981** Released tiger and crane video.
- **1982** School in Utah opens.
- **1983** Published third book entitled, *Tiger & Crane*.
- **1985** Expands his hung gar reach by opening a school in Tulsa, Okla.
- **1996** School in Mexico opens.
- **1997** His *Gung Gee Fuk Fu* book is published in four languages.
- **1998** Las Vegas school opens.
- **1999** Releases the video "Gung Gee Fuk Fu."
- **2000** His 60th birthday party becomes an international event held in Los Angeles' Chinatown.

Gung Gee Fuk Fu Kuen

FORM: Ready position (1). Step back into horse stance with double claws (2). Lunge strike forward with both claws (3). Retract both claws to side as you move into cat stance (4).

APPLICATION: From a ready position (1), as your opponent throws a left punch guide the punch away with the right claw (2). Double claw strike forward and hook your fingers into his collarbone (3). Retract claws downward and to your side (4).

Tiger and Crane

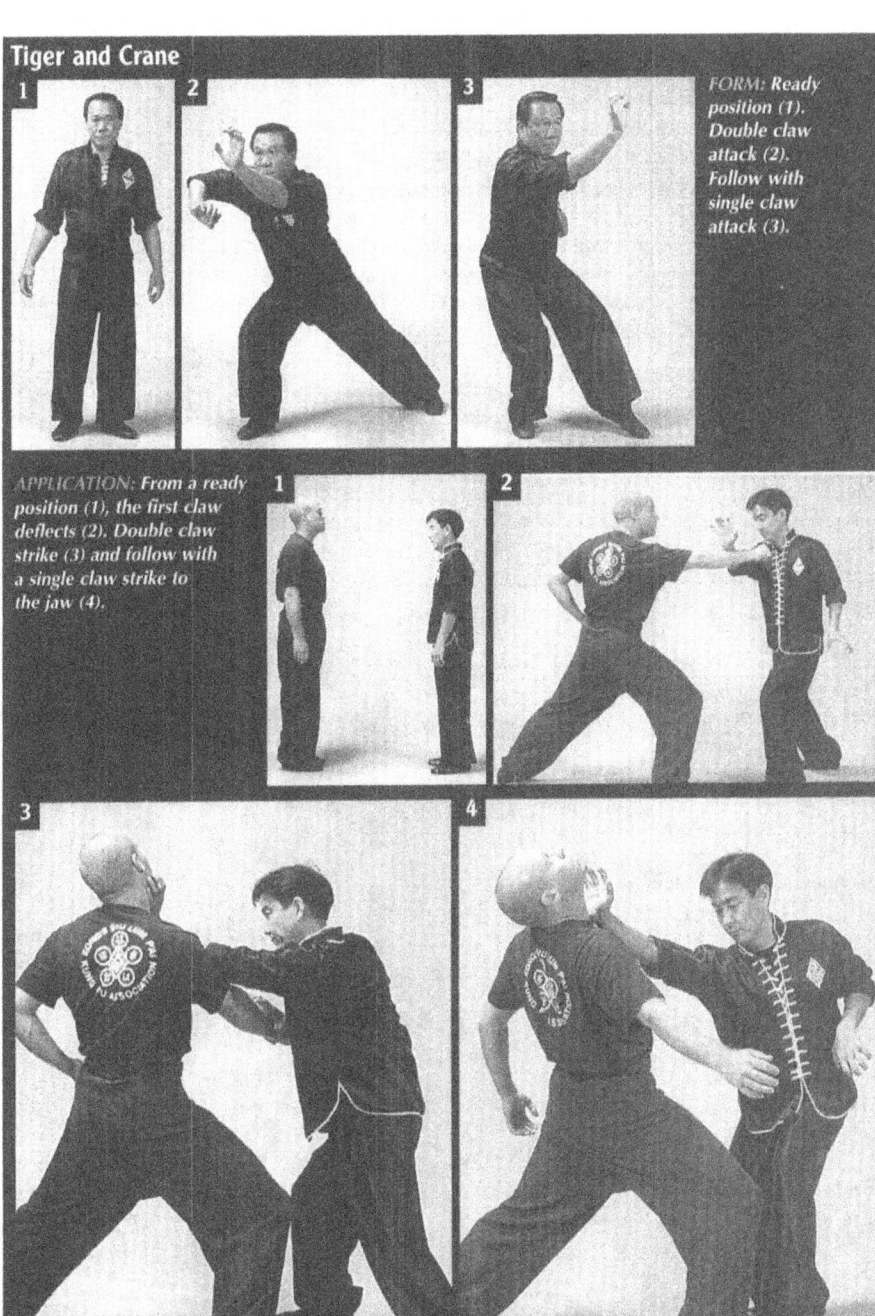

FORM: Ready position (1). Double claw attack (2). Follow with single claw attack (3).

APPLICATION: From a ready position (1), the first claw deflects (2). Double claw strike (3) and follow with a single claw strike to the jaw (4).

Tiger Applications

Tiger claws in hung gar are similar to a real tiger's claw in terms of movement and application. Some of the uses of the tiger claw include:

- Striking an opponent using the heel of the palm.
- Raking the finger down a persons arms or face.
- Grabbing and closing the grip on impact, then pinching the muscles, flesh, or vital parts like the groin or neck.
- Trapping an opponent's arm while simultaneously striking him with a claw to the face or chin.
- Using claws to tear ribs or hooking behind the jaw and ripping joints and bones from the body.

A powerful tiger claw attack can easily maim or kill an opponent and therefore should only be used in extreme cases of real danger.

Move Like a Tiger

A tiger's strategy is simple. A tiger first uses surprise, then force against force to overpower the prey. Within this strategy, if the prey puts up a fight, the tiger uses a counterattack. Counter-attacks, surprise attacks and tiger mechanics require a great deal of agility. Sifu Kong teaches the agility of a tiger through the famous hung gar form fu hok kuen (the tiger and crane set).

As the name implies, the tiger and crane set is a synergy of both animal styles. For the purposes of this article, we will only discuss the tiger. Contained in the form are the ten directions of the tiger's attack, which use both single and double claw attacks, as well as counterattacks. From continual practice of the form and a lot of patience, the student attains the agility of a tiger.

A Tiger's Attitude

When practicing the form sifu Kong stresses proper spirit. The spirit of the tiger is understood through the tiger's attitude. A tiger is at the top of the food chain in his natural habitat. Nothing eats tigers. A tiger attacks without fear. His stature is one of confidence. When practicing the form, project that confidence. Move without hesitation using good posture. Think of how people relate to tigers; they like tigers because they are beautiful but also fear them because they are dangerous. When the form is performed correctly, it too is beautiful—but dangerous. Incorporate the tiger's attitude and stature into your gung-fu and you too will project the true spirit of the tiger.

Internal Tiger Training

Two kinds of strength exist within the hung gar system—hard external strength and soft internal strength. External strength can be observed on the outside of the body and defined by strong, well- developed muscles and powerful movements. Not so obvious is internal strength. You cannot see internal strength. To be truly strong like a tiger you must possess both internal and external strength. For a student to gain internal strength he must learn the iron thread set (tid sin kuen), considered the highest and most guarded set in the hung gar system.

Sifu Kong only teaches this set to students he deems worthy. The student must be of good character, loyal, and disciplined in all previous forms. Although few students in his system have made it this far, those who have should be commended for their tremendous effort and years of dedication.

Hungry Like A Tiger

A student of hung gar must be hungry like a tiger to succeed. He must really want to learn. Hung gar training is no easy task. Many attempt to learn, but few actually do what it takes. Stance training alone is enough to stop most people. However, if your legs become strong enough, it is just the beginning. A hung gar student endures years of intense training. This student must be hungry for the secrets contained within this beautiful and effective style. Are you hungry like a tiger? ®

For more information or training schedules, contact Buck Sam Kong's Siu Lum Pai Gung Fu Assn., 1723 Hillhurst Ave., Los Angeles, CA 90027; (323) 664-8882. Joseph Plante is a martial artist and freelance writer based in Southern California.

Turning Fear into Power

Fear can be your greatest enemy but, if channeled and directed correctly, it can also be your greatest ally.

Dr. Will Horton

You're in a situation with your wife that makes you nervous. Your car has broken down, it's dark, and you're in a bad part of town. Your try to tell yourself to relax. You're a martial artist with years of training. A shabbily-dressed man approaches you. Your stomach tightens. He asks for "spare change" for a drink. You refuse but he persists. You start to walk away and he follows. You can smell the alcohol on his breath. He starts to reach out to you and you pull away. You back up, your wife behind you. You do not want trouble. Does he read this action as fear? Predators feed on fear, you remind yourself. He stalks closer, he eyes moving behind you to your wife. He has crossed your safety line. You get feelings you tell yourself you should not have—doubt and fear. You tell yourself to be calm but it worsens. You don't know what to do. You're frozen in indecision. Fear overcomes you. Your heart races and you have trouble catching your breath. Your hands shake, your vision narrows, your hearing shuts down, and your mind races with negative thoughts. Where is my Zen-like peace? Where are the techniques I've worked on for so many years? Why am I afraid? You pray your skills will kick in, but will they?

> "The physical states of fear are intended to help you. Just accept these states, then let the mind take over and channel the extra energy from the adrenaline to your own use."

Every martial artist's deepest fear is that when they need their combat training to defend themselves or their loved ones, they will hesitate or freeze. Most martial artists spend years sharpening their physical skills, yet spend little or no time developing their mental ones. They fall into the trap of thinking that physical techniques alone will ensure peace of mind in a violent encounter. Then when a real fight occurs, they are shocked at their response. Many quit training in the martial arts after such an experience, thinking their art failed them, or that they failed their art. In reality, though, they only neglected to train their brains as well as their bodies.

Mind Training

To train the mind to resist fear, you must first be able to realize the difference between an "adrenal push" and its physical effects, and the psychological state we label as fear, and make friends with both.

Only then can you put them to good use. The first part is to separate our physical responses from our psychological interpretations of them.

Fear is defined as a strong, often unpleasant, emotional and physical response to real or perceived danger. Adrenaline is a natural hormone secreted by the adrenal glands that are nature's response to stressful environmental triggers. Its only job is to prepare the body for action—be it fight or flight. Fear should be your ally. The process of fear comes in basically four steps.

1) Pre-Event Adrenal Drip: This state occurs often. Many people refer to it as a stress reaction. You're tense, slightly nervous and on edge. If this state is prolonged it can exhaust you. This is why stressful jobs "burn" you out. This state is intended to put you on alert—physically and mentally. It also releases neuro-transmitters for heightened mental focus. Fear of fear can increase this.

2) In-Event, Primary Adrenal Dump: This occurs rapidly and very intensely. It is when your adrenal glands "dump" large amounts of the hormone into your system. This is to prepare you for major physical activity.

The effects of adrenaline are varied, but it is important too remember that this state is the ultimate survival tool. Adrenaline can cause a variety of effects to the body. It can tighten the muscles in preparation for trauma. It will cause visual exclusion or narrowing of vision, which causes you to lose your peripheral vision, creating tunnel vision. It leads to auditory exclusion, in which you lose a high percentage of your hearing—this is why athletes can't hear the crowds at athletic events. Adrenaline can speed up the heart rate. It can release ATP to give extra physical strength, but it can also cause rapid exhaustion, giving you the shakes. Mentally, it can cause rapid cognitive activity, giving you an overload of thoughts—usually negative—which can flood your mind, making you feel overwhelmed. It can also increase your breathing rate.

These things, in and of themselves, are bad and are not to be feared. They prepare your body for action. People that channel this into productive use excel in tense and stressful situations. These are the people who do better on rank tests, fights and other events when most people go down a notch.

3) In-Event, Secondary Adrenal Dump: This is a second dump which increases the effects of the above, as well as blocks pain, gives a secondary rush of energy, and creates extra negative thoughts.

This state is intended to give you that "second wind," of extra physical endurance, strength, and power to finish your task. This state explains why some people get better as a game, or fight, goes on. This is why in football, some athletes go out of their way to get hit a few times, in order to "get into the flow of the game."

4) Post-Event Adrenal Drip. After an event, the adrenal glands secrete small amounts of adrenaline. This causes slightly higher physical tension and leads to mentally repeating the event and reliving the fight. This state is much like the first and is intended to help your body readjust to the effects of the stressful event. This leads to physical and mental exhaustion.

Channeling Fear Into Power

Once it is understood that the physical states of fear are intended to help you, the importance of not labeling these as "good" or "bad" is obvious. Just accept these states, then let the mind take over and channel the extra energy from the adrenaline to your own use. To learn to harness fear, the first step is to recognize that it is normal. Insight and knowledge opens the door to channel this wonderful, power-packed state into something that can give you an edge in hostile situations.

The first step is to find and identify the first feelings of fear—the pre-event adrenaline release: How do you feel? Where do you feel it (stomach, chest, shoulders, back, et cetera)? What is your state of mind? To do this exercise, think of something that makes you fearful such as a confrontation with your boss, an IRS audit, or stepping onto the mat for a tournament fight. Relive the situation, note the above sensations, label the information, and store it.

Next, think of a time you were at your very best and were physically and mentally sharp. It could be a tournament you did well at, an academic test, or a business deal. Now imagine a circle on the floor. This is your circle of excellence and power. What color is this circle? Does it have a sound, a taste, a smell? Do this until you've established a recognizable and identifiable presence for it.

Now, think of your positive event and step into your circle—pull the circle into you. Throw your shoulders back. Feel the focus and the power. Repeat this twice. Now step out of the circle and access your fearful state. As you begin to feel the fear (the adrenaline state), step back into your circle and breathe in deeply. Do this five times. This is the first step in turning fear into power. Now, when your body starts to access the state of fear, it will naturally go into the circle of power. The more often you do this training, the more automatic the response will be when confronted by a stressful situation.

As Tsunetome Yamamoto, an 18th century samurai, said, "The realization of certain death should be renewed every morning. Each morning, you must prepare yourself for every kind of death with composure of mind. Imagine yourself broken by bows, guns, spears, swords, carried off by floods, leaping into a huge fire, struck by lightening, torn apart by earthquakes, plunging from a cliff, or as a disease-ridden corpse."

It may sound morbid, but if you can imagine your deepest fears, death, humiliation, loss of pride, and step into power, you will be in a better position to face whatever comes your way. It will help you to develop the heart of a warrior. $

Dr. Will Horton, a martial artist and the founder of The National Federation of Neurolinguistic Psychology, is available for consultation, speaking engagements, or seminars by calling 800-758-4635, or visiting www.niptoday.com.

Paul De Thouars' Serak/Bukti Negara

In an age where many people claim to have mastered ten or 20 arts pendekar Paul de Thouars is still busy trying to learn one.

Danny Huybrechts

If one was to meet Paul de Thouars, he would find him to be a man of honesty, humor, and deep religious conviction. One would never suspect him of possessing a deadly martial skill. Paul de Thouars has been described by well-known and respected martial artists as one of the world's most skillful men. He is the "pendekar agung" of the Indonesian martial arts system of pukulan pentjak silat serak and creator of the subsystem of pukulan pentjak silat bukti negara.

The title of "Pendekar" means "champion" or "spiritual leader." The word "Agung" was added to the title to distinguish his earned title from those which are inherited or given as favors. In an age where many claim to have completed several arts in one lifetime and mastered all its complexities, pendekar Paul de Thouars claims only one art, the art of sera (or serak) and still contends he is not finished learning. He is the only living lineage holder of the original system of serak from his predecessor guru John de Vries.

History of Serak

The founder of the art of pukulan pentjak silat serak was a man named Ba Pak, "the Wise One" Sera. Pak Sera was a member of the White (inner) Badui tribe, an Indonesian people who live in the forest region of the Gunung Kendang. These people were isolated from the outside world for over 400 years because of their fearsome reputation as warriors, and because the neighboring tribes believed they possess clairvoyant and magical powers.

The Badui tribe is made up of two distinct cultures—the Blue Badui and the White Badui. Their village takes the form of a circle within a circle, with the White Badui residing in the inner circle, and the Blue Badui residing in the outer circle. Because of their strict religious culture and demand for secrecy, entrance to the inner Badui by outside visitors is strictly prohibited. Only the Blue Badui are allowed to communicate and trade with the outside world.

Pak Sera had the use of only one arm and one leg on opposite sides of his body and was said to be knowledgeable in nine different styles and proficient in three. Despite his physical limitations, Pak

ighting With Short Sticks. Danny Huybrechts and Louis Campos face off with batangs pendek (short sticks). Campos attacks with a backhand strike to Huybrechts[1] face (1). Huybrechts moves, using silwa (square) footwork to enter, deflect and trap Campos' stick as he tomaks (thrust) to the earth points on the neck. Huybrechts attacks Campos' outer gate and metal points (2) with his shin and buntut (short end of the stick) to weaken and unbalance. Huybrechts dempoks (cross-over step) to bizet (back-sweep) as he strikes to Campos' face with his batang (stick) hand and uses Campos' own stick against him (3). Huybrechts maintains control of Campos with right knee (4) pressure to the alarm points on the torso and the left knee trap of the weapon hand as he strikes the temple with his buntut

Unique, Devastating and Deadly

The serak system is unique because it was developed from Pak Sera's unique physicalness. Try to imagine his perspective; limited to the use of one arm and one leg. How would you move? How would you fight an enemy? Pak Sera somehow developed a unique leverage system that integrated his particular disabilities into an efficient method of combat. The physical characteristics of the leverage system can be seen in the combative posture and application of both serak and bukti negara.

Occasionally de Thouars will demonstrate the art through the use of one hand. It is during these demonstrations of "one-arm lever" that I can sometimes envision the founder, and marvel at Pak Sera's inspiration and creative genius.

The serak system is devastating because the leverage system is applied very efficiently. It translates to speed in offense and defense. Structurally fast, serak's movements will stop you in your tracks. Rhythmic movements seen in training, but not in application, develop timing. But in terms of rhythm, pendekar Paul may go "one" maybe, "one-and-a-half beats" at normal speed during application and that's about all you will ever see.

The serak system is deadly. Within the system exists a sophisticated method of nerve striking and pressure point manipulation generally referred to as "pukulan" or "poekoelan." "Poekoelan" is a Dutch-Indonesian word whose root is pukul, which means "to hit." It refers to those styles that place a heavy

Kepla Menguruan. *Huybrechts faces off with master guru Larry Watanabe (1). Guru Watanabe launches a right punch to Huybrechts' face. Huybrechts deflects the punch by attacking pressure points on the arm and then the jaw of Watanabe as he steps forward to foot trap (2). Huybrechts attacks with an elbow and knee*

(3) to wood points on Watanabe's thigh and back of head. Huybrechts left palm strikes to Watanabe's forehead as he begins to sweep. Huybrechts adds a right palm heel to Watanabe's lower jaw (Stomach-5 Point) as Watanabe begins to fall (4). Huybrechts finishes Watanabe with a stomp to dislocate the hip (5).

emphasis on hitting. Serak/bukti negara's maneuvers were engineered to place the enemy into positions of vulnerability where the tools of the system have their greatest effect. I have seen the results of serak/bukti negara maneuvers and I am constantly amazed at their precision and lethality.

Information regarding striking points, striking sequences, and direction are contained within the curriculum. This information was designed to cause severe damage, unconsciousness and/or death to the opponent. All true combative systems possess this information, but very few teachers share this with their students unless they have proven themselves worthy.

Along with the vital point and anatomy curriculum, there exists a secret internal training, which is similar to ancient yoga breathing practices and extends the practitioner's capabilities into areas of which I have yet to experience.

Mas Djut's Role In Serak

In the oral history of the art, the next major player was Mas Djut, the only man Pak Sera was said to have taught. A member of the reclusive Badui tribe, Mas Djut already possessed skills in Indonesian combat. Little is known of Mas Djut's training, but his contributions to the system are of major importance. Based on the system as it exists today, Mas Djut's creativity and insights seem incredibly farsighted and would most likely place him ahead of his time. Based on research from various sources we believe Mas Djut took the original method and restructured it into a progressive curriculum. He added to the system of levers a progressive footwork training.

These additions were based on experiences he had while serving as body guard for the Sultan of Pontianak. These people were known to be skilled in evasiveness, and it is said that it is nearly impossible to hit a player skilled in their styles. Mas Djut's creativity continued to fruition and produced the "guardian system," a unique method of using both hands cooperatively to protect the serak practitioner from an opponent's attack while simultaneously providing an unstoppable bridging method to ensnare, control, and pummel the opponent.

He has childhood memories of the man he describes as intense and brutish. One vivid memory concerns Mas Djut's killing of an irate water buffalo, which attacked young Paul. He describes Mas Djut confronting the animal and killing it with one blow to the skull. Whatever the limits of this man's abilities, they were most certainly of a very high order.

Enter The de Thouars Family

A missionary of Dutch descent and grandfather to Paul de Thouars, Johan de Vries befriended the Badui people and was the first European to be allowed to live among them. Johan eventually married a Badui princess and sometime thereafter befriended Mas Djut. Johan de Vries trained in the entire serak system under Djut, but for some reason declined the inheritance of leadership for the art. Instead, he brought his two nephews John and Ernest (Ventje), both of whom were trained to carry on the system.

John and Ernest de Vries were trained as adolescents under Mas Djut. Both grew into manhood thoroughly trained as highly skilled martial artists. Ernest eventually gained a reputation as a fierce fighter who "at the drop of a hat" would not hesitate to confront and fight anyone. John, though equally fierce, was the more intellectual and scholarly of the two. He understood the mechanics and depth of technique within the art. It is from this depth of understanding and skill that the present inheritor of the system, Paul de Thouars, gained his outstanding teaching and fighting abilities.

Paul de Thouars

Paul de Thouars was born in East Java, Indonesia in 1930, and was raised in West Java. In 1936, at the age of six, he began his martial arts training under his uncle John de Vries. The training regimen consisted of two hours in the morning and two hours in the evening seven days a week performing djurus and langhkas over and over again. In the beginning, pendekar Paul describes the training as being boring and repetitious. He was required to train the djurus and langhkas to perfection; very little explanation was given. At the time, he did not understand what he was doing and why he was doing it. But with time and maturity, he began to understand the value and wealth of information contained in the curriculum.

The art of serak is so dense with information, it normally takes a person 15 years to complete the physical curriculum. To this day pendekar Paul de Thouars maintains, "I am still practicing and exploring the one art of serak." In 1971, his teacher, John de Vries, gave him ten keys or principles to help him achieve a deeper understanding of the art. With this gift of understanding, pendekar Paul is eternally grateful. In 1971, de Vries appointed Paul as his successor before his death in 1972.

The Birth of Bukti Negara

Being that the art of serak requires a lifetime of dedication and training, and is a closed system, de Thouars had no way of sharing or teaching it publicly without violating the Adat & Hormat. As man of deep religious conviction, he asked God for a solution. After one month of prayer, a voice told him to look to the book of "Genesis" for a passage that read, "And the world was without form." From this passage, he understood that the world existed but was covered by water, so too was this new system of bukti negara emerging from the mother system of serak. Bukti language means, "evidence" or "witness." Negara means "country" or "continent." The system of bukti negara is evidence that the system of serak exists. Components from the djurus (forms), principles, and langkahs (footwork) were taken from serak and condensed into an easier-to-understand format, all of which came to him in one night. In 1985, after a long period of meditation and prayer, the art of bukti negara was born.

Bukti negara has been described as being direct and to the point. One of the main characteristics is the close range in which the fighting takes place. When a practitioner is involved in a confrontation, he immediately charges forward into the opponent at close range where strikes, elbows, knees, foot sweeps and the entire body is used to tenderize, off balance or temporarily tie up the opponent before a technique is executed. Bukti negara finds its safety in the heart of the danger. Because the art is based on physics, physiology, and anatomy, the practitioner is expected to produce maximum results with minimal effort. Timing and efficiency are valued above speed and muscular strength. Here are several basic assumptions about the opponent that the bukti negara practitioner is taught:

- Your opponent is always stronger and faster. One cannot depend on strength or speed.
- Your opponent is always armed. Expect the worst.
- Your opponent is not alone. One must be prepared for multiple attacks.

With these basic assumptions, timing, efficiency of technique, and exploitation of angles are of primary importance. Pendekar Paul de Thouars has said many times, "Speed and strength are garbage," "timing is everything."

Basic Curriculum

There are eight (8) djurus (forms) and eight (8) sambuts (two-man sets) in the art of bukti negara. Everything a student learns originates from the djurus and sambuts. When a student has questions about particular principles or more efficient ways of applying technique, he is always referred back to the djurus and sambuts. They provide a complete vocabulary of motions in which the student can extract and combine to create his own interpretation.

When the basic body mechanics and technical principles are internalized and understood, the student discovers his solutions to a variety of situations. Before this can be accomplished, a student needs a qualified teacher to help him unlock the hidden meaning in the forms. Djurus must be trained to perfection. Without diligent practice, the meaning of the motions are lost and hard to define. Pendekar Paul often says, "Before you can control your opponents body, you must first learn to control your own."

With each djuru, the complexity and number of motions increase. The first djuru, for example,

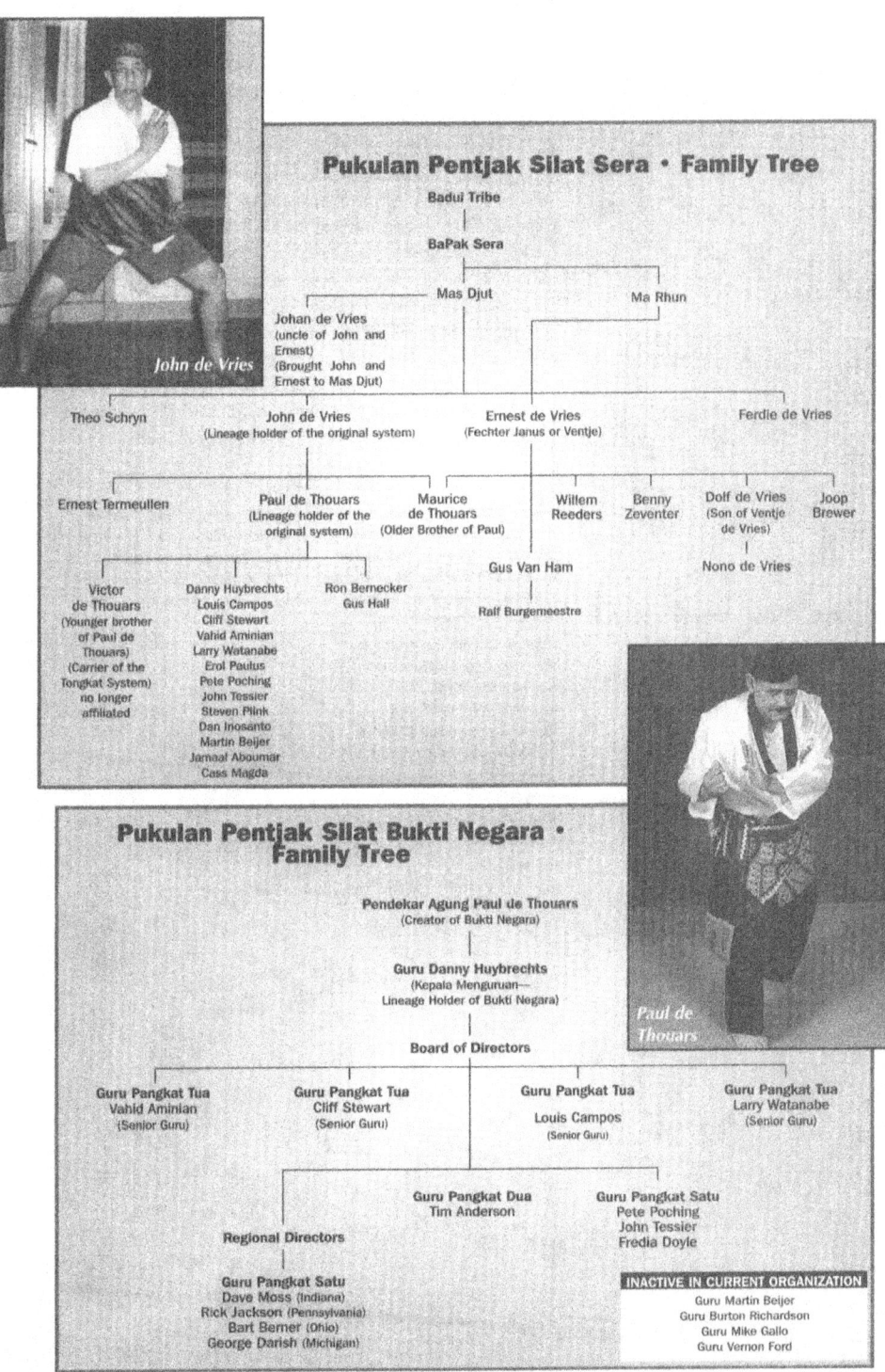

Pukulan Pentjak Silat Sera • Family Tree

Badui Tribe
|
BaPak Sera
|
├── Mas Djut
└── Ma Rhun

Johan de Vries
(uncle of John and Ernest)
(Brought John and Ernest to Mas Djut)

John de Vries

- Theo Schryn
- John de Vries (Lineage holder of the original system)
- Ernest de Vries (Fechter Janus or Ventje)
- Ferdie de Vries

- Ernest Termeullen
- Paul de Thouars (Lineage holder of the original system)
- Maurice de Thouars (Older Brother of Paul)
- Willem Reeders
- Benny Zeventer
- Dolf de Vries (Son of Ventje de Vries)
- Joop Brewer

- Gus Van Ham
- Nono de Vries

Victor de Thouars
(Younger brother of Paul de Thouars)
(Carrier of the Tongkat System)
no longer affiliated

Danny Huybrechts
Louis Campos
Cliff Stewart
Vahid Aminian
Larry Watanabe
Erol Paulus
Pete Poching
John Tessier
Steven Plink
Dan Inosanto
Martin Beijer
Jamaal Aboumar
Cass Magda

Ron Bernecker
Gus Hall

Ralf Burgemeestra

Pukulan Pentjak Silat Bukti Negara • Family Tree

Pendekar Agung Paul de Thouars
(Creator of Bukti Negara)
|
Guru Danny Huybrechts
(Kepala Menguruan—
Lineage Holder of Bukti Negara)
|
Board of Directors

- Guru Pangkat Tua Vahid Aminian (Senior Guru)
- Guru Pangkat Tua Cliff Stewart (Senior Guru)
- Guru Pangkat Tua Louis Campos (Senior Guru)
- Guru Pangkat Tua Larry Watanabe (Senior Guru)

Guru Pangkat Dua
Tim Anderson

Guru Pangkat Satu
Pete Poching
John Tessier
Fredia Doyle

Regional Directors

Guru Pangkat Satu
Dave Moss (Indiana)
Rick Jackson (Pennsylvania)
Bart Berner (Ohio)
George Darish (Michigan)

INACTIVE IN CURRENT ORGANIZATION
Guru Martin Beijer
Guru Burton Richardson
Guru Mike Gallo
Guru Vernon Ford

Paul de Thouars

utilizes the upper body only and isolates the upper from the lower body. Basic tools for defense are provided in the first djuru such as parries, blocks, elbow strikes, short punches, grabs and traps. With understanding and proper guidance, students learn to defend themselves with the first djuru. As the djurus progress, the direction of strikes, level changes, kicks, sweeps, weight distribution, body position and level of difficulty become more apparent.

Just as the djurus were designed to provide deeper understanding with each progressive level, so too must the understanding of the practitioner. Students are not given another djuru until they have fully explored its potential. They must demonstrate this by explaining and applying the djurus in a clear, concise manner.

The djurus are taught in conjunction with the langkas (footwork). The straight line (lurus) is first learned, eventually followed

Overhead Strike. *Huybrechts and Cliff Stewart square off (1). Stewart attacks with an overhead strike. Huybrechts deflects and traps Stewart's stick (2) as he steps forward along a silwa (square) angle. Huybrechts tombaks (thrust) to Stewart's neck with forward and downward pressure (3). Huybrechts steps to a new angle to shoulder strike the torso and knee Stewart's inner thigh to unbalance, armlock and throw (4). Huybrechts uses shoulder rotation to throw and break the larger fighter's arm by using Stewart's falling weight against him (5). Huybrechts knee drops to Stewart's gall bladder and liver points as he strikes behind the ear (6) with the buntut* (short end of the stick) to finish.

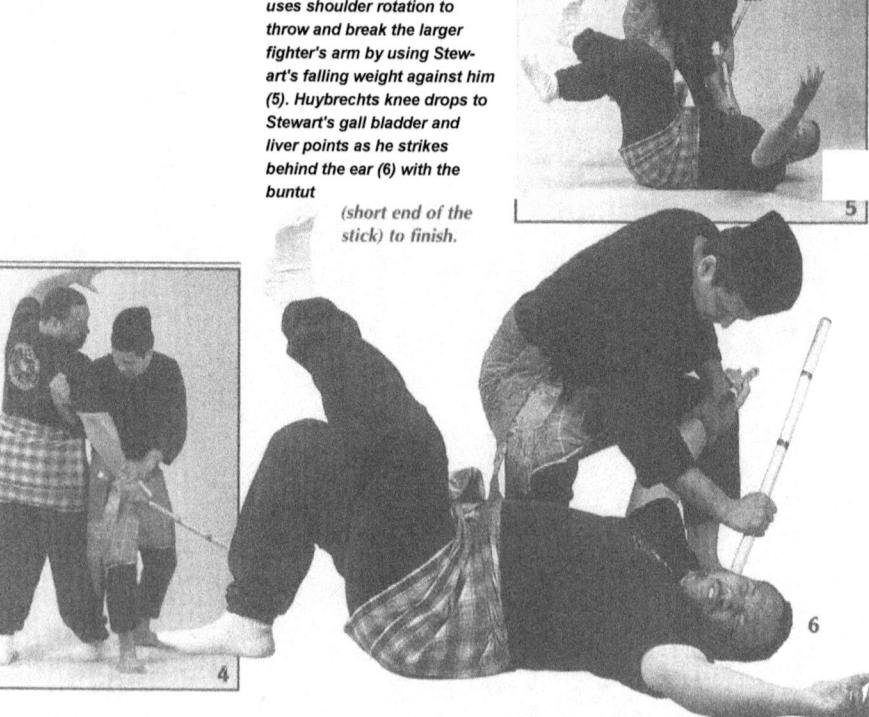

by langkah sudut miring (staircase), langkah tiga (triangle), langkah sliwa (square), tiga dua (two triangles) and sliwa dua (two squares).

Sambuts are a combination of techniques performed in a set sequence. They are trained with a partner to give the practitioner a sense of position and sensitivity. Similar to the djurus, sambuts are not meant to be set responses to attacks; rather they provide information about proper body alignment, position relative to the opponent, and basic body mechanics and technique. Lines of directing the opponent and sequential striking points are also defined within the sambut.

Drills

Bukti negara contains many different drills to help the practitioner improve various skills necessary for combat. One such drill is the sambutan or counter-to-counter drill. It involves two opponents in the practice of attacking and counterattacking in a continually flowing motion. For example, an attacker would strike his opponent with a punch. The defender would counter that strike by positioning himself in a position of control just before a technique can be executed. Immediately, a counterattack is executed and the other practitioner is placed in a position of control.

This attack and counterattack continues until one of the combatants can no longer counterattack. In the early stages, this drill is done slowly so students can learn proper body mechanics and timing. As their skill increases, so too does the speed of the drill. This leads to sparring at full speed.

Weapons

As with most combative systems, weapons are an integral part of a bukti negara practitioners education and training. Unlike other systems, weapons are taught toward the end of the physical curriculum. As pendekar Paul explains, "What you do with hands, you can do with a weapon with some modifications." The weapons utilized are the knife, bataan (short stick), tjabang (Indonesian sai) and long staff.

Conclusion

In an age where many people claim to have mastered ten or 20 arts in one lifetime, pendekar Paul de Thouars has always claimed to know one (serak). The family of serak players is very small. There are only four original players left who learned in Indonesia under the de Vries lineage—pendekar Paul de Thouars, Maurice de Thouars (Paul's older brother), Dolf de Vries (son of Ventje de Vries) and Guus Van Ham (student of Ventje de Vries). These individuals continue to train and teach in secrecy, adhering to the Adat and Hormat of the traditional system.

"Whatever one chooses to study, it is not done overnight," says pendekar Paul. "What you see on the surface is not really what you should look at. There are many more things hidden beneath the surface. It is deeper than what many are seeking; it is not only physical, but spiritual too."

Pendekar Paul adds, "There are two things we have to keep in mind. You have to have the heart to do it and the common sense to flow. Any art is good in its own right, but it is the man that makes it superior."

The study of martial arts is a long and strenuous journey for truth, which according to pendekar agung Paul de Thouars never ends.

"When you reach an end, there is a new beginning." $

Flying High with the Jet

Jet Li is more than a flash in front of the camera. He is a Beijing-trained, Hong Kong-honed wushu stylist with a plan to take the world by storm.

Dr. Craig D. Reid

It's super early in the morning at Los Angeles International Airport as I step onto a 747 heading to the cranberry capital of Canada, Vancouver, to visit Chinas wushu wonder Jet Li on the set of *Romeo Must Die*. It was an excessively bumpy flight but perhaps not as bumpy as what Li is experiencing when I get there.

Arriving on set, I see Jet precariously dangling from a thin, piano wire like a balled-up spider hanging from a single thread of webbing ready to vitiate its victim. Nodding his head in preparedness to Hong Kong fight director Yuen Kwei, the wire pullers yank. Bad guy Russell Wong charges in as Li rises up and from his closed-blossom position, plants his right hand on the cement floor, and while still crouching inches from the ground, lashes out with several venomous kicks.

However, he lands a bit too hard on his wrist and ankle. Injury is part of the game and there is no time for Jet to take a break or recover. They continue practicing the wire gag. Several takes and further sprains later, the timing is set. With shooting time running out and needing to finish the fight as well as keeping up his concentration over the pain, Jet regretfully requests a reprieve from the interview. With tight-lipped resolve, Jet continues fighting for the next seven hours.

Character Behind the Man

Months later and back in L.A., when I meet with Jet he is adamant in once again apologizing for not being able to do the interview in Canada. The apology is not necessary, but it does reflect on the character of a man, a martial artist with a conscience who chooses to remain considerate and respectful. These are virtues that many American stars lack. We open with a discussion of his latest alter ego, Han Sing, and why he did *Romeo Must Die*.

Leaning forward and in very deliberate English, he smilingly echoes, "Why? When I first come here, there is a producer Joel Silver and he says, Okay we need you to play this villain in *Lethal Weapon 4*. I say, No, no, no, I always play the good guy in Hong Kong. He said, 'Look, here is the deal, you play the bad guy then you can play a good guy.' So I didn't really choose this project, we had already decided."

"My character is Han Sing, the story is like Shakespeare's Romeo and Juliet—two families, one is Black, one Chinese family. They don't get along with each other. My father is bad guy also. When I was young with my younger brother in China, my father went away, so when my mum died I promised her I would look after my younger brother so this is why I eventually go to Hong Kong. Later on my character becomes a policeman and my family is the Mafia, so in times when my brother have trouble, I help him and my father, and that is why I go to prison, later on, I learn my brother dies and I want to find out what happened to my brother. So I come here, get information and revenge my brother's death."

Prior to our meeting I saw the first 18 minutes of the film, which showed a poorly edited fight scene of Russell Wong doing this bad Bruce Lee thing. But the saving grace was the next fight which featured Jet hanging upside down in a Hong Kong police beating room. As several cops are about to teach Jet a lesson, he pulls off some of his typical razzel-dazzle with some very interesting camera effects reminiscent of

210 **Best of CFW Enterprises, 2000**

Sonny Chiba's *Street Fighter* films. Inasmuch as I'm not a fan of hip-hop, Jet's presence definitely makes *Romeo Must Die* a must see.

"In this film, we have eight different fight scenes and it's important that they all don't look like the same water," he pensively reflects. "Many of the American audience can now pick out Jet Li style. Each movie decides what the character uses for fighting, not only physical movement but also the movement that helps the characters. We watch many Hong Kong and American films where they have those scenes where they hang you upside down and beat you, so we want to do something creative from that, So Yuen Kwei and my fighting crew want to do something different. It's never been done this way (acts like he's hanging upside down), and then the key thing (while laughing, he mimics how he steals the keys from one of the guards while beating up the others at the same time). This takes us five days to do that small part. In Hong Kong we have use action a lot and we put a lot of time into the action parts. It is normal to use seven days for ending fight but here when you talk to American producer and director and say we need ten days for the ending they go, Are you crazy? Ten days for the ending? That's a lot of money.'

"Also in America when they shoot action sequences they use few cameras from beginning to end (master shot), but with the kung-fu fights you can't do that just from beginning to end; need to show power in the movement, detail of the technique.

"We actually had little time to prepare for this. We need to work on new movement everyday because the audience can catch on very fast. First time see something they go, 'Wow!' See it a second time from different shooting angle they say, 'Hmmm.' See it third time they go, 'Hey, whafs new, whafs new?' Must always have something different and different angles."

The Jet Files

For those who came in late, Jet was born in Beijing as Lee Lien Jie and at age eight was enrolled in the Beijing Amateur Sports School for wushu training. His mentor, coach Wu Bin, a sort of surrogate father since Jefs real father died when he was two, designed extra training for Jet because he demonstrated the talent and perseverance required for wushu. After three years of intense instruction, Jet became the national junior champion of the Beijing Wushu team and for the All-Around National Wushu Champion. As part of a world tour in 1974, he performed for President Richard Nixon at the White House.

Jet Li, Mel Gibson to Produce Martial Arts Pilot, Television Series

ATLANTA, Ga—Hong Kong movie sensation Jet Li will join forces with Lethal Weapon 4 co-star Mel Gibson to produce "Invincible," a martial arts-related series for Turner Broadcasting System.

Li, who joins "Martial Law's" Sammo Hung as Hong Kong stars entering the American television market, may also appear in the pilot, which will premiere in late 2000 or early 2001. A possible series premiere is set for late 2001. There is no word on whether Jet will display his talents for the camera or whether his involvement will be in a strictly advisory role.

"Invincible" is the brainchild of Li and Oscar-winning actor/producer/director Mel Gibson, who conceived the idea while working together on *Lethal Weapon 4*. Utilizing the ancient martial art of wushu, this adrenaline-pumping movie pilot and subsequent series will pulsate with spectacularly choreographed, death-defying action sequences in the distinctive Hong Kong style of filmmaking.

"Introducing wushu through the medium of television will allow us to reach a wider audience than we could with film," noted Li, who has starred in more than 25 motion pictures. "And we can use each episode of the series to expand on the martial art's complicated but profound philosophy.

"In addition," he explained, 'Invincible' will feature awesome sequences that go beyond the light-headed bang-bang action often found on television. There will be a healthy underlying moral theme, emphasizing control, discipline, and the balance of good and evil."

Li, who recently completed *Romeo Must Die*, made his movie debut at the age of 16. He was an immediate sensation and went on to star in a number of hit films, including *Once Upon a Time in China, Tai Chi Master*, and *My Father is a Hero*.

Jet briefly recalls those times. "I learned many kinds of martial arts, pick up many styles of kung-fu, different names but foundations are the same. I learned for ten years since I was young in school. Martial arts are like a tree, different punches, and different style. So if you want to be a champion competitor then you go to one part of the tree and if you go into film you go into a different part of the tree, for health, then another part.

"My mother is in China, I've got two older brothers and sisters. I didn't serve in the army because I went to that special school to learn martial arts and travel the world demonstrating. When I come to Washington, many things were different for me, because in China we're taught things would be a certain way in America, but it wasn't that way when I got here. Things are different from the way you see things and what you learn. So coming to America help me learn this and grow up. I learned America has a lot of good things and trouble. China had a lot of good things and trouble. Different people and countries have higher percentages of trouble for different reasons. So when I come to America I start to think about things in this way. I also remember lots of food and policeman.'

Obvious Choice

Director Chang Hsin Yen soon discovered Jet and in 1982, an 18-year-old Li was the obvious choice to star as monk Guer Yuen in *Shaolin Temple*, China's first kung-fu movie since the Communist takeover.

"I had no idea what I was doing, I just followed the directors orders and did what I did." The films success spawned two inferior sequels.

Although portraying legendary folk hero Wong Fei-hung in *Once Upon a Time in China* (1990) (plus three of five sequels) launched him into Hong Kong superstardom, many critics believe that his sword skills featured in *Swordsman II* made Jet's career soar even higher. It's wild and wooly to witness. Some of his other must-see fant-Asia spectaculars include *Fong Sai Yuk* (1993), *Tai Chi Master* (1993), *Dr. Wai and The Scriptures With No Words* (1996), and *Black Mask* (1996), the actual progenitor to *Matrix*. Tapes and DVDs of these and many other of his far-out action films are only available through Tai Sen Video—(888) 668-8338.

"I, of course, enjoy doing those kind of films playing Wong Fei-hung and Fang Shi Yu, but I'd like to one day do something different," he explained. "But right now it's what I'm known for and no producers or company will hire me to do something else. Many audiences know me for what I do so why would they pay money to see me do something else?"

The Other Side of Jet

I close by asking some questions concerning his personal philosophy. With his growing fame in film, does he see himself as more of an actor than a martial artist? Also, since he is so busy, does he still find time to practice martial arts?

Jose Fraguas, Curtis Wong, and Jet Li at CFW Enterprises offices in Los Angeles, CA.

He looks me in the eye and with a gentle smile nods and shares, "Me busy? I'm not busy right now, I need a job." A jovial laugh later it's easy to see why his looks are as charming as his wit.

"No, just joking. I still train everyday at different times of the day based on the air. And of course I train inside (internal), which we call chi gong and taiji. With the martial arts you have to train outside and inside, not just your mind.

"I am a martial artist. My situation cannot change because from the beginning I learn martial arts then later on I change into acting, but it's because of martial arts that people invite me into acting, so I do a lot of martial arts first but now I do need to learn a lot of acting, because in real life, a Chinese saying is, I'm not sure how to translate, 'Life is acting and acting is life.' Because I never kill people in real life (laughs) no really, and then I never hurt people on the screen on purpose. I still want to learn more about acting and still learn martial art everyday and use that for my different characters."

Does he have a personal philosophy, something that drives him through life?

"My personal philosophy? Nothing is 100 percent wrong or right—only have different percentages and angles and one must see things from these different angles. If you look at the world, in the beginning it is nothing, then if you have a ball, like taiji, before taiji there is the wuji (translates as "no limit"), but now we have taiji and it is the yin and yang. So we had nothing, but now we have the ball, we know the sky, we know the ground.

"The yin/yang become the East-West and then they cross to become one. In my opinion, anything that happens you need to read both ways; you just can't use one ear or listen to one person. Just like you can't say that this style or that is the best martial art in the world. Things are all different.

"I'd like to close by mentioning that in my heart there's big troubles in the world and I'm looking for the best way I can help. Gang people streetfight, why? They're young and think it's cool. They play video games with fighting without learning new things. I'm working on developing video games that don't glorify violence and hurting people. So a video character that's a good guy, he doesn't need to kill his enemy, maybe he can help him, like Wong Fei-hung. So if you show mercy you get a higher score. Children who play these games can learn something from that. So it's not just all punching and blood, sometimes if you lose, you really win, it's not all about take, take, take." $

Dr. Craig D. Reid is a frequent contributor to Inside Kung-Fu *magazine.*

Gerald Okamura, Damage Control

Gerald Okamura's success in martial arts, movies, and charity fundraising is a result of his Kung Fu San Soo training which taught him to do the most damage with the least amount of effort.

Todd Hester

Gerald Okamura is an ominous figure. With his long flowing moustache, intense piercing eyes, and deliberate challenging stride, he is someone you would walk across the street to avoid passing on the sidewalk at night. A master of kung-fu's most feared fighting style, Okamura learned his craft from San Soo master Jimmy H. Woo—a fighter whose fighting prowess, to this day, is still spoken about in hushed whispers. One of the most adept practitioners of Woo's win-at-all-costs combat style, Okamura is an expert at applying San Soo's devastating organ strikes, disabling pressure-point attacks, and flesh ripping-and-tearing maneuvers designed with only one purpose in mind—to seriously injure an attacker in the shortest possible time. "When you control the focus of your effort, you control the amount of damage you do," Okamura says. "A small amount of effort, properly directed, will do more damage than greater effort which is spread out."

But Okamura is more than "just" a master of destruction. He is a surprising, funny character who is more likely to slip a whoopee cushion under your seat, than rip your heart out and show it to you before you die. Starting out in Hollywood by pure chance, in the first season of the *Kung-Fu* television series, the easy-going Okamura has played heroes and villains ranging from a God-like warrior in *Big Trouble in Little China*, to a Chinese singing Elvis in *Day of the Warrior*. "As long as people are laughing with me and not at me," Okamura smiles," then I'm happy. But there's no way to laugh at me, because I'm always laughing too. So I guess that means I'm always happy."

Q: What was it like training Kung Fu San Soo with the legendary Jimmy H. Woo?
A: More important than anything else to Jimmy was the ability to execute the techniques. Forms were kind of secondary for him. He felt that is was a sort of isometric exercise. The biggest difficulty was his language. His used to call the "temple," the "dimple." And I couldn't figure out why the hell we

were hitting the guy in the dimple for. What if the guy doesn't have a dimple, then what do you do? But he always got his message across. Many times he would pick me to be the dummy to demonstrate moves on, and I always felt that I was honored to be his dummy. Now that I think about it, I've gotten a lot of mileage out of being a dummy over the years.

Q: How often did you train?

A: I used to go there 4 days a week, and I'd be there from right after work to about 9 pm, or about 3 or 4 hours. Jimmy's mindset was that as long as you had a toned body that you didn't have to be muscular. You see, the whole philosophy behind the application of San Soo is to get the work done the easiest and the quickest. Do as far as endurance went, it was up to the individual. He felt that as long as you could pinpoint your target that you don't have to worry about how hard you hit it. Most of the things that other people emphasize we didn't worry about so much. We stretched, for example, but we didn't take it to the extreme. Everything went around the individual's physique. So I always say that in the beginning you might imitate Jimmy, but he didn't expect you to fight like him. You would just learn the basics and then combine them how you want.

Q: Was there any emphasis on philosophy?

A: The only philosophy that he ever really stressed was that you should build up self-confidence, but at the same time he also said you needed to add a little humility or you would become arrogant and fall over the other side of the fence. But you had to build up self-confidence—he always stressed that. The other thing that he stressed on the arts was that the art is there for any application for anybody. You don't have to look good to get the job done, you just get the job done the easiest way you know how. You have to be mature enough to use the art in the sense that it's not for show. If you get into a confrontation and kill a person, he said that you still had to face the laws of society. So were you the winner or the loser?

It's funny that he said that because his way of life when he was younger was just the opposite. He didn't care who he hurt. He was very dangerous. So I guess he got mature enough to pass onto us a more mature outlook on life, but at the same time never giving up self-confidence.

Q: Jimmy Woo taught techniques out of books that were passed down to him from the Shaolin Temple. Do you feel that this makes San Soo a pure art?

A: I thought it was originally, the way he taught it. But I have since talked to other Chinese people just to interpret the words "San Soo." And they say it is more like "garbage disposal." It grabs everything and anything and it's you that decides what to use. So to me it's very generous and I think it

GERALD OKAMURA

1940—Born in Hilo, Hawaii
1953—Began training in Judo
1958—Graduated High school
1958 to1961—US ARMY (Trained in Taekwondo in Korea)
1961—Discharged from Army, moved to Los Angeles to attend Aircraft mechanic school.
1963—Began working as a Jig & Fixture builder at Douglas Aircraft in Santa Monica.
1967—First original weapon designs: Mace—Medieval ball & chain type weapon, and Sai—To fit larger hands.
1967—Started training under Jimmy H. Woo in Kung Fu San Soo.
1969—Received his first Black Belt in Kung Fu San Soo.
1975—First TV role as a Shaolin Priest with David Carradine in "Kung Fu."
1976—First movie role on "Killer Elite" with James Caan.
1977—First magazine cover — Inside Kung Fu Magazine.
1979—Role in the "Octagon"

takes a mature mind to grasp what you want from it. And that's the beauty of the whole thing. If I don't want something then I just move onto something else.

Q: How did you get started in the movies?

A: The way it happened was that Jimmy Woo was called by David Chow, who was the technical advisor for the *Kung Fu* series the first year. David said he wanted someone to play in the series. Jimmy didn't know the industry so he requested that someone come to pick him up in a limousine at his house. Then when he got to the office he asked for a lot of money. So when Warner Brothers couldn't come up with the money Jimmy declined the offer and the next day came into the class and told me that I should go in his place. Not knowing the business and being naive at the time, I just went over to Warner Brothers and I introduced myself to David Chow, who could have just as easily sent me home because I wasn't Jimmy H. Woo, but I guess he thought I fit the role so I got a job. I worked on it for one day and played a Shaolin monk in one of the flashback scenes, and that's how I got started in the business. I had hair at that time and I had to wear a scull cap all day and it was as hot as hell. I came in at 6:30 am, stayed in make-up all day, and then didn't get in a shot until 12 hours later. That was my introduction to the limelight. Glamorous, huh?

Jimmy Woo stressed that "you don't have to look good to get the job done, you just get the job done the easiest way you know how."

Q: How did long did you work on Kung Fu?

A: Just that one episode—it was pretty much at the end of the first year. The next year another instructor in kung fu got hired in a movie called *The Killer Elite* with James Caan. It was a good movie but it could have been better. It was too early in the martial arts movement for people to understand and appreciate it. If you get a chance to rent it, you should. It was ahead of its time.

My audition came about when my friend asked if he could borrow some of my weapons for his. So I said, "They're my weapons, and if they go on an audition I'm going too." So I took two suitcases and a couple of duffel bags and went to Samuel Goldwyn Studios and met Sam Peckinpah and the stunt coordinators. I took out my array of different weapons and did a little show for them. I even had a cane that was a blow gun. But it was too ninja-like for the times,

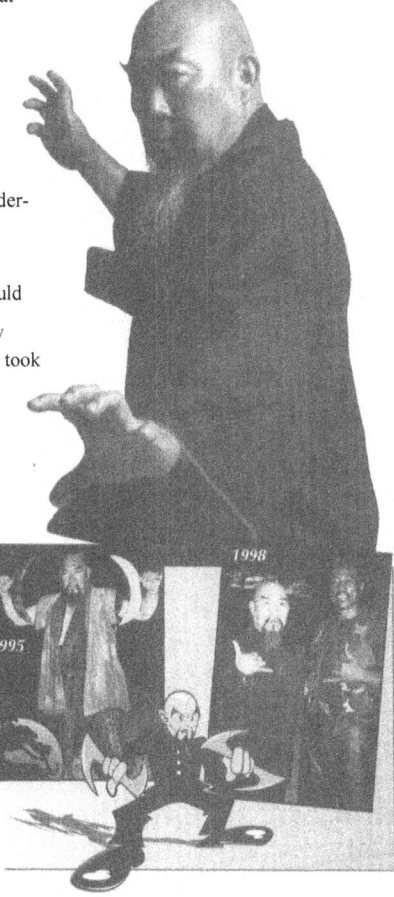

with Chuck Norris and Richard Norton.
1986—Cast as Six Shooter in "Big Trouble in Little China."
1991—Role as the executioner in "Showdown in Little Tokyo" with Brandon Lee.
1994—Cast as the corrupt referee in the classic fight scene with Charlie Sheen & James Lew in "Hot Shots Part Deaux."
1995—Played the demon warrior in "Mortal Kombat".
1996—First Martial Arts movie awards- Winner for the Scowling Face of the Year!
1996—First Annual DRAGONFEST
1998—Role as the elder vampire in

Martial artist and actor Aleong poses with Alec Baldwin and fellow martial artists on the set of "The Shadow" (1994). Warrior" (1996) and, left,

and so they didn't use it. Instead they used me!

But a few years later when some of the ninja movies with Sho Koshogi came out, things like that became hot. So *Killer Elite* was just too much ahead of its time. I don't think the stunt coordinators had very much experience in that kind of fighting. They interviewed a lot of top martial artists from a lot of different styles. Yet, if you couldn't sell a punch or a kick then they sent you packing. Sterling Siliphant wrote it and he had experience in the martial arts, but people just didn't get the concept. But in a way it was good for me because in 1978 movies weren't as tough for martial artists to break in.

Q: So back then it was easier to get into the movies?

A: Oh, yeah. There just wasn't that many high-level martial artists in L.A. that were going after acting parts. Now it's tough. After *Killer Elite* I met a lot of big people including Burt Young. He gave me a bump on the head and I still remember that bump. But then the following year I got a part in a B-movie called *Chesty Anderson*. A lot of girls and lot of big boobs—and I guess the biggest boob was me. But I was working, you know? Then I did a lot of small things like *Matt Houston, TJ Hooker,* and *Knight Rider*. Just things where they needed a pretty face.

Q: So how was your training going all this time?

A: Well, just around the time I really got into the movies I got promoted to 5th degree by Jimmy. And after the 5 th degree I got out of the organization and never got tested again so that's where I stand right now. I started my own school when I was still with Jimmy, and I've been there for 30 years, since about 1970. When the first article came out about me in *Inside Kung-Eu,* in about 1975 or so, I think there was a little jealousy from Jimmy, not that I was ever a threat to him or disloyal to him in any way, but that seemed to start a gap between us. I have nothing but good feelings and the highest respect for Jimmy.

Q: But during this whole time you kept a regular job, right?

A: I would take vacation to do all the movie parts. In the beginning I worked but a lot of the parts got cut. So the joke was always that my part came on during the commercial. So I guess the family life was a little tough, but the wife did a good job of keeping us together. But I would work for a whole week and then only be on for two or three seconds. So when you would have to watch an hour show just to see yourself for a few seconds a lot of people would laugh—but, hey, I was proud of it, you know? And it still excites me.

Now my stuff appears on all the cable channels so I get seen a little more. I've done things like *Blade, The Shadow,* and *Lethal Weapon 4*. I shot that last one for 3 weeks and then I'm hardly ever seen in it. My family had to watch the tape 10 times, back and forth in slow motion, just to finally find me. And out of everyone I was the only one out of focus. But I didn't care because at least I was in the movie! Same with *Blade*, I didn't have a speaking part and I didn't get to fight but I got to sit around a table as part of the Elder Vampire Council so I got a lot of screen time.

During this whole time, I've had this on-going character in a series of B-movies, as a CIA agent named Fu. I started out being the bad guy, then turned into a good guy. On one of the movies, *Day of the Warrior*, I play an Elvis impersonator in Las Vegas. I think I make a pretty good Elvis. One day a man called me and said, "I hear you do a bad Elvis impersonation." I said, "You got that right. I'm as bad as they come." So it comes down that he's looking for an Elvis and he says, "Now you've got to be bad—bad bad—not good bad." And I say, "You've got your man." So they rented out the lounge at the Maxim in Las Vegas and I did my Elvis moves to lip sync—they wouldn't let me sing. I thought I was pretty good up there, but I had guys calling me just laughing like crazy. Some people just don't appreciate art. But all the exposure is good for the kids at the tournaments I go to, because when I go they come up and they ask for autographs and it gives me a chance to tell them to stay in school, stay off drugs, and never, ever put on a white suit and sing Blue Suede Shoes.

Q: Is that where the idea for Dragonfest came?
A: I saw how much the kids liked to meet the people that they watch in movies. So my son-in-law, Gabe Frimmel, and I got some tables and we rented a hall and got these guys to come down and sign autographs. So since we're not paying them anything and it's for a charitable event, Pediatric Aids, they can sell their products, pictures, or video tapes, etc. The people can talk to the stars just like I'm talking to you. And we have vendors who sell their martial art supplies, movie memorabilia, and an array of collectors.. And that's it. Just an informal get together to give something back to the public and help out kids by doing it.

Q: Do you think that your years in the movies gives you an in with celebrities?
A: I have a good rapport with many of them. It seems like most celebrities are trained in some kind of martial art—so they are receptive. Erin Gray, for example, attends each year. I found out from speaking to her that she also teaches tai chi. So the first year we started small, but got good response. Then the next year was bigger and we moved into a bigger place, and then we went into the Glendale Civic Center with just one floor, and 2500 fans showed up. And now the traditional masters, such as Tak Kubota, Gene LeBell, Fumio Demura and many others are getting involved. And some of the rivalries that exist—such as the karate/kung-fu rivalry—can all be put aside for a day and we can laugh with each other and share knowledge without any politics involved. So it makes me feel really good that the martial arts community, as well as the public, come together as one each year at Dragonfest.

Q: What would you say to people who say that Kung Fu San Soo is dirty fighting?
A: My philosophy to that is that I will not turn the other cheek. I will throw the first punch if it requires it. In the past it used to be that if you were a martial artist you shouldn't throw the first punch. Well, the first punch that the other guy throws might be enough to put you down. So my philosophy is that if I have a chance, and if the situation warrants me—if my life or my family's life is threatened—I will take him out first. Call it whatever you want, but it's going to keep me safe. So whatever adjective you want to use for San Soo—call it clean, dirty, smooth, rough, whatever—it is an art that will keep you safe. $

For more on Gerald, visit his websites at www.dragonfest.com *or* www.geraldokamura.com

Qi Gong: The Power to Cure Cancer

Cancer patients around the world are discovering the amazing curative powers of qi gong.

Wen Mei Yu and Theresa Marie Hoff

Qi gong is an ancient Chinese healing art used to improve health, prevent and treat disease, and prolong life. The Chinese have long considered qi the vital energy of life; through the daily practice of qi gong, students of this internal art learn to build, assimilate, and store qi within the body.

The different branches of qi gong are Taoist, Confucian, Buddhist, medical, and martial. Within each branch, there are many different sects and schools. This article will consider several medically related effects of qi gong as well as the art's general application in mitigating some of the consequences of cancer. The observations contained in this article are derived from experiences in teaching qi gong to a broad range of students, including those suffering from cancer. Pertinent case histories are proffered, in the patients own words, in the sidebars accompanying this precis.

Qi gong is an exercise system that emphasizes soft, flowing motions synchronized with controlled breathing. These movements contain form, meditation, walking, and breathing techniques that condition the mind to heal the body and relieve the daily tension that accompanies modern life.

Health Plan

The movements facilitate blood oxygenation and greater control of cardiovascular functions. This improves the body's strength and, thus, facilitates recovery. In China, these exercises are performed as a simple regimen for health.

Medical qi gong involves different types of healing therapies, which include exercises, specific movements, and forms that are directed at bodily problems. The medical establishment in China holds that qi gong can help prevent or heal disease; indeed, patients throughout the world credit qi gong with extending their lives by disrupting chronic ailments.

Qi gong combines coordination, balance, and flexibility techniques into harmonious motions and gentle exercises. Qi gong includes slow, concentrated isometric movements and elements of self-defense that release pressure as well as increase energy and well-being.

Considered a medical internal art, Guo Lin qi gong is practiced to improve the body's natural immune system. It derives its power from energizing the same system of internal meridians that acupuncturists use. This system uses the mind to move energy throughout the body. The energy can then be stored within the body for future use.

Stress Relief

Qi gong permits practitioners to handle life changes in a state of relaxation by helping lower anxiety and stress levels. The process of body mastery can be learned through this ancient Chinese art as well as its modern forms.

Guo Lin qi gong was introduced 30 years ago by its namesake as a practice designed to confer distinct benefits to cancer patients. Guo Lin contracted uterine cancer and used both Eastern and Western treatments without effect: cancer spread throughout her body. Having been a master of the wu qinxi (five animal play) style of qi gong as well as a painter affiliated with the Beijing Art Academy, Guo Lin turned to qi gong to help herself combat cancer. In the aftermath of her disease, Guo Lin and her family credited her development and use of qi gong as the principal treatment that prolonged her life.

Guo Lin qi gong stresses scientific theory in its application of forms and exercises for therapeutic purposes. Guo Lin qi gong may be construed as a type of walking exercise that couples motion with stillness and meditation. It consists of five regulatory movements: control of mind (meditation); control of posture; control of respiration; control of voice; and control of movement. These five aspects can be combined in a myriad of ways by teachers and students to treat particular ailments.

By 1979, after a decade of public teaching, Guo Lin qi gong was credited as an agent in the remis-

Guo Lin qi gong, "one-step touch" section.

Master Wen Mei Yu (left front) leads Guo Lin qi gong, "walking section."

sion of cancer in 20 cases. These successes inspired the creation of a cancer survivor's club in Beijing, which has had more than 50,000 members. The Chinese government, in recognition of the phenomenon, began the scientific study of this new healing art. Following this period, master Wen Mei Yu taught this internal art in China as well as internationally; she also held special workshops in the discipline to disseminate the instruction she had personally received from Guo Lin.

Clinical studies were conducted to demonstrate the difference in treatment outcomes between a control group, which received only standard care, and a group that also practiced Guo Lin qi gong (two hours a day for three months). Chinese researchers noted significant differences in strength, appetite, liver function, and immune system response between the two groups; Guo Lin qi gong dramatically improved the health of the practicing group. Further studies demonstrated that benefits may be obtained by adding the practice of Guo Lin qi gong to the suite of treatments for many kinds of cancer.

Group Therapy

The psychological, emotional, and spiritual effects of practicing qi gong in a group setting are sometimes as important as the material effects of the art. Feeling empowered and being able to share personal information during cancer therapy with people undergoing similar experiences promotes stability and confidence, which are essential to recovery.

In the United States, research recently began on the use of qi gong in fighting cancer. Dr. Garrett Yount, a cellular biologist at the Geraldine Brush Cancer Research Institute at the California Pacific Medical Center in San Francisco, has been working with a qi gong master from China to assess the medical effects of certain applications of the art. In one series of experiments, Dr. Yount separated cancer cells from a cadaver. The master treated two clusters of cells differently: in the first group, the master willed the cells to die; in the second group, the master bombarded the cells with neutral intentionality. It was the use of neutral intentionality that had the most dramatic effect on the diseased cells—they died

Patients Cindy, Eiko and L... exchange conversation and sup...

Case Studies

"In Nov., 1997, I was diagnosed with breast cancer. I had surgery, eight cycles of chemotherapy, and radiation. The cancer treatment wiped out the cancer, but left me feeling fatigued with aches and pains throughout my body. I was referred to physical therapy for two months, which provided little relief. My internist felt I might benefit by complementing Western medicine with Traditional Chinese Medicine.

"I was referred to UCLA's East West Medicine Center. With their recommendation in August, 1999, I began practicing qi gong. I have more energy now and feel so much better, physically, mentally, and emotionally. The aches and pains have lessened, my sleep patterns are back to normal and I have been able to eliminate some of the medication. My blood counts are back to normal and blood draws are so much easier now. In fact, it is easier than it was before the cancer treatment!

"I practice qi gong five times each week. I prefer to practice outdoors in the sun. Some weeks I am able to practice every day. I can feel the qi in my hands. With more practice the sensation increases. Furthermore, if the duration of the practice is extended, I feel the qi even more. Without question, I am doing something very good to take care of myself."
—Claris Shimu-Luke

"Being diagnosed with breast cancer was devastating and scary. Working with alternative medicine and the addition of qi gong has enabled me to beat my breast cancer with increasing health and energy. I'm stronger everyday, cancer free and there is no fear of the cancer returning. Qi gong is a wonderful, nurturing, healing energy that has enhanced my life and healing."
—Sue

"I had an operation for colon cancer Sept. 25, 1998. A month later I began extensive chemotherapy for six months. At the same time I started participating in a qi gong class once a week, offered at the Wellness Community in Redondo Beach. My teacher inspired me to keep coming back.

"I also continue to practice qi gong every morning by myself. After each practice I feel so great, it gives me soothing energy from the inside out. I have made this exercise a daily part of my life. Along with the meditation that I learned from Terry, eating the right foods and supplementing my diet, I am hopeful the cancer will not return.

"After three months, my killer-cell activity improved from 30 percent to more than a 60-percent level despite the chemotherapy. And now my tests after the chemotherapy didn't detect any sign of cancer.

"This experience has changed my life, I believe that qi gong is the right type of exercise and has certainly helped me to restore my good health."
—George

George practicing "rock back and forth."

rapidly, seemingly influenced by the actions of the qi gong master. That neutral intentionality was more effective than willing death in destroying the cancer cells was predicted by the master, who stated that the enshrining of an intent to kill would disrupt his natural healing field.

It appears that by balancing his energies, the cells died more expeditiously than through other, more negative thought processes. The results of this test are still being assessed and considered.

In China, ongoing clinical studies, also using control groups, seem to support the distant effects of mental intention, with no physical contact, on disease as well as cellular biology. In the future, researchers are hoping to measure changes in the manifestations of genes that control cell growth or in genes that mediate cell death. Currently, the application of group intentionality in supportive and adjunctive qi gong treatments for cancer is being considered in California by your authors.

Research Shows Promise

Los Angeles-based groups presently meet at the Wellness Community in Redondo Beach and at UCLA through the Rhonda Fleming Mann Resource Center for Women with Cancer. The classes at the Wellness Community began in November, 1996; the classes at UCLA began in July 1999. The mission of the Wellness Community (in Redondo Beach) is to help people with cancer and their families fight for health by providing free psychological, educational, and social-support services. These approaches are in addition to prescribed treatment plans, which are based on the application of Western medicine.

As a result of teaching Guo Lin qi gong at the Wellness Community for three years, long-term, anodyne results are now being documented. Continuing classes at UCLA and at the Wellness Community offer cancer patients in the Los Angeles area diverse, complementary, and innovative tools to patients quality of life and sense of well-being is a goal at both centers.

Harold H. Benjamin, M.D., an innovator in the treatment of cancer, noted, "If you participate in your fight for recovery, you will improve the quality of your life and just may enhance the possibility of your recovery."

The Rhonda Fleming Mann Resource Center is an integral part of the UCLA Center for the Health Sciences (UCLA has, over the course of several decades, earned an esteemed reputation for advanced medical care and research). The resource center itself is part of the Jonsson Comprehensive Cancer Center at UCLA. The staff at the resource center believes it is important to treat the whole person and not just the disease; comprehensive psychological care is an important part of complete care.

Mann explained the work of the center, which was named in her honor, this way: "My prescription for all women with cancer: caring, compassion, communication, commitment." One of the programs offered by the Rhonda Fleming Mann Resource Center is a free monthly lecture series called Insights into Cancer; experts in their respective fields discuss topics relevant to patients and to their families.

After master Wen Mei Yu and David

> "I believe qi gong has helped me feel better physically and mentally and emotionally, understanding energy flow, etc. The teacher has been an inspiration, fun, and participants have lent support, all being in the same situation, experiencing basically the same thing—camaraderie."
> —Millie

Pat practicing "rock back and forth."

> "Diagnosed: February, 1999. Treatment: Six weeks and one day of pelvic radiation, plus six weeks of Cisplatinum every Monday, plus eight weeks of 5FV, all simultaneously.
> I attended about seven classes of qi gong.
> Benefits:
> • More relaxed after qi gong;
> • Increased muscle strength, especially in the legs;
> • Increased stamina;
> • Learning more effective breathing;
> • Increased positive attitude."
> —Pat

> "I have taken qi gong since September, 1998. I am really fine doing it every day. It helped me so much—very well. Qi gong really works."
> —Lourdes

> "I feel much better while attending qi gong. I like the support the class offers. Helpful with my mental attitude."
> —Cathy

> "I have definitely felt much better physically and emotionally ... just a general sense of well-being. I have also lost five pounds without too much effort. Coupled with yoga exercise once a week I could feel my body and my internal organs, muscles, etc., much better. I have also experienced more spirituality and could feel better the energy within me and the world around me."
> —Dan

Sylvia practicing "opening form."

> "I started taking classes with master Yu in July, 1999. I was a breast cancer client. From the first time, I was impressed with master Yu and her approach, her philosophy, and the inherent warmth she displayed to her cancer clients. I feel I have been greatly helped by the qi gong classes —both physically and psychologically. I look forward to attending the weekly classes, interacting with other "cancer survivors," and absorbing the teachings of master Yu."
> —Sylvia Franklin

Cancer July 13, 1999 regarding the use of acupuncture and qi gong to help restore health during and after conventional cancer treatments, your authors began teaching Guo Lin to a group of cancer patients at UCLA. Although the work is ongoing, master Yu and Hoff are gratified that they have provided assistance to patients. Many patients report feeling more relaxed and stronger after their participation in the groups that practice medical and Guo Lin qi gong.

We look forward to future progress as well as clinical support for master Yu's pioneering efforts to integrate Eastern practices of health and recovery into Western medicine. ®

Master Wen Mei Yu is an internationally recognized leader in the teaching and development of taiji and qi $S^{on}S$- A member of the Inside Kung-Fu *Hall of Fame, master Yus books and videotapes are available through Unique Publications/Video. Theresa Marie Hoff studies the internal arts under master Yu and for the last eight years has taught tai ji and qi gong to promote health and fitness.*

www.ingramcontent.com/pod-product-compliance
Lightning Source LLC
Chambersburg PA
CBHW070942230426
43666CB00011B/2533